Contents

Dorothy Hall's
Herbal
Medicine

Dorothy Hall's Herbal Medicine

Lothian Publishing Company Pty Ltd
Sydney · Melbourne · Auckland

First published 1988 by
Lothian Publishing Company Pty Ltd
11 Munro Street Port Melbourne Victoria 3207

National Library of Australia
Cataloguing-in-Publication data:

Hall, Dorothy (Dorothy Graeme).
Dorothy Hall's herbal medicine.

ISBN 0 85091 310 1.

1. Herbs – Therapeutic use. I. Title. II.
Title: Herbal medicine.

615'.321

Typeset in Sabon by Bookset
Printed in Australia by
Australian Print Group

1 *Herbs and people*

*H*ave you ever puzzled over exactly what is a 'bloody flux', a 'quartan fever', or 'the running of the reins'? No wonder the accusation of 'mediaeval nonsense' bedevils today's herbalists! Let's see how much real knowledge of health care, hidden under the language of past centuries quaintness, is to be found in these often-quoted herbals of the old masters.

As a small child, learning about the plants from my botanist–gardening–agronomy family, I pondered for hours with a child's bewilderment over the differences between early botanical drawings of the plants in books and the actual plants growing outside in the garden of our family home. My wise old grandmother, as always, gave me the clues, 'Man can only copy imperfectly what nature produces perfectly.' I have never forgotten her words. (It makes for better tolerance of humankind too!)

It was not until much later, in high-school years, that it dawned on me that the same comparison could be made about those 'weird and witchy' words in the old herbals. It was the period when 'witches' were pronounced on by the church, when heretics were stoned and tortured. It was the Dark Ages, when God and the Devil became members of the family and a personal decision to align oneself with one or the other was necessary. The mediaeval world was a hellfire and brimstone time and there were no half measures. You were either on your way to Heaven, by conforming, or on your way to Hell, by objecting.

Perhaps things haven't changed much! But the *language* of those days, exaggeratedly strong, still remains to bug today's herbalists and naturopaths every time another glossy 'Herbal' of bygone days is reprinted. Then came the idea that perhaps a useful exercise might be accomplished in *today's* language and symbols. By all means, look back to those mediaeval geniuses, with all their 'tertian fevers' and 'black biles' but once and for all put herbal medicine into the context of today. Humour, that terrible sin of laughter, may also help get the message home. The serious de-personalisation of today's science may be the reason why ordinary humans are rebelling against, even laughing at, much of its pomposity.

Herbalists in this century have been misrepresented as either 'trendy' or 'alternative' in some way to the now established new areas of pharmaceuticals and high-tech medicine. In truth herbalists are ultra-conservatives! The type of medicine they practise has continued, without a break, for over twenty-five centuries, even through the mediaeval 'nonsense' ages.

The earliest known written manuscript of herbal medicine no longer exists or so we are told by many who have searched in vain for its whereabouts. All we have left of the genius Pedanius Dios-corides of Anazarba (near Tarsus) is what a later female writer, Juliana Anicia, daughter of Avicius Olybrius, one-time Emperor of the West, gleaned and collated in a Codex form, about 512 AD. The Anicia Codex is now preserved in the Austrian National Library at Vienna, and translations have appeared down the centuries, the most recent from Spain in 1970.

A much-travelled man, a Greek physician to Roman armies about the time of Nero, Dioscorides spoke briefly in his writings of his 'travels' and of what he had learned from many nations of their medical practices using plants and simple naturally occurring sub-stances as their healing agents. It is generally accepted that his teachings were adopted by the Syriac and Muslim systems of medi-cine but I believe the contrary to be the case. Some of the earliest medicinal uses of plants like garlic, onions, aloes, etc., were record-ed on the steles and obelisks of Egypt centuries before Dioscorides was born. The Phoenicians also have much earlier records, and the Indians, and the Chinese. It seems Dioscorides may have *learned* some of his medicine in Arabic and Indian countries rather than *taught* it to them. Certainly, Arabic surgery and the knowledge of anatomy and physiology that its records show was highly devel-oped and accurate long before Dioscorides gathered his plant knowledge. Whichever way the knowledge flowed, I am grateful that the information has trickled through, albeit over some stony pathways.

It took me twenty-six years to find my own copy of Dioscorides's teachings. In Oxford, in the largest bookshop in the world, I dropped my perennial throw-away line just as we were leaving, 'I don't suppose you've got a Dioscorides in English?' Modern met ancient when a computer-screen flashed up the title, a 1932 translation by R. T. Gunther re-published in 1968 — and there was *one* copy left on the shelves! This work is a translation of a translation, but I believe the manner of its setting out to be the most accurate available. You see, another English herbalist, John Goodyer, of Petersfield, little known to us now, translated Dioscorides's manuscripts quite literally, line by line, into English between 1652 and 1655, and it is on Goodyer's translation that Gunther based his work.

Who knows how the Goodyer translation found its way into Magdalen College archives at Oxford, where it lay, unopened, until the 1930s. Although there is not much written evidence to support my theory, John Tradescant the Younger (1608–62), an extraordinary scholar of the natural sciences, would have numbered amongst his circle of botanical friends and acquaintances all the well-known adepts in the subject. He also collected antiquities and oddities from all over the world for his marvellous Museum of Curiosities in Lambeth. Did he acquire the Dioscorides Codex — or even the *original* Dioscorides manuscript? Did John Goodyer translate it, and Tradescant then bequeath it together with many other marvellous objects, to Elias Ashmole? Did the Dioscorides translation find its way into Magdalen College via that same old scoundrel Ashmole, pilferer extraordinary, whose name today graces the cool galleries of the Ashmolean Museum at Oxford?

And what does all this have to do with my work? Veracity, that's what! Truth is hard to come by when word of mouth and generations of students and teachers have tended to place individual interpretations on basic accuracy. 'How do you know this is *accurate* information on medicinal plants?' I'm often challenged when I lecture to students or to professional and community groups. The only way I can answer, with my own conscience comfortable, is to refer back to an ancient primary source of information rather than trust a secondary, later interpretation. If I want to know the essentials of the philosophy, theory and practice of homoeopathy, I read Samuel Hahneman, not a book written five minutes after graduation by the top student at the Homoeopathic Institute last year. If I wish to learn herbal medicine accurately, I refer to Dioscorides's factual, simple, practical application of plants to illness conditions which was the medical text for 1,500 years afterwards. I'm astounded at every re-reading to find how much of what I have learned in over thirty years experience in the practice of herbal medicine was set out by Dioscorides (via his verbatim translators) in much the same words.

More great early herbalists followed Dioscorides's lead. Turner, Gerard, Parkinson, Blunt and many others reverently cited Dioscorides and then proceeded to cloak the simple empiricism of the master in the religious mediaevalism of their day. Even the Englishman Dr Thomas Culpeper (1616–54), viciously condemning his medical teachers and the medical establishment of his day for losing the substance of great medicine in Latin declensions and pedantic nonsense, pays homage to Dioscorides's simple effectiveness.

Let's see what Culpeper's instruction to 'pick the herb on the south side of the hill, with a clear heart just before the summer sun touch the mid-point' is *really* trying to tell you. Is it superstitious magical nonsense, or is it sound phytopharmacy, even though couched in the language of the Middle Ages?

In England, Culpeper's home, the 'south side of the hill' faces the equator and gets the most sun. Therefore any aromatic oils, resins, etc., that the plant manufactures in its growth are in greater potency and concentration with this southerly aspect. As the morning sun begins to strengthen towards noon, the dew on the plant evaporates rapidly. Just before noon, the plant is dry enough to pick, without later mildew from excess moisture affecting its medicinal quality and its drying time. 'With a clear heart?' Surely this is a fanciful instruction? Only recently have we measured pH changes in acidity/alkalinity when emotions make us tense and distraught. Jealousy, envy, resentment, hatred, all can be triggers for changes that can now be measured, monitored and graphed. The same emotions can keep muscles super-tense and movements abrupt and jerky. *Tearing* a plant from its soil or *yanking* a stem from a bush can bruise soft cells and damage the plant; skin which is too acid or too alkaline can make your hand's encounter with the plant a chemically 'bruising' one too. Did Culpeper have the wisdom but not the words? When his *Herbal* is quoted to me as an example of herbalist's nonsense, I quickly remind my critics that the popular edition of Culpeper takes only one slice from a whole loaf. I own a magnificent old edition including chapters in which he takes his teachers to task for trying to bamboozle the public, and their own college students, with long words, arrogant statements and treatments that don't work. One of the first writers of a herbal in ordinary English (rather than in Latin, the doctor's language then and now), Culpeper provoked a storm of vilification not only against his writings, but against his person, from his fellow doctors. I'm often criticised just as vehemently today for speaking and teaching in a language the lay-person can understand! 'It's a myocardial infarction, Sister' sounds much more worthy of respect than 'Gee, your heart's stuffed up and has blown a gasket', but that heart-patient *understands* what I say.

Culpeper's 'fellow *doctors*'? Yes; don't forget that the plants used medicinally for tens of centuries comprised the Pharma-copoeas of yesterday. Until the 1930s the British Pharmacopoea (still used in Australia) was mostly composed of plant substances, simple compounds from nature, and some animal products. *All* world Pharmacopoeas, depending on the cultural background of their country of origin, still contain some plant drugs. The word 'drug' itself means 'dried plant material'. It was not until the 1949 revision of the British Pharmacopoea that plant substances were elbowed out as 'unscientific' and non-standardisable, and removed in bulk to minor listings in other reference works. Synthetic new formulations appeared year by year and the multinational phar-maceutical industry boomed. Much of the advance in pharma-ceutical new products kept pace with developments in those other multinationals, the petro-chemical giants. Man-made chemistry had arrived. Unless a substance could give predictable and control-lable results on double-blind crossover trials on laboratory animals, it was out, out, *out*! What had been a very fine dividing line between the substances medical doctors and herbalists used became a bottomless chasm. Formerly the only difference had been that in more recent times a doctor had gained his skills at a university while a herbalist had been taught traditional remedies by older family members or cultural teachers and built these skills on a natural aptitude and ability to bring plants and humans together in a way that produced health benefits.

In more recent centuries it was a professional sin for a university-trained doctor to work with an 'untrained' person at all. Do you know it still is? 'Unqualified' still exists as a prohibition in this country today. Officially, university-trained practitioners are forbidden to have anything to do with 'unqualified' persons. Per-haps the term itself needs re-defining. Unqualified at what? To do what? Perhaps 'non-university-trained' may be a better term — and less discriminatory in today's world! As recently as 1978 I wanted to buy a small private hospital to provide live-in monitoring for any very ill patients of herbalists who needed temporary round-the-clock care. An excellent young doctor applied for the position of superintendent and medical practitioner: his professional association threatened to de-license him if he worked with 'quacks'. My plans came to nothing and patients missed out on the benefits from two different areas of medicine working together.

Henry VIII, famous for his wives, perhaps deserves more lasting fame for his law-making and his willingness to settle arguments between warring factions of any kind by giving equal legal standing to *both* practices in contention. His 'Herbalist's Charter' of 1544 is a monument to commonsense and problem-solving. In essence it states, 'Let those who understand the uses of herbs use herbs, and those who understand surgery use surgery.' No mention at all was made of any teaching institution for either! He capped it off with one of those 'unto time immemorial' statements only a king or queen can utter and get away with.

A more recent statement in 1986 by the Traditional Medicines Group in the UK recognises the same right of one system of knowledge not to be ruled over and regulated *only* by another system of knowledge. It states 'medical doctors are *inappropriately* qualified to regulate and control the practices of herbalists, homoeopaths, etc.' who do their professional training in colleges and teaching institutions outside the university system and, of course, outside the experience of any medical doctors concerned.

China, formerly a closed book of knowledge on things medical and herbal, is today demonstrating its competence in, and indeed its right to maintain and implement, *two* systems of medicine side by side, the traditional one and the newer pharmaceutical one. The Chinese Herbal Pharmacopoea has been in continual use for thousands of years. Today there is respect and dialogue between newly-Westernised and traditional practitioners. Both have a place, but quite different philosophies, and training in both does not prevent mutual interaction while maintaining professionally different standards and types of health care.

A question of racial differences also arises when comparing, say, the Chinese system of herbal medicine with the Ayurvedic Indian system, equally as old, or even the Egyptian plant knowledge from the incised stone walls of Karnak, Kom Ombo and Deir-el-bahari. The plants indigenous to any country or continent were, by constant usage and familiarity, acceptable to the metabolism of particular racial types and groups. A plant which could produce mild purging in an Egyptian may cause repetitive diarrhoea and vomiting in a newly arrived Greek with 'traveller's constipation'.

Marco Polo undoubtedly had trouble with jasmine tea for a while, and I have personal memories of an excellently regarded 'mild' indigestion cure from Sri Lanka that gave me lift-off from the toilet-bowl for several weeks after one single dose. Racism it's not: but culturally and physically different human racial groups cannot easily and quickly interchange their medical and herbal systems one with another. It takes both time and a *gradual* introduction of the substances of one group into another widely different group. A Japanese macrobiotic diet may suit the Japanese absorption and metabolism exceedingly well but its sudden introduction after an Australian meat-and-three-veg meal conditioning may be mighty uncomfortable. Common use gradually acclimatises a cultural group over time. To introduce Chinese or Indian medicines to a predominantly white Caucasian racial-origin group not only needs time, but an excellent knowledge of plant chemistry and its multitudinous changes from country to country, soil to soil, temperature to temperature, and human to human. What is one person's meat certainly is another person's fish! Tastes vary too. What is terribly bitter to an Australian palate may taste quite sweet to a Brazilian, Mexican or Mongolian!

This is a long preliminary explanation of why there is in this book a predominance of plants which have been acclimatised and used for medicinal purposes by white Caucasian and Mediterranean peoples. I have purposely not included Chinese, Indian, South African, Asian, etc., herbs unless they have been in common use here for at least a long enough period to establish their effects in a foreign culture.

Most herbalists just happen. Many do formal training later, tired of the constant, 'How do you know that? You're unqualified . . .' Some just keep on fixing people and going to gaol. Recently, in Spain, we heard of yet another 'unqualified' martyr to his lack of academic training, who spent several periods in gaol. One of our greatest living herbal and naturopathic pioneers, Dr Bernard Jensen in the USA, used to have regular visits from his local police. 'Bring your pyjamas and toothbrush, sir,' they'd say apologetically, 'it's the slammer again for a few days.' Undaunted, he fought on — and won. Culpeper had the same problem, and paid the professional price for it — death as a pauper at the age of thirty-eight. Not because of the *damage* he did, but because (as happens even today) he cured too many people and his contemporary medical brothers concluded it had to stop!

So herbalists tend to be professionally lonely. They also tend to be poor. Why then are some other areas of medicine so determined to get rid of them? Why are they thought by some to be so dangerous?

Over the years I've become accustomed to ridicule, then to attack and abuse. What a shame so few of the attackers stay to learn about what they're attacking. They're criticising their own history of medical practice! If you're as old as I am, you will remember your family doctor would write you out an individual prescription for salve, mixture or tablet, and your local chemist would take down from his shelves the big glass bottles with the cryptic names and brown-colour fluid of strong odour and taste that are on my dispensary shelves this very day. It's only quite recently that the chemist became a 'pharmacist' in name, but a label-changer in practice. Some of my older friends in pharmacy remember its golden age of low-cost simple individual prescribing, and deplore the waste of their skills today. But, like a Pharaoh whose name and history was erased forever from the stone records of Egypt because of his desire to revive an old simple religion, the use of plants in today's medical and pharmaceutical university courses is ridiculed and dismissed (often with naively *wrong* assumptions). The old gods must be buried, say the new breed of 'scientific' academics, but before they go they must be disgraced publicly and forever.

At a recent large pharmacy conference in Victoria, where I had been invited to explain the principles and practice of herbal medicine to a group containing eminent academically qualified people, I had the greatest difficulty in convincing anyone that the *part* does not have the same chemistry, effectiveness, reactivity, etc., as the *whole*. Taking one or two chemical entities from a plant, and discarding the remaining constituents as 'of no therapeutic use' denies altogether a basic principle, not only of nature but of the foundation principles of chemistry itself. So does finding an alkaloid in a plant, testing the alkaloid only, and discarding the plant as 'toxic' chemically without evaluating at all what the other chemical entities present may do to change, minimise, enhance or even block altogether, the alkaloid's potential 'toxicity' taken alone. 'Why aren't we all sitting here dead?' I asked this same gathering. 'Come to think of it, why were we born at all? Our parents and grand-parents should be dead also!' After all, doctors prescribed, and chemists dispensed, nothing *but* natural whole plants, minerals and animal substances for several hundred years past, with full know-ledge of a plant's *whole* chemistry and biological activity. How come we were not all poisoned *then*? Why should exactly the same formulations as I use today suddenly become such 'funny' plants, dangerous and deadly to the public?

At the same gathering, an eminent professor from London University, with a great sense of humour, placed between his slides of lists of 'terribly dangerous' substances in plants like Alfalfa, Chamomile, etc., cartoons drawn by his teenage son of witches, warlocks and wild-eyed 'herbalists'. He saw no relevance, apparently, to his own faculty, pharmacognosy (the study of the contents and extraction thereof from plants) of such a witchy image — no, *herbalists* were the witches. I could not resist telling the gathering that one of the revered pharmacognosy textbooks he used to train his students was also used by me to train mine.

So it seems that although pharmacy and herbal medicine used to be almost the same discipline, it is necessary today to deny this relationship. And what's more, any previous similarities must be either ignored or vehemently denied. Poor Dr Culpeper! I know just how he felt.

As Webster's Dictionary defines science, 'A *science* teaches us to know, and an *art* to do, and all the more perfect sciences lead to the creation of corresponding useful arts . . . Art is knowledge made efficient by skill . . . knowledge possessed as a result of study *or practice*.'

The root-origin of the word 'science' is '*scire*', to know. Unfortunately, it now seems only to classify and identify those who have been taught at an approved university! Does this mean the rest of us do know, or can know, nothing? Does it mean that all knowledge gleaned, observed and pondered over by mankind since it began is worthless without at least a Ph.D.? Does it mean we shouldn't practise what we know unless we hold a university degree?

Perhaps the clever wine merchant, testing how full or empty his wooden casks were with a small vibrating diaphragm to which he listened through simple tubes and earpiece, should never have invented that stethoscope and, worse, showed it to his friends, the doctors, explaining how different chest-sounds could indicate congested ('full') or sound ('empty') lungs. Medical history abounds with inventions and innovations by *laymen*, which all add to 'scientific' knowledge, and the *practice* of that knowledge as an *art*, a skill.

Even Louis Pasteur, adopted son of orthodox present-day medical thinking, was chiefly famous (again in the wine industry!) for his work with bacteria and micro-organisms destroying vines in

France. His major contribution to 'science' was the understanding of how enzymes and friendly bacteria worked together in fermenting grapes. Almost as a sideline, his 'germ-theory' impressed some medical minds. Could sudden illness onsets be caused by 'germs' too? Almost on his death-bed, Pasteur recanted. The human 'climate', he said, made a difference. In a *healthy* body 'germs' could not proliferate well. However, he set a trend in medical thinking for several generations to follow: illness had nothing to do with what *we* were doing with our lives; it all came from 'germs' outside us, waiting to pounce!

'Science' employs 'scientific method' our references told us. Would you believe how hard it is to find a practical definition of this method? It appears to involve 'controlled conditions' of experiments, and 'reproducible results' every single time the experiment is performed. But almost every recognised parameter of 'scientific method' ignores that most individual of all non-standardisable ingredients, the human being. A variety of animals, machines, flashing lights and different-coloured buttons to press tell us whether any 'results' obtained from the exercise of scientific method procedures are accurate or not.

I can't find out, nor has anyone else been able to show me, who invented or first implemented today's scientific method. To add to the puzzle, try finding out who invented the double-blind crossover placebo trial! In 1985 a professional new acquaintance, Dr W. W. Buchanan, of McMaster University, Hamilton, Ontario, suggested that Dr James Lind, an Edinburgh graduate who worked in the Royal Navy in the eighteenth century and conducted trials with lime juice to prevent scurvy may have been the first, but Dr Buchanan could not enlighten me about how the double-blind crossover placebo trial came to be accepted in the years after the 1939–45 world war. It seems some anonymous Swiss may have reintroduced and updated earlier models of this format. I would be delighted if any reader can provide a name, a date, even the pharmaceutical company involved, or the university, so that I may at least know who first narrowed real discovery down to such a sterile model for 'proof' of therapeutic efficacy.

Whenever I produce any human-benefit results from herbal medicines and display a well patient as the outcome, 'scientists' look at me with a withering condemnation. 'That's not a valid result without a double-blind crossover placebo trial', they say. It's no use at all producing a patient without migraines after ten or twenty years of weekly blinding misery; nor is it acceptable to 'science' to produce a child who now walks without a limp, or an asthmatic whose wheezes are gone permanently. Unless every other asthmatic sufferer can be given exactly the same measured amount of that herbal mixture and have their asthma disappear too, then the treatment is not a 'valid' one scientifically and, even worse, the original patient didn't get better either! Or if they *did* (and the possibility is squeezed out between clenched teeth), then it must have been from some other reason entirely. How desperately do we cling to un-truths, and how hard a *real* truth is to swallow!

Underneath this so-called authority of science lies a desperate human weakness, one of the most negative energies in our whole personality range of choices, doubt. We doubt whether we could really lose illnesses so quickly and permanently; we doubt whether a simple weed, growing at our kitchen doorstep, could do what all the multi-billion dollar sophistication of the best 'scientific' research has still failed to do. Worst of all, we wonder whether we have made ourselves look stupid, difficult or unacceptable to the herd by doing something *different* from what present authority has decreed. When we say 'Anyway, I'm better, and I don't care', will the God science strike us down for daring to be so, against all odds?

It's a strong human who swims against the tide, and a stronger one who helps others to do the same. It's very hard indeed to *begin* such a change of direction. Only when we suddenly find dozens, then hundreds, then many thousands all swimming 'the wrong way' has the tide turned.

It's as inevitable as are all the other natural cycles, night to day, summer to winter, season to season. Nature shows us what *real* science is all about. It's not about feeding nutrient pellets, all weighing the same, to inbred laboratory rats who all look the same and share brother–sister DNA. It's about observing the natural laws of the universe and using these. It's about working *within* those laws for our own benefit. It's about the efficiency of use of our human vehicles so the constantly changing circumstances of life can be predicted, known about, and dealt with, without our organism succumbing. It's swimming *with* nature's tidal rhythms, not insisting that intellectual science win some battle or other *against* the 'forces of nature'. Perhaps the human ego needs to feel on top, but any household cat can teach us more about survival than can a civil-defence master plan for contingencies A, B or C. It's a truly 'scientific' human who is willing to acknowledge our very minor contribution to the workings of nature.

The greatest single resistance to herbal medicine today comes from people who've never tried it! 'It *can't* work,' says angry science. 'There is no scientific reason for it to work,' say many 'scientists' who've never had their upset tummies soothed by Chamomile tea or their sinuses cleared by Horseradish. 'It *does* work,' say others who have given it the good old Aussie try, 'that's good enough for me!' It's astounding how many patients who come back for their second consultation start off with 'It didn't work; nothing's changed' and on closer questioning admit quite freely that they've *not* followed the diet or *not* taken the mixture! I don't accept criticism from those with no experience of what they're criticising. The Australian 'knocker' too often prevents the adventure of finding new ways, new directions, or the continued use of an old way that still works well. 'Do you expect me to believe that?' sneered one current affairs host. 'Not until you've *tried* it,' I replied (and my reply was edited out in the final to-air documentary).

'I believe in natural medicine,' say many patients; 'placebo effect' says science. I'm certainly not denying that the *energy* of a human thinking process is considerable, nor am I denying that 'energetic thinking' can help almost anything at all work better. What herbal medicine does is provide a 'shape' chemically and an energy structure of its own, which over centuries of use has been evaluated by results *in vivo*, not only by laboratory testing. Each plant used has an energy-identity which has been found to be either similar to, or empathetic with, the energies of various healthy body-structures and functions. It all looked like 'magic' perhaps to those mediaeval minds. Now the new true sciences of bio-physics, bio-energetics, quantum mechanics, polarity reflexes, geo-magnetics, resonance frequencies and space-data evaluation have begun to show, and to *prove* even to the satisfaction of the most die-hard conservative knocker, that yesterday's 'magic' is today's 'scientific breakthrough'. What a shame all those witches and heretics had to die for it first! What a pity I still receive jeers and sneers today because my plant-knowledge was not gained at a university.

But now I'm no longer swimming upstream in a minority group. Now there are millions all over the world who want simple and less costly means of maintaining and improving health and well-being.

An official (Geneva) World Health Organisation (WHO) publication in 1978, 'The Promotion and Development of Traditional Medicine', states it very clearly:

'**Traditional medicine** . . . the sum total of all the knowledge and practices, whether explicable or not, used in diagnosis, prevention and elimination of physical, mental or social imbalance and relying exclusively on practical experience and observation handed down from generation to generation, whether verbally or in writing.

'Traditional medicine might also be considered as a solid amalgamation of dynamic medical know-how and ancestral experience.' (p. 8)

'The traditional healer . . . a person who is recognized by the community in which he lives as competent to provide health care by using vegetable, animal and mineral substances and certain other methods based on the social, cultural and religious background as well as on the knowledge, attitudes and beliefs that are prevalent in the community regarding physical, mental and social well-being and the causation of disease and disability.' (p. 9)

'Reasons for the promotion of traditional medicine . . . Approach — unique and holistic . . . Traditional medicine has a holistic approach — i.e. that of viewing man in his totality within a wide ecological spectrum, and of emphasizing the viewpoint that ill health or disease is brought about by an imbalance, or disequilibrium, of man in his total ecological system and not only by the causative agent and pathogenic evolution.' (p. 13)

'Guidelines for integrating traditional medicine into primary health care

'(1) Giving recognition to traditional practitioners and incorporating them into community development programmes. (p. 14) . . .

'(4) Educating the community to believe that the provision of traditional remedies is not second-rate medicine.' (p. 15)

In 1985 a recent WHO Bulletin contained the following paragraphs:

'Critics of the use of galenical products rather than pure active constituents should consider the following simplified example, which illustrates the value of galenical preparations. A chemically standardized tincture of *Atropa belladonna* for use in treating stomach ulcers has a therapeutic efficacy at least equivalent to that of a standard dose of atropine sulfate (the major active principle of *A. belladonna*). The plant itself can be cultivated easily in almost any country and the manufacture of a stable, standardized tincture would require little in the way of hard currency, which would be needed to import tablets of atropine

sulfate. Other similar examples of efficacious galenical preparations that could be promoted in developing countries can be
identified from the information presented in Annex 1. There is
therefore much in favour of establishing programmes for producing standardized and safe galenical traditional preparations for
potential use in primary health care, with the eventual aim of
discovering their active principles.

'Even if the active principles have not yet been identified in
some of the plants used in traditional medicine, historical
evidence of the value of such plants could result in useful preparations, provided they are safe. Evaluation of safety should therefore be a prime consideration, even at the expense of establishing
efficacy of the preparation.'

'Medicinal Plants in Therapy', N. R. Farnsworth *et al*,
WHO Bulletin, no. 6, vol. 63, p. 968.

As the health cost for Western nations soars, and high-
technology medicine costs the individual more in tax-dollars for a
place even in a public hospital let alone a personal consultation,
herbalists appear again to be a rational well-proven 'alternative' in
the thinking of some people, and 'complementary' in the minds of
others. The developed nations' love affair with chemistry is over.
We have outsmarted ourselves with our clever plastics, our brightly
coloured synthetics, our imitation-food and our sprayed and over-
fertilised crops. Our greed for short-term apparently easy ways has
turned forests into wastelands and agricultural land into deserts.
Our need for an immediate 'quick-fix' pill has produced a snow-
storm of tablets and capsules of every conceivable shape and colour. Our bathroom shelves and kitchen cupboards bulge with half-
used panaceas. And when we throw out the lot in a fit of righteous
willpower, where do all these 'Take only as prescribed' drugs go?
Down the toilet and off to the ocean to pollute fish, seaweeds and
the continental shelf. We can't get rid of our chemistry love affair
quite as easily as we thought we could. No wonder Japanese sea-
weeds show high levels of arsenic; no wonder country rainfall
catchment lakes show massive pollution levels from agricultural-
chemical run-off into them. The ocean, our last comparatively
unpolluted area until recent years, is becoming a garbage-bin for
chemistry.

Plants, on the other hand, are real alchemists. Plants can
change the chemistry of breakdown and decay in a compost heap

into the chemistry of life and living when that compost is added to their environment. Plants breathe *in* what we breathe *out*. Animal excrement is changed by plants into a nitrogen-carbon circle of creative chemical change. We can eat the products of decayed manure, rotten vegetables and dead flowers *after* they have been recycled through a plant's metabolism. What a waste-disposal system plants are! If we hadn't been so blinded by our new infatuation with *in*organic substances that last forever unchanged, we might not have such a dirty waste-ridden planet! It may not be too late.

Herbal medicine is not so remote as many of its critics portray it to be. Even as recently as our parents' generation people had close and intimate experience of plants used to improve health. Perhaps it's only the translation from mediaeval to modern that's difficult. A herbalist today needs not only botanical and pharmacognosy understanding, but a research doctorate in mediaeval history! And it takes one to know one! Much that is lost in translation of old documents, manuscripts, papyri and stone records is because the translator may have had an excellent knowledge of the ancient *language* concerned, but little theoretical, and no practical, knowledge of the *subject* being translated.

As an example, the Biblical 'rose' of Sharon, the 'rose of the brook', is not a rose but a pink oleander! 'The pink open flower head that bursts forth in Spring' may have meant, to a translator in England or Europe, a 'rose' — especially if the translator was not a gardener. It took a visit to Petra, in Jordan, to show me the truth. There, up and down the gravel creek-beds in early spring was a river of pink. Oleanders, supposedly from Greece, had been here not only since biblical days, but perhaps long before. Our Jordanian bus-driver, a keen gardener, was a mine of information on plants from then on. 'We call it traditionally "Rose of the Brook",' he told me. A long-standing question in my own mind was resolved. Roses don't naturally grow well with wet feet, or around rivers and low-lying shady ground. As a gardener, I had known this since childhood when my mother's 'Black Boy' rose climber and 'Etoile d'Holland' bush rose suffered in wet or humid weather or when I over-watered them. That biblical phrase hadn't made sense before; it did now.

The 'lily' wasn't our present-day lily either. It was what we now call an *iris*. Those earlier biblical translators followed the current common names again. The Flag Lily was well known to the population at large, as well as to herbalists — the common field iris.

Blue Flag, one of the herbs discussed in this book, is still used today in my dispensary. The 'fleur-de-lis' of the French — lily-flower — is the same common mauve iris family. The biblical 'lilies of the field' were white and mauve *irises*. All those good ladies who decorate churches may want to use oleanders and irises now, for accuracy; but instead be as careful as that Jordanian bus-driver. 'For looking at, not touching,' he chided me when I bent an oleander branch down to look at the pink flower cluster. Luckily, we *both* knew that the sap, even the touch of its leaves, can cause violent skin irritation for many people. Our common bond became greater. When I picked a small stem of a Spurge variety later on to show my husband, my new friend refused to let me into the bus with it. 'The Milk of the Snake,' he commented, losing all confidence in my abilities. It was several grumpy hours before I could convince him to talk to me again. '*You* may know its sap is dangerous, even if only touched to the tongue,' he finally conceded, 'but what if someone else in the bus touched it and didn't know?' He was quite right, of course. When I found the wild Hemlock in the weeds behind a desert Coke-and-Hamburger stand the next day, I made sure he saw me throw away its flower I had picked to look at before I re-entered the bus! His next comment made us friends for life: 'Poisons grow near poisons,' he remarked quietly, as all the empty Coke bottles were returned to the counter.

Common names given to medicinal plants from many different localities and countries of origin also cause headaches for today's herbalists, in two ways. Common names for the *same* plant may be different, even from one valley to the next and *different* plants may be called by the same name. Botanical accuracy in identification can become a nightmare! There are at least three different plants whose common name has been 'All-heal' (Yarrow, Prunella and Valerian), then there is 'Self-heal' (*Sanicula europa*) and, to complicate matters further, there's 'Heal-all' as well! No wonder there are so many instances of so-called 'severe reactions' when some enthusiastic newcomer to plant medicines picks the wrong plant; some other plant entirely often gets the blame for the reaction. Thank goodness for Linnaeus (1707–78) and his orderly mind. His system of plant classification makes accuracy easier to achieve. Still, those newly converted to plant medicines should be wary indeed of joyfully picking some pretty little flower or other, making up a 'herb tea' from it and doing themselves all sorts of mischief because they picked the wrong plant in the first place.

WHENEVER YOU PICK A PLANT FOR HUMAN
USE, HAVE IT ACCURATELY IDENTIFIED BY
YOUR LOCAL NURSERY, AGRICULTURE DE-
PARTMENT BRANCH OR BOTANIC GARDEN
STAFF. Even for this to be accurate enough, you will
need at least 150 mm (6 in.) of plant stem, with some
new and some older leaves, and if possible unopened
buds as well as open flowers; if another near-by plant of
the same kind also carries seeds or seed-pods, these also
should be supplied. It's impossible to identify a plant
accurately enough without *all* these plant parts. One
leaf, often brought to me with a query, 'What's this?
Can you tell me what it's from and whether it's useful
medicinally', is just not enough. It's a very unwise and
unwary herbalist who will identify from less than *all*
plant parts.

Another pitfall lies ahead for the would-be medical botanist. Plants,
like people, grow differently and look different too in different
localities. The coarse, strong dark-green dwarfed leaves of wild
Yarrow growing in the icy winds of the Snowy Mountains of New
South Wales granite cliff-paths bear little resemblance to the pale-
green, long and slender, thousand-floret softer leaves of the cultivated herb-garden-pampered Yarrow grown in Sydney or even in
Canberra: and yet both are botanically identical. It's intriguing to
find, however, that the much hardier *wild* Yarrow has a measurably
greater medicinal effect than its city-bred twin. Like the traditionally different energies of hardy tough peasants or effete lazy so-
called aristocrats, the medicinal plant world tends to become
dependent and attenuated if over-fed and over-indulged.

The wild plants, the weeds, often figure largely in Pharmacopoeas. These plants self-sow, and therefore only grow in positions suitable for them. They struggle and fight sometimes to retain
these positions against some other plant that threatens to overrun
their domain. They hang on grimly through searing heat, pelting
rain, snow and winds. They *survive*. When such plants are measured on today's energy-recording instruments, like the Kirlian
apparatus or even the galvanometer, they show stronger and more
lasting energy-patterns than their cultivated twins.

The Kirlian camera photographs the energy-aura surrounding
living things. Using a particular type of charged photographic plate,

the peaks and rays of energy which surround the leaves of growing plants, the fingertips of humans, etc., can be seen to vary depending on the healthiness or otherwise of the living organism being photographed. A galvanometer is an instrument used to measure the amount of electrical activity passing through any living material. It also can measure any electrical system which doesn't involve living material.

Wild plants, growing in situations of their own choice, certainly produce the most obvious health improvement in humans. The recent well-advertised commercial plantings of Korean Ginseng and Aloe Vera species are good examples. In the wild, mountain Ginseng and desert-hardy Aloes develop the *energy* to survive: under commercial cultivation they can be fed, watered and lovingly tended, and may even show equal *chemistry*-equivalents to those grown in the wild. Using instruments of *energy*-measurement, however, those hardy wild-grown plants beat them every time.

So what are we gaining from plants used as medicine: better chemistry or better physics? I believe we gain both. I believe that what we can now measure quantitatively and qualitatively in terms of today's physics is what once produced the 'magical' effectiveness of some plants to prevent, treat and cure illnesses in people. After all, wiser people than I have defined 'magic' as 'truth for which we haven't yet discovered a reason'.

In the following pages you'll find my list of medicinal plants from A to Y, but realise now that almost every plant or weed, fern, mould, lichen and fungus can be said to be able to change the metabolism, the structure, even the homoeostasis of Man in some way, though it be to paralyse him, send him blind, even kill him! Whenever any sentimental herbalist, or would-be herbalist says to me, or to others, 'Herbal medicine is *safe* to use, you know; it's just God's good plants', I hasten to disabuse all within hearing range of this dangerous fallacy. There are just as many 'baddies' in the plant world as there are in the human world. There are plants that will strangle other plants; there are parasitic root-robbers and sapsuckers; there are plants in your backyard right now that are the 'Hell's Angels' of botany. *Don't* for one second believe that all of nature is kind, gentle and forgiving! Every plant, like every human, has times when it's 'very very good' and other times when it's 'horrid'. For example, during particular parts of the growth cycle of *Papaver somniferum*, the opium poppy, swallowing the white milky sap from the calyx will bring sleep, dreams, relief from pain, even the sleep of death; but three to five days later the seeds inside the same calyx can be baked in a German Easter cake and be highly nutritious and an excellent source of phosphorus and Vitamin B. Some plants, like Rhubarb, have 'good' stems but 'horrid' leaves. There's good and bad in all of us, and the plant world exhibits the same pattern.

One lady tried for years to get to sleep by taking a cup of Valerian-*leaf* tea each night. She gave up finally, criticising herbal medicine as 'rubbish' to anyone who would listen. Try the *root*, lady, try the root. And don't use it fresh from the garden either or you'll wind up hyperactive, possibly with schizoid patterns of behaviour and delusions of grandeur! Only after the Valerian root is *dried* for one to four years is its medicinal value best available, and *safe*, for Man. You see how generalities can be very dangerous in the use of plants for food or medicine.

Speaking of which, when does a plant cease being a 'food' and become a 'medicine'? This question has bugged me for years, because I can't answer it. What is the difference, say, between Celery eaten as a vegetable and Celery extract prescribed by a herbalist as a medicine to correct some malfunctioning body process?

If we had the instincts that animals have, we'd know the difference. 'Food' is something chosen to be eaten when 'well', and 'medicine' is something chosen to be eaten when 'sick'. The demarcation line is not so clear with humans. Our intellectual choices often ignore or override our long-neglected instincts. Children perhaps fare better, if only we would learn by their instinctive avoidance of a food, then great clamour for it, at an 'inconvenient' time for us perhaps. Your dog or cat knows when it's time to eat meat and when it's absolutely essential to eat only grass. The human thymus gland and pineal gland lag a long way behind. Too often we wait for some other authority to pronounce us 'sick' or 'well' and far too often we ignore our craving for a particular fruit, vegetable, herb tea or juice. That's when it's 'medicine' and may be required urgently. Until we all recognise our true instincts again, the herbalist continues to be necessary to prescribe, with an *objective* diagnosis, what you need in chemistry — and in physics — to put you back in harmony with yourself and the world around you.

Always get this objective view *first*. With the best will in the world, you can't step aside from yourself and see yourself. Someone else needs to do this part for you initially. Sure, after a while you can not only learn to be more aware of *you* and your particular chemical and physical patterns, but you can turn up the volume on your 'still small voice' and listen to it more clearly.

There is always a friendly neighbour or a family member with a story of what 'worked' for them in improving their health. While such advice is well-meaning, sometimes over-enthusiastic and convincing, it must always be carefully edited by the listener. Are you exactly the same as your friendly adviser? Is your sniffle or cough from the same causes? Are your previous illnesses the same too? Are you even the same age, the same sex and the same weight? If not, what works for them may not be applicable to you. Self-diagnosis is inaccurate enough; friends' and neighbours' diagnoses are well-meaning but perhaps not applicable; family members' diagnoses can be disastrous! Too often a mother, husband, grandparent or child gives you 'health' advice which will make *their* life easier in being around *you*; it's seldom an impartial or objective view! As I've exhorted you previously, take the step first of a consultation with a professionally trained herbalist who has no axe to grind, who doesn't have to live with you and who has no *personal* connection with your daily life. You'll get a fairer and more accurate assessment this way.

You'll also save money and time. Far too many converts to simpler and more natural ways of health maintenance and home treatment of illnesses read a book, diagnose themselves, trot off to their health store and become a captive customer. 'Try this, it's great stuff'; 'You need to take this with that and five of the green and two of the red'; 'Rub this on and sniff this up.' You wonder whether you've left a too-complex, too pill-ridden medical regime for an even more complex herbal and naturopathic one. I have a continuing professional disagreement with over-the-counter diagnoses given in a couple of minutes in a busy shop. Such 'help' can be no help at all! How can the sales assistant know your past medical history, your living circumstances, your job stresses, emotions, and even your ancestry? How can such advice be accurate enough to be effective? Even worse, you may be so carried away with the anticipated improvement that you buy a bundle of teas, pills, potions and creams, blowing your budget for the entire week. Your conclusion? 'Natural medicine is too expensive for me!'

The herbalist's relationship with a health store should be that of a doctor with a pharmacy. Get your diagnosis done *first*. Then you can buy what is advised, save all that experimentation, and also save money! Do-it-yourself health is fine *after* you have had the initial help and evaluation from your professional herbalist, part of whose function should be to educate you about yourself, so that any *later* self-help can be effective and accurate.

There are three different ways to think of illness removal:

1   Wait until you get sick, see your herbalist, take your mixture, and recover.

2   *Don't* wait until you get sick; see your herbalist for a general consultation and evaluation of the illness history of your whole life, your circumstances, emotions, environmental factors, etc., and seek removal of the *causes* and the *results* of previous patterns of illness.

3   Have an *educational* consultation which can establish for you what you need, and what you *don't* need in teas, tablets, lotions and potions.

In a good professional visit, some aspects of all three above should be explored together. Most people tend to wait until symptoms of illness appear before they think correctively. When they attend for their first herbalist's visit, some of these symptoms may be improving already (especially if they've had to wait a week or two for an appointment). 'Getting better' is quite a slow business for bodies. Most people feel 'well' again long before the process of the illness has been completely overcome and removed permanently. Herbal medication is excellent for cleaning up and cleaning out. Many of the plants used are concerned with the removal of waste products of illness and of day-to-day cell-metabolism. *Completion* of any past or present illness-process is a prime aim.

2   *Fresh, dried, powdered or extracted?*

Fresh

I am sometimes at odds with other streams of herbal thinking when a decision must be made by the practitioner on the *form* of the plant-material to be prescribed. We must here blend theory not only with excellent pharmacognosy knowledge, but with commonsense. Ideally, and theoretically, the *fresh* plant, straight from the garden or the roadside or field, would seem to have the most effective and pure applicability to human health. Theoretically, too, such a plant would be unspoiled by any processing, and intact in its contents.

Many medicinal plants *are* best this way, amongst them most of the culinary herbs. The aromatic oils and oleoresins are actively present, and any water-soluble vitamin loss is minimised. It *sounds* fine.

In practice, there are pitfalls. There is a class of substances called alkaloids which are found to a greater or lesser degree in most medicinal plants. It is these alkaloids which orthodox pharmacy decided to call the 'active principles' of each plant, and in the latter part of the last century these alkaloids began to be chemically isolated and extracted from medicinal plants. Once they were chemically identified, it became possible to synthesise the substance in the laboratory and manufacture this chemical identity far more cheaply than it could be extracted from plant sources. Modern pharmacy had begun: phytopharmacy (the chemistry of whole real plant parts) began to decline. As I've mentioned earlier, other chemical identities in the plants were discarded altogether as not being involved in any beneficial effectiveness at all — an astonishing conclusion! These alkaloids, as the name implies, are alkaline nitrogenous compounds, and because of this are capable of producing quite severe new body reactions of a damaging kind if over-used. I'm sure you know some of them by name already. There's heroin, morphine and codeine, from the opium poppy; all able to cause severely discomforting symptoms, even death, if over-used. There's atropine from Belladonna (Deadly Nightshade); there's reserpine from Snakeroot (*Rauwolfia serpentina*) and ephedrine from Ephedra (*Ephedra chinensis*). There's a whole host of others. Extracting these alkaloids or making them synthetically breaks one of the first rules of nature: nothing in nature works alone. There is a measurably different effect in a human body between the use of an alkaloid alone and that of the whole plant in which the alkaloid is one part only.

In *fresh* plants, these alkaloids can be very lively indeed! It is a principle of botany, as well as herbal medicine, that the drying of the plant-portion used attenuates the alkaloid activity, weakening it further the longer the drying proceeds. In this way, some plants which otherwise would be far too active to use at all become 'tame' and safe. I am alarmed at a recent trend to produce 'fresh plant tinctures' almost as another 'breakthrough', this time in natural medicine. Such tinctures will be, what's more worrying, *differently* active in humans from the long-established uses of tinctures made from the dried plant material. It takes a lot of reading, ancient and modern, to see who's right. I'll stick to the old way every time! It's been long established, by trial and error, which plants are best and safe when fresh, and which need some of the bounce taken out of them by drying. With each herb in this book this point will be clearly identified.

Dried

So 'fresh' may not always be the way. The next simple process is to dry the plant, not only to ameliorate its stirring effect, but also to bridge another of nature's provisions so that we sick humans can have help available all year round. Fresh herbs are only available in their season of growth. Since the world began, Man has always preserved food for later out-of-season use by drying it. Bundles of herbs were tied to the rafters, with the strings of onions, the smoked hams and the dried fish. This is still the best way to dry herbs today; small bunches hung upside down near the rafters, under an overhanging veranda or terrace, in cool air where *no sun* reaches to leach out the aromatic oils and evaporative contents. I have discussed more of this in my first book, *The Book of Herbs* (1972), so my concern here is more with commercial drying before making tinctures and extracts for professional use.

Some plants like Cascara (*Cascara sagrada*) need four years of drying. The bark of this South American tree is laid out, skin down, so the warm air can gradually tame the virulent chemistry found in the fresh bark. Valerian root (*Valeriana officianalis*) needs twelve months of drying. Many other plants need just a week or two. The commercial preparation and manufacture of herbal tinctures and extracts is not only handed down often in a family firm or from parent-phytopharmacist to child-chemist, but also from the experience of herbalist to herbalist down the centuries. To get it all accurately and safely, all patients' comments must be listened to, as well; all adverse effects noted as well as all benefits.

Dried plant materials come to specialist phytopharmacist manufacturers from all over the world at their various seasons. Every manufacturer has their own developed method of percolation, titration, filtering and diluting, extracting and standardising, and these secrets are guarded as jealously as are the formulas for Coca-cola, Southern Comfort whiskey, and Chanel No. 5! No one, but no one, easily gives up their methods for achieving better 'fresh' odour, better preservation and keeping qualities, and a better shelf-life and colour. However, most manufacturers make and standardise to the BPC (British Pharmacopoea in this country) requirements. These are also rule-of-thumb and traditional in origin. Some plants are standardised at one-to-five dilution, others at one-to-eight or even one-to-twelve. Mostly, the dilution reflects their relative liveliness when introduced into a human body. Such rule-of-thumb standards didn't impress the stern new mistress, science, at all, especially when the plants themselves were not all 'standard' to begin with! Worse yet, they were not sterile à la Pasteur! The final indignity was that they were not always available! A bad season for Sage, or a drought in Turkey, or a hailstorm in Yugoslavia, and there went a whole year's supply of raw materials. Science tut-tutted, and looked elsewhere for medication. Herbs were *out*!

But the dedicated phytopharmacist kept going; using the old processes, the patience, the careful selection, the worldwide buying in season, and the concentrations appropriate to each batch of plants delivered. It certainly is inexact and non-standardisable by today's criteria — but so are people. Infinitely variable plant medicines and uniquely different humans take some cross-matching!

This is why the *arts* of the herbalist are so essential in training. The 'feel' for which plant is appropriate to which person is something that cannot easily be taught. I've tried to do with pictures what is difficult to do with words alone, and introduce an appropriate 'person-picture' with each herb. This way, the student's observation can be trained and diagnostic puzzles minimised. There are thousands and thousands of herbs to choose from in treatment. Any means of narrowing down the choices is useful.

Tinctures and extracts

Our discussion on dried herbs has developed already into the next step; in the form of fluids for introduction into the body. Again, the specific rules vary widely, but the general rule is as below.

Tinctures

The oldest form of adding dried food or plant material to a fluid is via alcohol of some kind. Who knows how ancient Man and early physicians first decided to add other plants to grape-wines and other naturally fermented liquids? Perhaps it was for flavour only, at first; then a perceived health improvement which followed may have been repeated in others who used the same plant. In any event, the first herbal medicines were taken in an *alcohol* base. Steeped in wine, or later in distilled 'spirits of wine' (or brandy), the dried plant material remained effective not only that week or that month, but that year, and even years later. Alcohols were found to 'freeze' natural decay processes otherwise inevitable in even the most carefully dried materials. Now it was possible to keep the 'goodness' of the original plant for years, and far away from its country of original growth.

The methods of passing alcohols through a tightly packed vessel of small-cut and pulverised plant material came later. In Dr Albert Vogel's original clinic at Teufen in Switzerland I saw his first tall glass cylinders, still in active use, and watched the drip, drip, drip of the alcohol through the plant material; over and over and over again, until all that was left was the white skeleton of the plant with all its physical and chemical properties transferred now to the fluid, ready for final filtering and bottling. 'Mother'-tinctures are made this way, then diluted with water, more alcohol, sometimes even a little glycerine, to the appropriate BP standard.

Of course, the only chemistry extracted this way is the range of compounds in the plant which will come into solution with alcohol. Many plant-substances will only extract into water. The phyto-pharmacist must decide here too. Does he or she want only some compounds and not others? Or are all the ingredients required? Water may be mixed with the alcohol in some tincture-making. It's much more likely, however, that an *extract*, a slightly different means of processing, will use this water-alcohol mixture method.

I tell my students each year a simple rule to decide whether to use a tincture or an extract ingredient in a compound mixture for a patient. In general, alcoholic tinctures are more rapidly absorbed, more finely distributed quickly, and more deeply penetrating in their action. They are best for *chronic patterns of illness* or inter-mittent return of the same illness-patterns and symptoms. They are best used when the patient's story goes like this: 'I've had my usual bronchitis back again recently, and I can't seem to get rid of its remains', or 'I've got more aches and pains in this ankle I injured years ago; they come back every so often when I get over-tired or worried', etc., etc. The patient's story is of a *weakness* left unresolved and incompletely repaired. (We'll see shortly how an *extract* is used under different circumstances altogether.)

Tinctures have a long shelf-life compared to that of extracts. Tinctures can, and should, show improvements on tiny doses com-pared with extracts. 'Ten drops three times daily in a little water an hour after a meal' is a commonly used dose for tinctures; extracts may need 15–30 drops every few hours, as described now.

Extracts

Although theoretically a tincture can be described as 'extracted' from the plant, the commonly used term 'herbal extract' has a different and distinct meaning of its own.

Extracts can be made under reduced pressure in a vacuum extractor: they are mainly water-extracted after previous macera-tion and standing in either BP alcohol or alcohol and water. Some of this extraction process may involve heat; some of it may involve pressure-rolling to squeeze out juices from the fresh plant or to pulverise the dried plant before further processing of both the juice and the squashed plant pulp. Spagyric extracts go one step further; after all the active chemistry is transferred to the fluid passing repeatedly through the plant material, the plant skeleton is dried, burned, and the ash returned to the final liquid. This last method extracts virtually everything from the plant, even heavy minerals and metallic compounds, so you get the lot. It's the way the 'alchemists', so-called, extracted 'all-chyme' — *all* the chemistry of the original plant — to recover the trace of gold or silver they hoped to find in the crucible. It's startling to find that today's newer gas chromatographs which can measure plant contents prove that there are in fact minute traces of precious metals in them. It's even more surprising to find that sea-water, even sea-weeds, can be made to give up noble metals under specific kinds of extraction processes. How astonishingly foresightful was Paracelsus, the father of 'alchemic' extraction.

Boiling in water is another method of 'extraction' of various plant contents, bearing in mind that much of the chemistry is changed by this process. There is loss in steam, in heat changes, and in the fragile Vitamin contents, so obviously this is not a recommended *medicinal* extraction process where contents are required intact.

Extracts contain much more fibrous material, more mucillage and more chlorophyll, more enzymes, and many more reasons for going 'off' in storage. The recommended shelf-life of a herbal extract is no longer than twelve months. Each time the bottle is opened and air enters, shelf-life is marginally reduced. It's a well-made lively extract that grows a little mould, or crust, around the bottle's stopper. In effect, it's still 'alive'.

Extracts are prescribed when symptoms of illness are present right then and there. When you're actually sneezing, coughing and blowing; when the arthritis is actively painful; when the migraine is present; when the sprained ankle is a lovely purplish-green colour. The much more rapid results of extracts can be a relief to patient and practitioner alike! More concentrated in many ways than tinctures, extracts are also given in larger doses and probably more frequently, especially initially. Perhaps the best way to describe the difference *in activity* between extracts and tinctures is that the tinctures change slower, older and deeper illness patterns; extracts change present symptoms, new symptoms which have not occurred before and which one hopes will most likely not occur again. If you break a leg, it's extracts you need; if a broken leg ten years ago has left you with intermittent arthritic pains ever since, tinctures are more applicable.

I am very much in favour of the commercially prepared tinctures and extracts over and above those a herbalist can himself or herself prepare after professional training. Many herbalists disagree with me, but in Australia we have great difficulty in walking out into the paddocks or the waste-lands, even into our own gardens, to find medicinal plants *where they grow naturally*. In Europe, in Asia, in India, in Sri Lanka, and in North and South America the local people do have access to locally grown and traditionally used plants. Ours is the only country in the world where the traditional plant-medicines of the Aborigines are part of their religion and have always demanded secrecy in their use. The small amount of local knowledge that's filtered down to us over more recent years is frustratingly incomplete in the 'how much?', 'when?', and 'for what illness?' departments. Even when any useful piece of real information filters through, it may not work on Europeans, Mediterraneans, even Asians, in the same way, or with the same effect in illness, as it does with Aborigines. A herbalist's life is sometimes *not* a happy one! It's sadly true that dandelions growing in Scotland, or Greece, differ greatly in their contents from those growing near human habitations in Sydney or Adelaide. Plantain in a Sydney North Shore rock-path really doesn't do what European plantain does for coughs, chest colds, and respiratory congestion. My answer is the commercially-prepared herbs, processed *here* but gathered from the habitats in which their pharmacological activities are well proven. After all, all of us are 'transplanted' to Australia too in the beginning, except those Aborigines whose tribal secrets of the indigenous flora used as medicine may be lost to us.

Extracts and tinctures may be mixed together in an individual prescription to correct some present, and some longer term, symptoms together. (See Prescribing, pages 313–14.)

Infusions and decoctions

Aren't they romantic, these mediaeval terms? Can't you see the Lady Guinevere sipping a decoction of lime-flowers? Or the Virgin Queen with her infusion of elderberries and cowslips? In practical terms, there are important differences between a tea, an infusion and a decoction.

A **tea** is made by pouring just-off-the-boil water onto dried or fresh plant materials, letting this steep for a few minutes, then straining the fluid before drinking it. A tea can be made from any part of the plant, but is more usually prepared from the flowers, buds and leaves. It is drunk hot or cold.

An **infusion** is a super-tea, extracting slightly more of some substances but less of others. Boiling water is poured over the herbs (fresh or dried) in a heating vessel, and this mixture is simmered for a few minutes then let stand, with the herbs still in it, for a further 30 minutes, then strained. Infusions can be drunk lukewarm or cold, and can be stored in a covered jar in the refrigerator for a few days, so you can make more than you need immediately. They are not much used today, but can be made from all the green parts of the plant, the flowers and sometimes the berries.

A **decoction** is made from tougher parts of the plants; from roots, bark, rhizomes, etc., and from hard seeds or woody parts. Because of this, decoctions take longer to make. Cold water is poured over the cut or macerated plant material which is then simmered over heat for 30 minutes or more. Not a good method to retain vitamins! But the heavier minerals, like iron and copper, extract well.

The old 'wineglassful' dose applied here, and these were often taken before bedtime. They, like infusions, are not much used today.

All three classifications are prepared using similar related quantities; a 'handful' of the fresh herb, or a rounded teaspoonful of the dried herbal material, to one cup of water — far from exact or scientific! Anyone who wants measured milligram doses, don't become a herbalist! Every single patient will be given individually different amounts, too. Unless you trust your own judgement, and it gives you proof over and over of accurate assessment, perhaps you'd be more comfortable as a computer operator!

Infinitely variable is the challenge of herbal-medicine manufacture and use. You *need* to learn it from Grandma as well as from study courses or books, because it takes the combined experience and verification of more than one lifetime before you get it right. Even then, surprises are common. It's a continuous all-day and half the night learning process.

Ointments and oils

*S*alves and liniments; perfumed sachets, pomanders and potpourri: every herbal giftshop knows the appeal of wonderful odours and soft textures. Fragrant soaps and scented notepaper; Mary Poppins please park here! Don't overlook the medicinal value of appeal to the senses! As well as being pampered and soothed, you'll also be receiving tiny doses of medicinal substances.

Ointments take the chemistry of the plant in through the skin, an excellent organ of absorption which bypasses the digestive tract. Oils go one better. The delicious perfumes of aromatic plants penetrate even the most stubborn human resistance to treatment. You'd be astounded how many people don't take any needed medication or undertake any herbal medicine programme — *in case they get better*! Sometimes the brain decides the body should remain 'sick' as a polite and acceptable way of legitimately avoiding some of life's challenges and responsibilities. Brains can be dodgy dictators to the body! The human will can override almost anything in the universe — except perfumes. Chanel, and all her sisters since time began, knew a thing or two about overcoming (or overriding) sexual or emotional blocks holding back a hesitant lover.

Medically, oils can be used when there's a steadfast refusal to 'take anything' by mouth. Even the most stubborn migraine can weaken in a warm bath with a few drops of Lavender oil added: the most tense aching muscle will give way and relax a little, lessening the pain, if Rosemary oil is rubbed in gently. Skin and nose work together here: rubbing-on and sniffing-in can be powerful herbal medicine indeed! Use the oils described later in the Materia Medica section as a way of bypassing those self-damaging refusals some folk insist on. The olfactory bulb high in the nasal septum carries any aroma straight to the brain itself. The hypothalamus translates the tiny molecules of the plant into nerve-signals which go back almost instantaneously to the whole body. Massage with appropriate oils, and aromatherapy, are powerful parts of herbal medicine practice.

Tablets, pills and capsules

Tablets are, classically, compressed dried plant materials, with a lactose base to aid the absorption of the herbal material in the stomach and small intestines. Tablets are not usually coated, and they tend to break down faster in storage than pills do, especially after the sealed container is opened for each dose.

Tablet doses are different from extracts and tinctures as they retain the properties of the simple dried plant materials they're made from. The leaves, roots, bark, etc., are dried, then pulverised and mixed with the lactose filler, then compressed into shape. Many people believe the lactose is to 'make up the weight', or dilute, or adulterate, the plant material in some way, and feel they've been robbed. Not so. The amount of lactose is necessary for the tablet to be large enough for you to handle and to take. Otherwise some tablets would be pinhead size! Quite small amounts of dried plant material will give a satisfactory therapeutic change.

Pills are preferred by manufacturers when the plant materials are either sticky, strongly-smelling or unpalatable in taste. The previous tablet-form is coated with some relatively impervious material so that contents are better preserved intact. A natural shellac 'varnish' was traditionally used, or a gum or resin from various trees; today, protein-coating makes the former difference between tablets and pills harder to define. Protein-coating of various types can turn a tablet into a pill quite easily. Now we also have 'slow-release' tablets — or are they pills? — where the covering layer breaks down gradually as it passes various digestive system landmarks. I often wonder how such slow-release tablets are 'timed' to suit all digestive tracts! I have seen patients with irises with stomach-zones so hyper-acid they would digest rusty iron and old razor blades in an hour, almost. Protein of any kind would be quickly broken down and all tablet contents released in the first stages of digestion. On the other hand, a *hypo*-active stomach would pass a relatively intact tablet through to the intestines. If this individual human-difference can be taken into account in manufacture, I would be happier.

Capsules

Don't despise *all* technological change! Sometimes we can work *with* nature to use her rules even more effectively for today's living styles. Since the gelatin-capsule is made by a machine, I can only applaud this excellent example of nature and Man working *together* for mutual conservation of resources in a stable form. Dried plant material can be well protected, kept stable, and delivered into the appropriate digestive area by this means. Gelatin is a naturally occurring substance in the 'gristle' and sinews of animals and will melt well at body-heat, removing the worries about under- or over-active stomachs. Capsules can be filled with the dried powdered plants, or with oils or sticky substances. They should not be stored in high-heat areas, nor on a sunny window-sill, but in a cool cupboard away from the stove, and capsules will not oxidise or discolour.

I like this form of medication for travellers, and for city dwellers in units with little or no garden space and relatively small kitchens and bathrooms. Too many larger herb-tea packets, and your storage-space bulges! Capsules take relatively little room in their containers, and will stack well.

Dried plant material, often subject to deterioration if opened and stored too long, can be protected well against contamination from air, airborne bacteria, moulds, etc., and insect depredations, in capsules.

Teas

Perhaps the best way to begin your acquaintance with the plant world is via a herb tea. 'I don't like them,' some people say. 'They are dangerous,' say others. I then walk firmly towards them and remove from their hands the cups of tea or coffee they are drinking!

'Horrible stuff!' I agree. 'Dangerous when over-used,' I continue. They stare at me, wondering what I'm on about now. 'Oh no,' they say as they retrieve their drinks, '*these* are all right; we're *used to* these.' Therein lies the answer. Humans tend to distrust mightily what they personally are not used to.

If you were a Peruvian, you'd be 'used to' *maté* tea as your everyday drink. If French, you would have known the soothing taste and odour of Chamomile since you were first teething as a child. If you were German, *Hagenbuten tee* (Rosehips tea) would be a regular tipple. We've learned to *eat* Italian pizzas, Greek honey cakes, Chinese pork and Lebanese houmus and tabouli, Japanese raw fish, and Indonesian curries. We've swallowed sake, French champagne, and Rheinwein; we've even tried soy milk! Surely we could be more accepting, and more adventurous. But when it comes to *teas* made from dried plant material, too many of us refuse uncomfortably. I often wonder why.

Of course, there are teas and *teas*. Some can taste quite foul, like your first sip of Valerian or Sassafras tea, but there are so many that taste terrific that a range of them provides many *different* tastes through the day. You may need advice at first (see *The Herb Tea Book*, [Pythagorean Press and Keats, USA]).

Start with the more pleasant-tasting ones, especially if you're trying to convert your household. Begin with Peppermint, say, or Spearmint. Almost everyone has already had experience of this flavour, and acceptance is easier. Rosehip tea with a slice of lemon and a pinch of ginger could be next. Jasmine could slide in unobtrusively at the Chinese restaurant on Saturday night, and apple-tea could be a good weekend change drunk icy-cold with a sprig of mint in the glass. I always enjoy the hot sweet teas of Lemon Balm in Egypt or Jordan, but I also enjoy the new blended American herb teas available in convenient tea-bags for even the most rushed of office-workers.

There are all sorts of individual cups, pots and infusers to choose from now, and these make the sampling of different herb-teas an aesthetic pleasure in their preparation. There are French infuser-mugs with lids which double as stands for the wet filter before drinking. There are small and large teapots with built-in strainers so you won't get a mouthful of woody stems or sappy leaves in your first mouthful. There are sachets and bags and even solid cubes of concentrated 'instant' teas. Recognise, though, that it's best to buy any dried herb teas from reputable manufacturers who put their names and addresses on the packet or jar. Be very wary if buying from local weekend markets in unmarked packets. Even with the best intentions, anyone new to the plant world may mis-identify the original plant, or may even — Heaven preserve us — adulterate one plant with another one until you're not quite sure what you're drinking. Yet another headline 'Dangerous herb' may hit the Sunday papers!

The packing of herb teas is most important. Never buy them in *plastic* bags! Cellophane, a more natural cellulose product, suits dried herbs really well; glass, of course, is best of all because it's chemically inert and won't react in any way with the contents. Glass containers can also be re-sealed, even kept in the refrigerator. If you *must* buy herbs in plastic or any other synthetic material, transfer them to glass jars straight after opening.

Herb teas can be the beginning of 'health from the kitchen' again. What all our grandmothers knew about health maintenance in the home may need to be resurrected as government health budgets begin to rival defence budgets in size. Surely it's time for commonsense health measures to be promoted again! They're well-known substances involved, tried and tested by time and experience. Do we really need another three-million-dollar research fund to have 'science' tell us that Rosehips tea perks us up, and Chamomile relaxes mind and body? Surely human experience is worth more than what those poor suffering laboratory rats must endure, especially when their *natural* diet has never included herb teas!

Other ways

Nature does not use hypodermic syringes! These are man-made, and have absolutely no relationship to herbal medicine. We don't give garlic intravenously, nor an intra-muscular shot of Valerian to relax lumbago or tennis elbow. All herbal medicine is *absorbed* in one way or another; through the skin, the digestive tract, the nose, and the other senses. Is it possible that by just looking at and handling the plants we get a message from them which will improve our well-being in some way? Every gardener will tell you of an 'uplift' of some kind after touching the hibiscus flower, smelling the roses at dusk, seeing the colouring hyacinth spikes long before spring has begun to open the other flowers. Even the mouth-watering crunch into fresh beans straight from the vine, or a golden orange eaten from one's own tree, skin and all, sends a message, subtle but strong, of *renewal* of some kind. Admiration at the beauty, and at the continuing cycle of seed, plant, flower, fruit, reassures us in some way of the continuum of life. It is certain that without plants Man could no longer inhabit this planet.

What happened to all those 'plant-a-tree' campaigns? They were left to nature, after their original start, and now look at how green our *cities* are becoming! When I fly in over Sydney after some overseas visit, I can scarcely see the red roofs for the *green* that's grown up to cover and shade them. I know of no other resource that pays such great dividends with little or no cash outlay and almost no maintenance. It's a *free* resource, the plant world.

Medicinal plants are not only free, but also embarrassingly abundant. As so many of them could be classed amongst common 'weeds' they don't even need the minimum care of planting and watering — let alone fertilising! And I've never heard of anyone buying dandelions from their nursery, so there's not even an initial cash outlay. Give it serious thought when looking with new eyes at the unweeded garden and the waste-ground. Amongst the tangle of weeds may be the remedy for your aching back, your irritable colon, or your underfunctioning left kidney.

Plant a herb garden. Don't think all medicinal herbs begin and end with Thyme, Sage and Marjoram. Be adventurous — and save money! It might not be too many years before those health mega-budgets begin to dwindle, and we spend less living time learning how to 'adjust' our lives to accommodate an illness, and more time actually *living*. A healthy human gets things done, and *enjoys* doing them. There is intense personal satisfaction in achievement, in physical strength used to the full, in taking Mankind *forward*. Right now, too many of us spend more and more of our energy just running furiously on the spot to avoid slipping backwards!

Books to read

In the 1980s there are too many instant 'experts'. No sooner has someone finished a weekend course in something than there they are teaching; within a few months they've written a book telling everyone else how to do it!

There are herb books and herb books! There are those publishers who commission professional collators to 'do a herb book', and after some time in a reference library, such a task is not hard. Unfortunately, those excellent collators of information may have little or no knowledge of the subject matter. They may also have too little experience to judge which reference book is reliable and which has been put together by yet another collator. It's not hard to achieve garbled nonsense in any subject when one collator works from too many other second- or third-hand sources. At best, the information will be bland and general; at worst it can be wrong! The first requirement in choosing a herb book is to find one written by a long-term professional practising herbalist. These are not many. There are all too many of the other kind.

Look at the title page for the qualifications of the author. Check the back cover for autobiographical information. Scrutinise your mentor's record of experience. See if the author really should be believed and his or her advice closely followed.

When there tend to be more pictures than text, I begin to worry. Full-colour photographs can lend visual authenticity to a modicum of information. Watch out too for the 'quickies' — 'All you ever wanted to know about Herbs' — in thirty-six pages!

Potentially even more of a problem are those specific-illness books, 'Herbs for Asthma', 'Herbs for Migraines', etc. These can convince you that it's not only easy but absolutely safe, to use Lobelia or Hawthorn, and your symptoms will quickly disappear. In this book, I have deliberately avoided the 'herbs for named disease' absolutes, and chosen the professional herbalist's way of 'herbs for the *person*'. It is potentially *un*-safe to take any advised herbal mixture in such a book for a disease as it assumes you have only this disease and no other. It also assumes that you have diagnosed yourself accurately in the first place. Many symptoms of 'indigestion' don't respond to indigestion mixtures because they are early heart symptoms, or pancreatic tumours, or even anxiety pains: and sadly yet another patient may say, 'Herbal medicine doesn't work.'

But it's difficult to write a herbal medicine book *without* advising on specific illnesses. Many writers, even practising herbalists, overcome this problem by giving only *general* information. 'Feverfew is used for migraines' you read. Yes, but how? Do you rub it on the forehead, swallow the flowers, or perhaps the leaves, or even the seeds? Do you do any or all of these procedures before, during or after the migraine, or do you take it three times a day in water for three months, or in the salad-bowl once a week? Such general information is often deliberately given, and for very good reason. Without a full case history of each patient, the careful experienced herbalist is unwilling to give a *partial* remedy only on a few specific facts. Holistic medicine must be practised always. Consider *all* the facts of each case before prescribing the mixture. As a lay person reading this book, there are facts you won't be told, and diseases with only *part* of their relevant treatments discussed. This is done for your safety. It's still *essential* to have the objective diagnosis done first by a practitioner trained in anatomy and physiology, in biochemistry, in emotional counselling and differential recognition of mind-body circumstances; in short, *self-diagnosis can be a health hazard*.

Be wary also of herb books that *insist* the author has the 'only' way to cure some illness or attempt a recovery pattern. Some fixers of sick people fall heavily into the ego-trap. They *like* to feel a little above their patients: sometimes they blend an almost religious fervour with a 'message' of some kind which is to save mankind as well as remove headaches. It is not coincidental that many of the most fervent herbalists, whose names have lasted down the centuries, were also clerics. William Turner, one of the earliest writers (*The Grete Herball* — 1526), was often actually in prison, let alone in disfavour, with Elizabeth I. The Queen's religious battles with Scottish Mary saw Turner on a dizzying ride of grace and favour, only to slump into ignominy when he coached his students — and his congregation! — in how to knock Bishops' caps from their heads in the street!

Religion claimed many herbal 'cures' via its monks and its monastery gardens. Abbés and Fathers abound in herbal literature. In Egyptian papyri the physician was recorded as a mixture of priest, sage, botanist and astronomer — with the emphasis first on 'priest'. Always there has been the religious impact of illnesses.

Your 'sins' were catching up with you! This intermingling has harmed not only the practical ordinary use of plants in sickness and in health, but has also kept the practice of herbal medicine a quasi-religious one, even today, in the minds of many authors. Even the orthodox and highly regarded Harley Street doctor and researcher, Dr Edward Bach, gave his own philosophy of the flower remedies and their uses a highly religious, almost divine, framework in his book *Heal Thyself*. Many would-be users of plant medicines feel that in some way they deny their own religious faith by consulting a herbalist who claims to work with God in a slightly different context. For this reason alone, many feel *guilty* about a herbalist's medicines. I suggest that you leave the religious-dogma connotations out of such herbal books you read, and look at the other aspect of real religion depicted therein — nature. Not until recent years have we observed, recorded and, most importantly, integrated together the dependent interlocking systems of that new true science, ecology. Once you glimpse how many systems of energy interlock, resonate, ebb and flow, balance and thrust, you will wonder no longer at the divine control of nature. *Any* religion can feel comfortable today with plants used as energy-sources to rebalance human cellular changes in the processes we call 'disease'.

There are also available textbooks of pharmacognosy that ignore altogether any integrated natural ecological relevance of a medicinal plant, and pull it apart cell by cell, physically and chemically, reducing it to a skeletonised chemical equation only. There is the plant displayed with its intestines laid out all over microscope slides, and out comes a 'scientific' estimate of its potential uses to Man. This is like cremating dear old Mrs Bloggs, putting her ashes in an urn, and labelling it only with its calcium, phosphorus, magnesium, etc., contents. You'd have no idea at all of the human qualities of Mrs Bloggs. Was she short, round, kind and funny, or was she tall, emaciated, crochety and depressed? Did she like the cold weather, or prefer summer? Did she love her family? Did she even have one? Was she ever loved in return? What was her job? How long did she live? What did she die from? You see how difficult it can be to extract *all* of the story of life from chemistry alone!

The books of the above kind are unfortunately the ones pharmacy and orthodox medicine use for their reference bibles: 'It's no use arguing. Comfrey has dangerous levels of pyrrolizadine alkaloids in it so it must kill people by changed liver-function.' 'What about all those who've consumed large amounts over a lifetime and whose livers are in perfect running order?', my reply continues to infuriate them, 'What about Comfrey grown on a compost-heap as opposed to Comfrey grown in the dry leached-out sandstone of Sydney's magnesium-depleted soils?' I continue. 'What about the young leaves versus the older leaves? What about it growing with a northerly hot aspect against a brick wall, or in a shady cool corner under a tree?' The battle is a fierce one, and still goes on. Chemical evaluation tells us much *chemically*; humans need a wider dimension, and so do plants, to appreciate fully the personality and life experiences of Mrs Bloggs or the reasons why *some* Comfrey plants cause *some* humans to react in one way and some in an opposite or entirely different way. Chemistry is, to me, even more unrelated to the *quality* of life and human experience than is mathematics. It can certainly provide for us *tools* of technology, but as a gauge for measuring living qualities and reactions of Man, animal and plant, its equations tell us little.

It begins to appear that our herbal medicine reading is to be severely restrictive! This is not my intention at all. 'Selective' would be a better description. Knowing what to discard from your reading is perhaps even more important than deciding what to believe and implement. A good rule to follow is to read *many* different herbal books first before following any of the advice given. When the same piece of information occurs over and over again, through many countries and cultures, ancient and modern, then that piece of 'truth' may well claim to be so.

The best herbal-medicine books, in my opinion, blend yesterday and today, and give clear *warnings* as well as laudatory superlatives. Like humans, plants can also fall from grace! What was fashionable and plant-of-the-month in Georgian England may not be relevant to a vegetarian single parent in northern New South Wales today. Plants enjoy periods of fashion and acclaim, and then depart, like captains and kings, from contemporary Herbals. New plants move from common usage in one culture to another where their impact can be not only different but hugely better or horrendously worse. South America is at the moment a source of plant material which may never have appeared in early European or Arabic, or Chinese or Indian Herbals. The occupation 'herbalist' requires constant reading in bed! It's about the only time a busy practice gives you to catch up on the billions of plants worldwide, and their possible interaction with humans.

I'm often asked 'How did they find out in the beginning what all the plants were useful for?' By trial and error, and by observation and recording, *any* human can learn much about the plant world. Any gardener can tell you how instincts become sharpened by use: any farmer, or sailor, watching the clouds and the wind can work with nature instinctively. But don't go out thinking beautiful thoughts, and eat a pretty weed on the footpath to see what it does for you! *All* the great herbalists of the past were men and women who spent lifetimes studying before they ventured to tell others, to experiment, and to come to conclusions. Many of these 'conclusions' were, in today's terms, *wrong*. People died quickly from Digitalis prescribed for a quinsy of the throat! Others dropped like stones from Ergot-contaminated Rye, and from Black Hellebore and Henbane.

> THERE IS ONLY ONE WAY TO LEARN HERBAL MEDICINE PRACTICE, AND THAT IS THROUGH PROFESSIONAL TRAINING WITH THOSE EXPERI-ENCED IN TRADITIONAL PLANT KNOWLEDGE.

Don't be a do-it-yourself experimenter unless you are prepared by training in the subject first. The human ego can be arrogant and wilful and, even as I write this, I know that some of my readers will go against the above advice. I hereby disclaim all responsibility for whatever hard lessons the plant world teaches you. I know that after thirty years in it, there are for me surprises still — good *and* bad — every day.

> CAUTION is essential.

Back to our recommended books, for a last summary:

- Is the author a practising herbalist? If so, for how long?
- Does the book give *specific* information enabling you to use plants safely; or is it a broad general-interest ramble that tells you little of actual practical kind?
- Is the book personally bigoted with other beliefs of the author, adding a particular dogma or 'Way' to the herbal information?
- Is it written from personal experience, or just collated from the experience of others? (Or is it perhaps a collation from other collations?)

3 *Plant ingredients*

Although I've stated that chemistry is not all, there are still some chemical terms to learn in order to put parameters around the types of reactions we can expect to find from certain herbs. Our instincts, visual impressions and feelings may alter this chemical framework, and should put flesh and personality over the physical and chemical skeleton as we gain experience.

We can treat the plant purely as a mass of water and *elements* (Ca, H, Si, etc.), or we can list certain *chemical compounds* found in the combined state already (e.g. $CaCl$, $MgSO_4$, etc.). We can further label compounds into *chemical* and *physical classes* of substance (e.g. alkaloids, glycosides, etc., and oleo-resins, fats, starches, etc.). We can then call all of the individual plants by *reaction*-names, (e.g., vulnerary, purgative, laxative, etc.). There is, right at the beginning, much discipline to be learned, and accuracy in identifying by quantity and quality. We'll start with the elements.

4 *Elements and compounds*

'High in calcium', 'low in sodium', 'potassium-rich', 'lacking copper balance': the elements are named in their free state, not in their actual combinations with each other. It's necessary to learn a little basic physiology to appreciate this method of categorising plant contents. All the chemistry of foods, fluids, etc., ingested daily goes through a rearrangement in various parts of the digestive apparatus and with associated organs like liver, pancreas, etc. What goes in as a food or plant rich in certain compounds may come out again for distribution through the blood after a game of chemical musical chairs. What goes in as potassium sulphate and calcium chloride may (although my chemist friends will cringe at my over-simplification!) come out into the blood as potassium chloride and calcium sulphate. Before every chemist and biochemist runs to put pen to paper in criticism, this is an *example* only, not a fact! Therefore, when a herb is labelled 'rich in calcium', there will be a predominance of calcium compounds available for breaking down by the liver, etc., into other calcium compounds. During this activity, the free ions of calcium cross the floor to dance with another chemical partner. The whole process introduces a calcium-rich environment as this changeover is taking place. Any calcium compounds *needed* by the body will be eagerly combined.

So a herb 'rich in calcium' will be expected to provide for bones, teeth, nails, hair, nerve fibres and digestive tract all the raw materials in the blood from which to extract benefit for these body components. When you read of a plant which improves the health and function of bones, teeth, nails, etc., you'd *expect* to find it 'rich in calcium', the mineral most needed for these body parts to function well.

There will also be mention of some compounds often called 'tissue salts'. These are compounds needed in particular body processes, and where they are already in a herb in this chemical form, they can be more directly absorbable unchanged. Compounds like sodium phosphate, silicon dioxide or iron phosphate are essential keys to various maintenance procedures.

When a particular type of maintenance is needed, these 'tissue salts', taken as part of a plant's chemistry, already exist in the needed chemical form and can ease the job of the digestive tract, liver, etc. They don't need to be manufactured; they are already present. Obviously, such plants are more easily digested, and quicker to have their contents available to the blood for distribution.

5 Chemical-identity groups

What follows is a classification of groups of plant substances more related to the theory of their body-reaction than to the pathological changes found in illness. There are many more of these classifications. The biochemist has one range, the industrial chemist another, and the chemical engineer yet another. Every day a new 'group' seems to be bred in a laboratory and be given a group-name. The man-made range of plastics and synthetics breeds 'groups' like laboratory mice! There are the polystyrenes and the polypropylenes and the polyvinyls, etc, etc. Luckily, the herbalist follows a simpler system. I'll mention only several group-names for the benefit of the untrained reader: there are a multitude of pharmacognosy reference works for those who evaluate knowledge by the number of polysyllabic words used to describe it.

Alkaloids

I often feel this word will be carved in letters of fire on my brow as I unroll my list of questions for God in whatever after-life there is for struggling herbalists. How it has bedevilled every communication between herbalists and pharmacists in the last half-century! How it still causes jaws to tighten and opposing sides to be drawn up on the academic battlefield!

The word itself is descriptive of a class of substances which are nitrogenous, crystalline or oily, and which have the potential to produce alkaline reactions in various body processes. The blood has only a limited acid/alkaline range: from 7.25 to 7.35. Any substance which can tip this pH more towards the alkaline can be potentially dangerous if consumed. I will never understand, therefore, why it is predominantly these alkaloids, extracted and isolated from the plants that contained them, that have found their way into orthodox medical acceptance and use! Even today, you'll recognise most of them.

There's morphine, heroin, and codeine, alkaloids from the Opium Poppy. There's Hyoscyamine and Hyoscine and Scopolomine, extracted from Hellebore, Henbane, etc. There's Reserpine, from Snakeroot (*Rauwolfia serpentina*), and Atropine from Belladonna, the Deadly Nightshade. A whole range of potentially deadly substances has been separated from nature's more balanced chemical partnerships and is now injected and ingested by humans in the name of health improvement! Worse, the effects of these alkaloids, unmitigated by the synergistic chemistry of the original plant (which has been discarded as 'useless'), can be proved by example and use to react *more* dangerously than the original whole plant! I marvel at the blind doggedness of science: perhaps it is this nebulous entity that should wear the blindfold and carry the scales — not 'justice'. How can we ever justify such myopic actions by 'science'? The part is *not* the same as the whole, and never will be, in any of the true sciences.

I have a lovely old book written by Dr Goodenough in the last century and recently reprinted. He extols the then new discovery that extracted parts of the plant work 'almost as well' as the whole plant. 'Why not continue to use the whole plant then?' I ask of his ghost in the wee small hours of my reading in bed. It beats me! Herbs worked 'too slowly': some people died before the whole Opium Poppy tincture could relieve the pain and shock of surgery or accident. Others couldn't relax at all and surgery for them was like hacking through tight bands of contracted leather. A draught (carefully measured!) of *Hyoscyamus niger* (the *whole* plant) produced floppy, flaccid muscles, a dreamy state of other-worldness, and an easier and faster job for the surgeon. Why try to improve yet again on what worked well already? In our attempts to 'save' lives have we lost all perspective on the after-effects such alkaloids leave the body to cope with and dispose of? I'm sure any of you who've had Scopolamine before surgery and have vomited all the way to the theatre and for hours or days afterwards would agree that your body is attempting to throw away the alkaloid poisoning you've suffered — and the surgery has also to be coped with as well.

So do we go back to draughts of Henbane before a spear-wound is sutured on the battlefield? I don't think any of us would choose to be *that* mediaeval, but *do* ask your physicians and surgeons for as light a dose as possible of any alkaloids they feel necessary.

In homoeopathy, infinitesimally small doses of the above plants may be prescribed, but in herbal medicine they are no longer used. Mindful of the very different application of medicine to today's living conditions, herbalists now use gentler and safer herbs. Wherever a plant described later *does* contain an alkaloid, there will be very clear warnings given on its use.

Glycosides

If alkaloids indicate 'handle with care', then glycosides cause the herbalist far fewer head-on collisions with pharmacists and pharmacognosists. Glycosides (sometimes spelled glucosides) yield various sugars on hydrolysis. Because of this, they are energy-producers and laxatives as well to some degree. Regarded as the 'goodies' in most plants, the tonic and restorative effects of glycosides are responsible for many of the good reports of patients after being prescribed herbs containing them.

A 'lift' of energy, physically and mentally, is often noticed and there is a stimulant effect present, especially in muscles, after this type of medication. The name 'glycoside' also refers to the muscle-sugar *glycogen*, which is made by the liver and distributed out to muscles for energy. It is necessary to have good dietary intakes of potassium in order to begin the processes of chemical change required to break down glycosides into their final state of use. As you will gradually come to expect, after further experience, nature has already put two and two together for us and most of the plants discussed later are already high in potassium *and* glycosides. Nature is always there waiting for us to catch up with her!

Sugars in general provide not only energy, but also waste-removal stimulus too. More energy to the intestinal tract and bowels produces a more positive peristalsis, the contracting rhythmical movements that propel food onward and wastes outward. Glycoside-rich plants will also be found in liver-herbs, laxative and purgative herbs, and in digestive-tonic lists.

Don't forget that the heart is also a muscle! Glycoside-rich plants maintain strong heart-function. Medically, even today, cardiac glycosides from plants like *Digitalis lanata* produce the drug

Lanoxin, a standby for many heart patients. The next time someone comments about herbal medicine's 'dangerous use of Digitalis' (Foxglove), reply, quite accurately, 'Oh no, they don't use that any more; it is used by orthodox medicine now which extracts and uses part of that plant only.' Let's set the record straight once and for all: I've heard it so many times: 'Herbal medicine? Oh yes, that's Digitalis. Deadly stuff!' Wrong! I've never used it, nor any part of it, in my life; nor do I teach about it or train anyone else to use it. I *hope* this will once and for all put this misconception to rest.

There are many glycosides whose names you will recognise. *Vanillin* is one that may surprise you. Yes, it's not just a luscious flavour, but a tonic and a stimulant to muscles and digestive system as well. Of course, this only applies to the *real* vanilla-pod soaked in a little milk, or soy milk, for an hour or two before use. The synthetic vanilla essence may fool you on taste, but your liver won't be fooled by its chemistry.

Amygdalin, from almonds, and from some medicinal plants and other stone-fruit kernels like apricot, is also a glycoside. Its use, either synthetically copied or isolated from other substances combined by nature with it, was in brief favour recently as yet another questionable 'breakthrough' for cancer prevention. Even from the short acquaintance you've already had with professional herbal medicine, I'm sure you can understand how amygdalin, like any other glycoside, can stimulate waste removal and improve general energy, and can therefore be used as an aid to removal of *any* disease-process from the body. Any means at all of raising energy and improving elimination will improve the body's ability to fight the *processes* which are the true nature of disease. In my explanation of Alteratives (pages 50–4) you'll find more about why this reaction-class contain glycoside-rich plants.

Steroids

We may think more of athletes and training regimes for them than of herbal medicine when the term 'steroids' is mentioned; or it may bring to mind the various pharmaceutical preparations of cortisone available. You may not have been aware of it, but steroids are hormonal substances and they are also found in the plant world. Phyto-steroids, hormones from plants, resemble our human hormones like twins resemble each other: they may do different things at different times, but they are virtually identical in characteristics and structure. As is usual with pharmacy, extraction of one or other steroid can be made and then prescribed on its own: herbalists prefer nature's balanced ingredients used together. Many medicinal herbs contain one or more of the steroids oestrogen, progesterone, testosterone, cortisol, and vegetable forms of these and other hormones which act like the human forms, although not identical with them. You may be surprised by the name of another animal hormone that is easily absorbed by human skin — lanolin. Lanolin may be used as a base with which to mix herbal extracts into an ointment.

Perhaps our most notorious steroid today is cholesterol. What a lot of fuss, fear and futile striving this hormone has brought into our lives! Every second human, male or female, seems to want to 'reduce cholesterol'. You should know that cholesterol is made by the liver, used in seminal fluid and vaginal lubrication, and is an essential part of nerve-fibre structure, strength and resilience. As soon as we realise that 'reducing cholesterol' may also mean lowering sexual activity and becoming nervously irritable and depressed, perhaps we'll return to the 'fat and happy' ideal. Add to that: 'fat, happy, *sexy* and nervously stable'. This may need to be our new standard *soon*, for our whole-health's sake. You'd be amazed at how many relationships have been ruined and how many large fit contented people have been turned into thin miserable impatient monsters, with poor sex lives, from the current craze to lower cholesterol. 'Science'-ism is again at work. Cholesterol *has* been found deposited on, and becoming part of, blood vessel walls, reducing the flow of blood through these vessels and putting the person at major health risk. However, it seems to do no good at all to point out to 'science' that cholesterol is a *necessity* in processes that make our lives not only worth living, but *fun*! If it is partnered by choline and lecithin in appropriate balance, it need *never* deposit out on to arteries but will remain in circulation in the bloodstream — and improve your sex life and your nervous system health. Mr Pritiken, you have a lot to answer for! Removing as many sources of cholesterol as possible may for a time cause the body to re-absorb and digest stored excess fats, but after between six to twelve weeks you'll have lost any excess, and now be seeking treatment for impotence, premature ageing and wrinkling, and marriage guidance or sedatives!

Keep your cholesterol balance as nature has arranged for you. Most of the food and plants that contain cholesterol also contain lecithin and choline. Chinese cuisine is an exquisite blending of this triangle in good natural balance. Most nuts, vegetable oils and many common plants like Fenugreek and Dandelion contain the balancing chemistry for cholesterol to remain in circulation — not depositing — as well as cholesterol itself. (Also see *Natural Health Book*, Nelson, 1979.)

Abnormally high intakes of *animal* protein and lack of physical exercise are the major offenders in cholesterol deposition problems. Dandelion coffee can be good herbal medicine! Think of all the *fun* you could enjoy again. I've never seen so many scraggy necks and sagging upper arms as I've seen on Pritiken-people. And the majority of them were cuddly, fun-loving and sexy beforehand! There's a worse problem ahead, too. If you cut out all those fats and vegetable oils, etc., you remove 80–85 per cent of your sources of the fat-soluble vitamins, Vitamins A, D and E. As these contain major anti-oxidants and protection for the immune system and cell division and cell reproduction, you may not die of heart disease, certainly, but of various forms of cancer instead.

Think well! 'Science' doesn't apologise or pay out damages to those who follow its latest 'breakthrough'. Stay with the strength! Nature is *never* wrong: nor has she changed her rules since the world began.

Tannins

'There's tannin in herbal teas,' I read just the other day, 'and you shouldn't drink them because tannins are carcinogenic.' I do wish some of these 'experts' would learn their subject before they rush into print and make fools of themselves! Worse; they produce yet another scare about using well-known ordinary plants and commonly-eaten foods or drinks. There's tannin to a greater or lesser degree in many plants. Oak bark is full of tannin, and so is Australian wattle: it is used industrially with the same result in mind as it produces in body tissues — it is astringent. The true definition of 'astringent' is a few pages ahead, but here 'drying, toning and tightening' will be enough to explain its body processes to you. All tannins are *tonic* in effect. Fluids are either retained better in tissues, or forced from areas of sluggish fluid retention and allowed to drain better through elimination channels.

A 'cuppa' contains tannins. In accordance with nature's unbending major law, one or two cups of tea (*Thea chinensis*) act as a tonic, a gentle diuretic and diaphoretic (see pages 62–5 for definitions). *Too many* cups of *Thea chinensis* and this process is *reversed* in the same body parts and functions. Eighteen cups of tea a day, and you're in big trouble — not from cancer because of tannins but at risk of any disease at all because of unbalanced consumption of any one kind of food or fluid. *Tannins* don't produce cancers: *people* do! Almost *any* given substance can produce the irritation → inflammation → immune response that can begin a cancer process. Tannins don't do it any more than peanut butter or hydrocarbons: too *much* tannin; too *much* peanut butter; too many petrol fumes, cigarettes or asbestos fibres; or too much of anything can cause imbalance and produce conditions where the random cells that everyone is born with can clump together and begin a cancerous process. The immune system's attention is elsewhere fighting off these too-often repeated assaults of a local inflammatory kind.

Most tannin-containing plants are sharp-tasting and refreshing. Like a 'dry' wine, the effect is to contract tissues. If you become violently thirsty after a dry Bordeaux 'red' or wake at 4 a.m. and drink water copiously to lubricate your dry mouth and contracted tongue, it's the tannins in the wine that produced this.

Tannins are complex compounds, capable of combining well with proteins. Sometimes they combine *too* well, making the protein somewhat indigestible; at other times, and in different quantity, they enhance protein digestion. Do you like to drink fluids *with* a meal? Or do you prefer a drink half an hour before or afterwards? Herbs containing tannins may be the corrective treatment if you suffer either way from too much, or too little, salivary and digestive fluids, especially if this is most obvious when eating or drinking.

Herbs which stop external fluid loss from bleeding, or plasma loss in burns, even severe haemorrhages internally or externally, are always high in tannins. So there really *was* some sense in that old wives' tale of cold tea applied to burns to 'dry' the tissue and stop fluid loss.

There are many other types of plant-contents, and our short list could become a very long one. There are starches and fats, oils and resins, saponins and enzymes, etc. As there are excellent textbooks available, full of long difficult names and biochemic chains of activity and interaction, I will recommend these to readers who want it all to sound difficult and technical. For those readers who look for commonsense and simple explanation, let's press on.

6 Reaction-names

If you've read any herb books at all, you've probably been suitably impressed with the writer's 'scientific' training when words like 'vulnerary', 'rubifascient', 'carminative' are used to describe a herb's medicinal qualities and body-reactions. Don't be. These names tell you bare essentials only, especially when even a passing knowledge of Latin and Greek roots will show you that the above three terms reflect varying degrees of 'hot, red and inflamed'. Academia must be served again. (Did you know the original 'Academy' of Plato was under a grove of Acacia trees? There he discussed *nature* and taught how to observe, understand and wonder. The degree 'Bachelor' (leaf or book) signified that his students had obtained a leaf only from the vast tree of knowledge. How today's academics have changed this simple analogy!)

I often wish it were still an obligatory requirement to study Latin and Greek before undertaking medical, pharmaceutical or botanical university courses. It would be then so simple to understand the true meanings and the real descriptions, to forget polysyllable arrogance, and to write or teach in people-language. Now follow definitions and long words, all of which have simple and very clear meanings.

Alteratives

You're to be forgiven if you've already assumed that herbs so classed should *alter* some body process or other. Mind you, I never would have blamed you in the first place for this assumption. But don't be complacent yet: these buzz-words get harder!

'Alterative' has become a word to describe the blood's processes of cleaning. 'Dirty blood' used to be a good, people's term for infections of many kinds, especially when any of the organs of elimination — skin, lungs, kidneys, bowels — were either infected themselves, or doing two jobs because one or more of their metabolic or functional partners was infected. So alteratives will be prescribed when infection is present, or the remains of an earlier infection have not been completely removed. 'Blood cleansers' they were often called. Their action in the body always caused *elimination* of some kind. 'It's better out than in' was stated grimly by many an early herbalist, even by general practitioners not so long ago, as extracts of herbs rich in iron, sulphur, chlorine and silica were mixed together in a dark-brown strong-tasting brew. Some of these compound mixtures contain so much iron and silica that they taste almost gritty, and metallic, on the tongue. It follows that, because elimination is their major effect, you will certainly know when you are taking them! You may also experience elimination processes in, or on, or through, the organs concerned. Urine may smell strong and be darker, bowels may be looser and there may be wind and some strong odours about. Skin may show new 'spots', or sweat may be strong or more copious. Lungs may cough out old mucus you never knew was there. You may have what many naturopaths call the 'healing crisis'. This sounds dangerous and worrying: it's not either. As every elimination organ works harder to expel rubbish it had grown used to and accommodated before, you feel better and better! Energy increases, eyes lighten and brighten, spirits lift, and an indefinable quality of recovery begins.

Alteratives as a class cause much of the hostile criticism of herbal medicine that impresses news editors searching for a 'sensation' of the week. 'Herb causes diarrhoea'; 'Burdock causes back-aches' (it's not the back, sir, it's the *kidneys* stirred into more active fluid elimination and protesting as lazy tissue will when first woken up again); 'Herb causes skin sores' (no; the skin hadn't 'breathed' well in years, and the pores were choked with all sorts of debris. The alterative herb began to *clear* and eliminate this waste matter outwards. In hours, days or a week or two, the skin would not only be clean again but the blood supply to it would be clear of infection causes and inflammatory debris.) You see how the phrase holds the truth: you certainly are 'better off without it'.

Until this fundamental principle of naturopathic laws becomes acceptable once again, as it was formerly, to medicine and pharmacy, we will continue to read and hear the academic cautions on the use of plants with such 'side effects'. Side effects they are not: they are the results of a cleaning-out process. The body has not done such necessary waste removal for a long time, for months or even years. Under the prodding of alterative herbs, lazy body systems stir into more positive activity, cell metabolism is more complete and efficient, and accumulated wastes depart somewhat obviously.

It is only since antibiotics have become the orthodox medical and pharmaceutical treatments for fighting various infections that body wastes have begun to be buried *in situ* rather than eliminated and removed. Any honest medical practitioner will tell you that most antibiotics don't 'kill' pathological invaders; they reduce the ability of the infecting organisms to proliferate and breed, and perhaps also reduce the likelihood of secondary infections of other types while your defences are down. But what about eliminating all the viral, bacterial and other toxins which are the waste products of the infecting organisms? The need to remove such toxic end-products of infection (and it's these that make you 'feel sick') appears to be ignored altogether in present-day medicine. It seems to me surprising that a patient who is taking weeks and months to recuperate from infections has no medical recourse at all to speed up waste-product excretion and spring back again to health with energy restored and the illness and its results removed, not buried. The naturopathic philosophy has as one of its basic principles that if a disease process, *and* its waste products, are removed from the body, it's as if that patient had never experienced the disease at all. Iridology bears out this principle: an iris can record a disease process, and perhaps gradually even the darker yellows and greys and browns will begin and remain in the iris afterwards if the illness-wastes are not removed. But the patient who is conscious of the need for alterative action to mop up the last sniper and flush out the last pockets of resistance back in the hills will record again clear iris colour as if the disease had never occurred. *Completion* of any disease process and total removal of left-overs is the task of the alterative herbs.

Once these principles are explained, most patients will rejoice mightily as their bowels become more active and perhaps the colour and consistency, even the odour, of faeces changes. Mrs Brown rings in great glee to tell you there's some action now in that sore neck where a 'lump' had appeared on and off for years ever since a tooth abscess occurred which had been treated with antibiotics apparently 'curing' the problem. The alteratives you prescribed for her had brought to the surface of the body the waste products of that earlier infection, never before removed. As the 'lump' finally discharges some foul matter Mrs Brown feels better and better! And the 'arthritis' in the neck, her reason for consulting you in the first place, is easing day by day too. She didn't have 'arthritis', you see, she had an old septic focus which had never been removed completely. Iris diagnosis had showed the tell-tale clouds of brown wastes covering the zones of jaw, teeth and even towards neck and shoulder — just where the 'lump' and the 'arthritis' were located. Iridology shows clearly when *elimination* is the process to be activated. As the old waste matter leaves through skin, bowels and kidneys, even through lungs, the brownish iris-fogs begin to lighten and fade. Surprise! Mrs Brown had had hazel eyes for years she thought: now they are blue and clearer every day and every week. Her energy increases relative to the elimination rate. By the time the 'lump' has seeped its last, the 'arthritis' has also left permanently. Mrs Brown sings your praises and sends you all her friends. But what could the story have been if you had not explained to Mrs Brown that signs of elimination were to be expected from the alteratives in her mixture? Muttering darkly about 'dangerous' herbal medicine, Mrs Brown may have contacted the media, or her now very unfriendly general practitioner, and the banner headlines would fly again! 'Dangerous herb causes boils' or 'Diarrhoea from panacea', or even 'Fake "cure" gives patient new illnesses'.

Poor alteratives! They produce some of the most positive and permanent improvements in health, but receive the worst press! Every student of herbal medicine must appreciate the difference between disease symptoms and elimination symptoms: such differentiation is part of the training. Remember, you will feel *better* and more energetic each day as elimination proceeds; you will feel *worse* and more tired, irritable and depressed as a true disease proceeds. You'll never confuse elimination 'symptoms' with getting sick if you remember this simple guideline.

Many of the hellfire and brimstone naturopaths begin every patient-treatment with massive elimination regimes before reconstruction and improvement treatments. In principle, this makes good sense. In practice, many patients cannot endure the experience equably, especially if it is not first explained to them. The desire of humans to seek an apparently 'easier' way, a short cut, a multivitamin, say, or a 'tonic', may need firm words from the naturopathic herbalist. 'I can't build a seven-storey concrete edifice on wooden foundations, infested and rotten with white-ants,' I said to one patient, a builder, who wanted a 'diet' for his painful back. He understood perfectly from then on. No way could he build better health on the shaky ground of an earlier streptococcal throat and kidney infection which years of antibiotics and pain relievers had never really beaten. As his back jabbed and ached even more, and his kidneys excreted brownish strong urine for the first few weeks of treatment, he rang joyfully. 'It's just like you said,' he chortled. 'Boy, there was a lot of muck there that I never knew about. I'm beginning to feel better and better as it all leaves.' First elimination, then the improvement can begin.

A forewarned patient will fare better — and will return for the second part of the treatment, the re-building and improvement. Neglect to explain, and the editor of the Sunday paper will have a field day on the subject of 'unqualified' and dangerous herbalists. *Differently*-qualified, is the correct term.

Garlic is possibly the most general and best all-round alterative in the herbalist's Materia Medica and the best for home use. Its praises have rightly been documented, inscribed and sung for some six centuries. No wonder jealousy and malice have dubbed it 'the witches' herb'! 'If you can't beat 'em, rubbish 'em' must also be recognised as a built-in human defence! When I first sang its praises publicly over thirty years ago, I was laughed off the stage. Now most people admit to taking garlic capsules, or cloves, from time to time, to prevent or to remove infections. More of its praises on page 72. As a dietary alterative, it is now in common use.

Burdock, Red Clover, Horsetail, etc.: there's a long list of medicinal plants classed as 'alterative' in action. Expect positive and necessary elimination when they're prescribed for you. The rule for alteratives is:

Small quantities over twelve weeks (blood cycle) for removal of chronic or long-term wastes.
Larger quantities over *shorter* periods of time for *acute* infections. (This can mean hourly or two-hourly, heavy doses, or medium doses 3–4 times daily over a few days.)

> Alteratives should be prescribed for you on professional advice only. Most of them act strongly and need training, care and caution in their application!

Anodynes (antispasmodics, narcotics, sedatives, etc.)

*F*rom both Latin and Greek, anodynes are pain-relievers. (It's perhaps macabre to note that a hangman's noose was called an 'anodyne necklace'!) *Relief* from pain is one of the most urgent of all human needs. Pain is the barometer of the quality of an illness. The more pain, the more human mechanisms of recovery and eventual survival demand *rest* as an automatic response. Are we really clever then to resort to anodynes of any kind, even natural ones, so that we may keep going, doing whatever we need to do, and not feeling so much pain?

There's a vast difference between *relieving* pain and *blocking* pain. Anodynes reduce the intensity: but narcotics block the recognition of pain signals, often by deadening nerve-messages to and from the brain and the organs or structures concerned. Anodynes make pain easier to bear. Many of the herbal ones reduce pain by releasing spasms in organs and muscles allowing blood to flow more freely and nerve-signals to pass unimpeded; so antispasmodic herbs, like Chamomile, Valerian, etc., can be 'anodyne' in effect. Wintergreen, Rosemary and Lavender oils, can be anodynes used externally by massage into the skin. Penetrating resinous and oleaginous substances from them warm the tissues by bringing blood quickly to the area, and in disease processes where warmth and relaxing reduce the pain, body massage with oils can be a pleasurable way towards pain relief.

However, especially if pain recurs in the same area, there may also be inflammatory processes at work where fluid accumulation, pressure and swelling produces local pain and the pain area enlarges and even is referred to other compensating body areas if not relieved. In these cases, the primary causes of pain may be from the blood (e.g. rheumatoid arthritis), and heat and friction often produce *more* pain.

As a herbalist naturopath, I teach that there is 'hot' pain and 'cold' pain, and both must be recognised as from quite different causes. Then there is *pressure* pain even from something as simple as too-tight shoes, or an uncomfortable armchair or car-seat. Pain can result from *immobility* too. Every hospitalised patient complains of pain in the lumbar spine, aching neck, etc. I'll have a neck-ache or sore right arm after several hours in the one chair writing this, so *postural* pain must be recognised too as a signal sent by the body to change position because various blood vessels and nerves are becoming posturally impeded and pressure-gradients in fluid flow are building up.

Every day, our bodies tell us in clear signals of flashing orange when parts of us have had enough, and changes are needed. When we persevere past such instinctive signals, pain of many kinds results. Nature slaps our wrists, adjuring us to listen more to her voice and less to our own almighty theories of what we *should* be like. All parts of our bodies need various forms of rest. Pain tells us when it's time — and over-due.

It follows then that herbal anodynes will be found relieving spasms, improving blood and nerve supply, sending us stronger and clearer signals on when to rest and when to be active again. Herbalists today do not use narcotics at all, in spite of all those mediaeval legends and Borgia-legacies. Narcotics *block* the body's recognition of pain-signals — a dangerous flouting of natural laws where pain is an inhibitory mechanism against further use in the same manner of the traumatised part. Today's herbalists diagnose to remove the *causes* of the pain, not the pain itself.

Sedatives are more often prescribed. These herbs calm the excitability of the physical nerve signals and, as overstimulation of the nerve fibres can also produce acid-waste, such a calming can reduce perceived pain-sensations. Sedatives like Vervain, Hops, St John's Wort, etc., calm the overreactive folk whose nervous systems work overtime, and whose perception of 'discomfort' as 'pain' is very real.

Accepting pain as a monitor of just how sick, over-tired, or over-strained is a body part results in better judgement on pain-reduction treatments. There are pains better for movement and releasing pressures, and pains better for rest: knowing the difference is the job of the trained professional herbalist.

I always cringe when I see sportsmen and sportswomen fight past pain. Our will-power (that incredibly perverse energy that must frighten God occasionally) certainly can make us do self-damaging actions which nature cannot contain without repercussions against us. Ice-water or a 'freezing' aerosol may block pain for a time, but when athletes take high doses of pain-relief medications just before a contest so that they can endure without screaming the self-torture inflicted, I'm sure many other earth-creatures must look at us with pity and sadness.

Antiseptics

As a partner with alteratives, antiseptics are also fraught with misconceptions and advertising hypes. Do you really want a germ-free bathroom? Then buy whiter-than-white cleanliness from a bottle perfumed with pine, lavender or surgical spirit. The image is not only clean but 'germ-free'. Nothing could be further from the true state of affairs! Not only is a germ-free environment un-achievable, but it's also undesirable! Big fleas really do have 'littler fleas upon their backs to bite 'em', and the littler and littler the organisms become, the harder it is even to know what's there, let alone remove them. Micro-bacteria, viruses and moulds and fungi, and even micro-organisms only just perceivable at the advance borders of our technology, have coexisted since life began. Ecologically, whatever eats up one form of life has another waiting to eat it in turn. It's the *balance* of micro-organisms in the environment that is desirable. If our technology could identify your private 'zoo' of organisms and display them stood end to end, you'd be amazed at the complexity of your passengers and parasites. And what's more, you *need* most of them! Scavenging jobs are done by such populations, and interdependence keeps your micro-climate going. In the intestines and the bowels, and in the stomach above them, live all sorts of 'friendlies'. In your nasal cavities and your sinuses and your throat live countless millions of micro-organisms sucked in with every breath. A nasal swab of any of us would make your eyes pop at the variety and number of harmless, as well as potentially harmful, micro-organisms for whom we act as the transportation vehicle. A *human* only has to walk into that shining bathroom and its 'antiseptic' state is ruined completely.

What we have tried so far to do is to kill off, or severely limit the numbers of, the *un*-friendly organisms whilst retaining those necessary to our own needs. *Streptococcus lacto bacillus* is a 'friendly' found in yoghurt: streptococci of less friendly types can kill us. How do we select which to retain and which to destroy as potentially 'infective' agents dangerous to our health? Why, even, do some of us succumb to an 'infection' by the bad guys and others of us carry the same organism aboard us without even the slightest signs of illness occurring? Much of our defence rests on 'clean' blood initially, so you can see how alteratives and antiseptics may not only be both necessary together, but one may not be completely effective without the other. Many of the severe infections we suffer most from are *secondary*. While our immune systems are busily engaging a primary ecological imbalance, secondary populations may proliferate unchecked. It would have been much harder to describe human homoeostasis years ago as 'interaction between synergistic populations': now we are more aware of environmental ecology. If a gardener removes all the weeds one year before they've seeded, he or she just knows that a different weed population, taking advantage of the altered environment, will spring up next year, and the one after that.

Our best way out is to support helpful bacterial and micro-populations which are known to be present in health, then there should be less likelihood of population explosions of a different and possibly less beneficial kind. 'Killing all germs' should not be our goal. It's impossible anyway. There are, however, various plants which are known actually to kill selectively particular dangerous attackers which we are better off without. There's Garlic for tubercular infections and there's Thyme to fight off harmful streptococcal throat and lung and kidney infections. Caster oil poulticing will draw out all sorts of possible nasties like soil-born tetanus from dirty wounds; and Calendula will clean and strengthen and oxygenate cuts and abrasions and burned tissue so the weakened areas will provide a less attractive environment for secondary passengers. One can *deter* harmful invasive populations: their complete destruction is virtually impossible.

When Dr Kildare scrubs up before surgery, don't you feel protected and safe? You're not, you know. Up the back of his neck is crawling a micro-world of seething tiny bodies; in his perspiration, wiped off by the theatre sister is a multitude of teeming tiny life. On his every hair growing from every pore are microscopic travellers. A sterile environment? No! *Humans* are present, with all their tiny friends — and possibly foes — aboard.

So think of antiseptics only as reducing the likelihood of abnormal population imbalances. Homoeostasis is a delicate and fragile process of interaction between 'good' and 'bad', or perhaps 'constructive' and 'destructive' energies. *Both* are needed for human balance. No one can, or should, believe all 'baddies' can ever be destroyed, or every human, and possibly the universe too, would fall clean over!

Astringents

I'm sure many readers know what 'astringency' means in the wine industry, but is the herbal medicine definition related? Think of a very 'dry' white or red, and the mouth-membranes contracting as you swallow. Think too of what many cultures do traditionally; they drink water and more water for every sip of dry wine drunk down. I'm sure many of you have become desperately thirsty in the wee small hours after too much 'dry' wine earlier. How can copious liquid make you *thirsty*? It's the astringency that does it.

Astringents tighten and tone and contract and bind: the result is often fluid loss from the area affected, causing what may actually be, or appear to be, a drying-out process. Fluids, even some fat-based fluids, can be forced out of the immediate zone by the sudden or strong tissue contraction. But a paradox exists here, another of nature's equalising action-and-reaction energy flows: fluids can also be *retained* when tissues tighten and bind and contract. Dabbing a cut with alcohol or covering it with a Yarrow leaf can cause blood flow to stop and prevent plasma loss. Perhaps the best double astringent action is seen in the fluid blister over a burn site. Astringents applied will stop further fluid loss into the blister, but will also cause reabsorption back into underlying tissues of the fluid present already. A *balance* of fluids in the tissue is re-established: fluid loss and fluid retention are equalised.

So astringents are prescribed for internal and external haemor-rhages, for diarrhoea and dysentery and cholera (fluid *losses*); but they are also prescribed for the oedema of swollen ankles and sprained wrists and pre-menstrual fluid gain (fluid retention in tissues). Somewhere in the middle is the ideal; excreting or retaining only the fluids necessary for optimum balance in the tissue concerned.

Is the word 'naturopathic' beginning to make more sense as we progress? *Balance*, self-regulating but constantly in movement, is the condition the naturopathic herbalist tries to regain for each patient. The ability of the body to regulate itself from within its own resources sometimes breaks down. We call it 'illness'. As we interact with our environment, our energies can become moulded, bent and re-directed by circumstances. The herbalist uses plants to re-establish our own direction and balance according to each individual's 'nature'.

Demulcents and emollients

If you're a 'softie' and don't fancy the rigours of elimination or the spartan efforts required to remove whole micro-populations threatening your health, then soothing and smoothing may be a more acceptable category of reaction for you. Demulcents comfort you *inside*, soothing soft organs like digestive tract, vagina, bladder, kidneys, lungs, etc.: emollients sooth you *outside* and most cosmetics, ointments, soaps and lotions contain this class of substance. The effect of both is comfort! Plants which contain mucillage, sticky and gluey, line and cover you internally or externally with a protective layer which promotes healing by reducing inflammation, roughness and irritation, thereby also reducing pain and discomfort. This mucillage also reduces damage by contact with any over-acid body fluids and mucous linings or skin. Perspiration acids can almost corrode sensitive skins, and hot dry winds, salt water, etc., can be abrasive too. Emollients reduce external friction, and the roughness resulting.

Stomach acids, and too great a pH change at the duodenum can erode the tissues away there and cause ulcers. In the intestines and large bowel, too, ulceration can occur. Demulcents, like Aloe Vera and Slippery Elm powder, line, soothe and insulate such painful areas so healing can begin and progress more rapidly. Bear in mind, though, that such treatments internally and externally should be continued until real healing has been established and completed, usually a six to eight weeks' daily-use course. Otherwise if treatment is interrupted the whole time may need to be begun again.

Externally, creams and oils often combine physical properties of covering and spreading uniformly, with medical ingredients to be carried into the body via the skin. A very large body organ, the skin needs its selective permeability and its expansion-contraction energy-balance maintained constantly. As your outside perimeter, it takes the brunt of many environmental shocks and contacts. Heat and cold, sun and rain, salt water and humidity, as well as its contacts with clothing, and with other people's skins in close encounters, make it peculiarly and especially vulnerable. Use soothing emollients with a free hand: there's no pain attached, not even any elimination!

Rubefacients   A working knowledge of Latin

helps to make sense of some of the deliberately difficult polysyllabic words sprinkled through medicine, pharmacy, biochemistry, and even anatomy and physiology — let alone botany! 'Rubefacient' simply means 'making it red'!

This activity group consists of irritants which bring blood to an area by over-stimulating either surface or deeper blood vessels and nerves. The area becomes red, and may experience heat, throbbing, even inflammation. With typical misapplication of the name, rubefacients are applied to *counter* irritation, heat, throbbing, etc., when the area has already been 'made red' by some other irritation or inflammation. Stinging nettle ointment applied to ant-stings, or mustard-plasters applied to a congested bronchitic chest, may both be called 'rubefacient' treatments when really two very different diagnoses apply. In the first case, nettle ointment will counteract one irritation by overcoming it with a greater irritation: in the second case, simple rubefacient effect is observed when an irritating mustard-plaster is applied to a *not-active-enough* chest. Both apply irritation in order to stir, stimulate and drain an affected area: but the first example reduces one 'red'-ness by causing another, and the second example causes only a single 'red' heat and irritation by its own application.

Rubefacients are used externally. They are rubbed on, applied on poultices or dabbed on as tinctures. 'Spanish Fly', always referred to when the subject of aphrodisiacs crops up around the dinner-table, is rubefacient in its action on the penis. It causes 'red'-ness, stimulation and increased blood supply to this organ — but there could be irritation and itching for days or weeks afterwards for the male, and extreme discomfort too for the receiving end of this sexual partnership!

Wintergreen oil is an excellent example of rubefacient action. Its glowing warmth, which counteracts and replaces deep-seated joint and muscular aches and pains, may also cause the skin at the site to redden quickly and obviously in sensitive people.

Be cautious with rubefacients! Keep these irritating substances away from body openings like nostrils, mouth, eyes, etc., and wash hands well after applying to yourself or others. There is always a price to pay when we try to exceed nature's boundary lines.

There can be medicinal need for rubefacient action when there is atrophy present in muscular tissue or after trauma to the spine, etc. The irritating effect is profoundly useful here, so that blood supply to the affected areas may be maintained and possibly even help to restore some proportion of use. Flagellation with stinging nettles was a mediaeval way of stimulating wasted paralysed limbs and numbed spinal nerves after accidents or trauma. Of course, there is a limit to how often a tissue area should be 'made red'. Continued application after the area has reddened may cause a 'burn' effect. Stop each treatment as soon as heat and obvious redness is achieved.

Diuretics and diaphoretics

These two terms must never be confused as, although they both represent fluid-excretion processes, one acts through the kidneys and the other through the sweat glands and skin. In an anatomical way, both are related, as the skin is often called 'the third kidney', and can assist the kidneys by taking over part of their job, especially if there is kidney slowness or malfunction. Those who urinate in small and infrequent amounts may sweat profusely and eliminate fluids this way: conversely, those who hardly sweat at all may urinate more often and in greater quantity. Those who do *neither* process well and effectively may have need of herbs which are both diuretic and diaphoretic.

Just as fluid is needed in order to transport nutrients into every body cell, fluid wastes from cell-metabolism must also be excreted and disposed of regularly. Failure to excrete fluid wastes well can cause many severe and long-term chronic illness-symptoms. Blood pressure may be elevated, heart overloaded, and energy severely reduced. There may be 'aches and pains', which rightly or wrongly may be classified as 'arthritis' or 'rheumatism'.

Diuretics

Diuretics from the plant world contain high levels of potassium and silica, and perhaps iron and sulphur as supporting partners. As potassium aids the excretion of fluid out of cells, and silica stimulates kidneys, bowels and nerve supply to both, any plant with appreciable amounts of both will have strong diuretic effects. Such herbs as *Equisitum arvense* (Horsetail), *Juniperus communis* (Juniper), *Apium graveolens* (Celery), etc., can produce obvious urinary changes and improvements. At the start of any diuretic treatment, be prepared for somewhat darker, more odorous, even slightly irritating urine, as fluid wastes are more strongly removed. There may also be 'chalkiness' or cloudiness, as gravel or tiny stones may be also sped on their way out from kidneys or bladder, because of the more powerful excretory energy now available.

There is no need to worry about potassium loss when using herbal diuretics, as the plants fitting this category are already high in potassium themselves. Because of this, most herbal diuretics also improve muscular strength and energy, and such better muscular tone also aids the 'pumping' action of excretion. Many of the commonly used diuretics also contain sodium to balance the potassium, and in close to the ideal proportions of three to one approximately. This balance ensures a maintenance of the body's own proportions of sodium and potassium, so that the upsetting one-way stimulus often created by pharmaceutical diuretics is avoided.

Diaphoretics

These plants cause increased excretion through the skin. Just as diuretics may produce some difference in quality, quantity and ingredients in urine when first taken, so diaphoretics may cause a change in the amount, the odour, even the colour, of perspiration initially. You begin to understand how all these smelly concentrated residues must have limited your waste-excretion efficiency. No wonder you felt that a good 'flush-through' was necessary!

Many patients taking herbal diaphoretics like Fenugreek (*Trigonella foenum-graecum*) or even Lemon Balm (*Melissa officinalis*) as a tea, throw a sweat almost within minutes of ingestion. If curry does this to you, and you break out in beads of sweat on lips, cheeks, chin and forehead, be aware that most curry spices are diaphoretic. Eating highly-spiced 'hot' curries in hot climates will actually cool you down! You will lose body heat as you sweat and mop your brow over a bowl of Vindaloo chicken or Madras beef. Traditional diets in different countries are often based on sound principles of good health for the local inhabitants. On the other hand, it might be positively dangerous to eat a curry meal at the North Pole or in Helsinki in mid-winter! There are inherent dangers in believing that a universal 'good diet' exists: there are also great health risks in a worldwide chain of hamburger and soft-drink outlets from Reykjavik to Timbuctoo.

It is necessary to perspire to some degree no matter where you live, but a healthy skin will acclimatise itself quickly to its surrounding air and temperature, and will sweat only as much as is necessary to aid the kidneys and to regulate body-heat. If this is not easily possible, diuretics may be prescribed to help.

There is an obvious need for diaphoresis when fever flares rapidly, and body temperature with it. Children can quickly race up a temperature. If this *remains* high, and won't break by natural sweating followed by sleep, diaphoretics may have to be prescribed quickly. (See Fenugreek, pages 159–63)

Have you wondered why people don't throw temperatures as often as they used to? The beginnings of a whole host of infective diseases were temperature elevation first, then malaise, sore throat, cough, pain, etc., following. One of the body's first defences under attack by harmful bacteria, viruses, bacilli, etc., was to elevate the temperature in order to bring oxygen-laden blood to the area and 'burn' out the invaders. How long has it been since you've seen a natural fever process, followed by sleep, and then complete recovery several days later? I fear that our constant reliance on antibiotics against infections (even *before* any infection is present, at times) has reduced our natural immune responses. In this present age when a 'non-specific virus' can keep us below par for weeks, months even, perhaps we would be better off *strengthening* our natural immune responses rather than relying constantly on anti-biotics to do our fighting for us. There's no defence yet against the AIDS virus: perhaps it might never have become so life-threatening if our own immune systems had been allowed to develop first the fever, then the sweating, then the sleep to speed recovery and *completion* of the disease process.

There are times when fevers rise alarmingly, remain high, and may do damage unless reduced quickly. To the herbalist, such cir-cumstances demand the use of diaphoretics as well as alteratives, both in accelerated dose-spacing and dose-quantity. This treatment does not in any way *block* the body's own immune mechanisms: there is just increase in the *speed* of the diaphoresis, so that the infection is more quickly dealt with and completed while the invad-ing population is comparatively small. If this fever-process does not occur quickly and naturally, there remains an increasing population of pathogens which are not 'burned-out' for weeks and months, if at all.

I do not like to hear of three-year-olds who've been on anti-biotics for two years already and who have been told to stay on them almost permanently thereafter for such diseases as middle-ear infections, bronchial 'wet' asthma, gastric upsets, etc. We hear this story far too often from our clinic patients. A good sweat after a fever is a natural body response. We interfere with or discard this process at our peril!

Plants classified as 'febrifuges' will include diaphoresis amongst their biological activities. Although not strictly interchangeable terms, they are often both applied to the same plant.

If you sweat heavily and profusely when active on a hot day, this is not only natural, but desirable. If, on the other hand, you do *not* sweat in such circumstances, diaphoretics may need to be pre-scribed for you. The skin should cool you down in its role as 'third kidney' while you drink at the other end to make good the surface fluid loss. If you *don't* sweat, *don't* feel thirsty, and *don't* urinate much at all, be aware that fluid wastes will be concentrating and irritating in tissues, and may set up next the inflammatory aches and pains previously mentioned. Frequent drinking and frequent fluid excretion through skin and kidneys will 'clean' your fluids by flushing them through well.

I always notice my iris colour to be bluer and clearer after a day's sailing or a bush-walk, or even mowing the lawn, when I have sweated profusely. Use the skin to help clean the body of liquid wastes, just as the bowels clean out the solids. Most of us place insufficient value on the former process, and too great a value on the latter. 'A good bowel movement each day, doctor' may not be the passwords to immortality unless you can add 'and a good sweat'. Exercise is, of course, diaphoretic in effect, so herbal diaphoretics may not need to be taken very often if sweaty exercise is a daily routine. Manual and outside workers often hold 'arthritis' at bay all their lives while they 'glow', perspire or sweat on the job.

Nervines

There is almost no person on earth who is not better off for a dose or two of their own particular nervine! As life throws at us today's challenges, tasks, emotional and environmental crises, and circumstantial pressures, all of us need *calm* nervous responses to these stimuli. Nervines may sedate or stimulate, but the end-result of their prescribing should be a nervous system which responds appropriately to stimuli with neither too much, nor too little, action. There should also be inherent after the nervous activity phase an ability to cease action, and to rest and recuperate. There are few people today who can balance accurately between stimuli responses and rest. Appropriate nervines are added with every patient's individual mixture at my own clinic as one essential ingredient no matter what illness is being treated. Nervines form the most used group from any herbalist's dispensary.

The action of any nervine prescribed should be a double one. Unlike pharmaceutical drugs, where one isolated substance is used when stimulation is sought for a slow or tired-out nervous system and another different substance is required for sedating an over-stimulated nervous system, the plant-nervines' job is to *balance* both the too-high or the too-low responses, and to achieve a calm two-way signal between action and relaxation. By this means, energy is still not being expended long after the stimulus has gone, nor is rest maintained too long when action is required again. What a lovely lot of humans we would be — and healthier for it — if our nervous systems remained calm and balanced, acting when required, and changing the action as the circumstances also changed!

The 'person-pictures' throughout this book can be easily related to nervine-types. Although every one of us is unique, general groupings can still be made according to the way our nervous systems respond. There are those who worry and plan *before* it happens (see Hops, pages 183–8), and those who live each day twice, as they act out the days' experiences again at home re-living their stresses (see Chamomile, pages 130–6). Then there are those tight-lipped controlled people who never let out a syllable of their day's doings, and whose poker-faced silence belies the pressure-cooked turmoil inside (see Valerian, pages 294–300). There are the sensitive souls who overreact to imagined slights, as well as the thick-skinned phlegmatic ones who never appear to hear you or change their path! There are chronically over-conscientious folk who die young, racked by migraines and rheumatism; and there are the perfectionists for whom every accomplishment is disappointing and every potential friend, lover or employee not quite 'right'. All of us are 'under' or 'over' in some way, our differing nervous systems never quite in the middle.

Because of this under- or over-activity, all of us use *more* nervous energy than is appropriate or efficient. Are there many people you know who are not 'tired'? There is no such disease as 'stress'; there is just *life*, and our ability to handle it all efficiently and well, or inefficiently and needing our nervine.

It is also true that when the appropriate nervine is taken as a tea, or prescribed in tablets, or in a mixture of liquid extracts, many other symptoms of illness disappear without even being specifically recognised in treatment. It follows a basic natural law that the more efficiently your energy is applied, the less other potential weak-spots may break down. If only we applied the same procedures to our bodies as we do to our car-engines! Tuning is essential for a smooth-running engine, reduction in wear, and a long useful life: this commonsense rule employs nervines from the plant world to fine tune our human 'motors', reducing the effort and increasing the possible loading-ability.

Plant-nervines do not become an addictive necessity, nor are they required in increasing doses to do the same job. Every time you drink a cup of Valerian tea your muscles will relax; and Chamomile tea will always calm the Vagus Nerve (10th Cranial Nerve) and all its branches. You don't need more and more — but you may require less and less! Nervines are in themselves corrective of causes as well as ameliorating symptoms. Before too long, your now calmer nervous system may indicate to you different ways of handling life, emotions, job, friends, study, decisions, etc. When herbal medicine is most obviously effective in producing a 'changed person' in the eyes of family, friends or workmates, that is when the nervines are prescribed accurately and wisely.

Who knows, those expensive 'stress management' seminars may not be really necessary! You could soon be managing life's experiences very well, thank you, and in a way which is most appropriate to your own character and personality.

All of us have our own mechanisms, both inherited and developed, for 'coping'. But it's far easier when our essential combination of particular nutrients is available. Most nervines contain varying amounts of magnesium, phosphorus and calcium, with silica and some zinc, and trace minerals like bromine, iodine, selenium, etc., as optional extras. It is the task of the trained professional herbalist to evaluate you from an objective distance, and to choose your most applicable nervine detachedly. If you recognise yourself in any of the 'person-pictures' following, bear in mind that this will be a *subjective* assessment: people around you may see you more clearly than you see yourself, and a non-involved observer like your practitioner will see you most clearly of all.

I regard nervines with the respect I give to alteratives in the massive improvements in overall health that they can produce. While alteratives do the cleaning out, nervines do the toning up, the balancing and the tuning which can make your body vehicle an extremely efficient mechanism in which to house a calm strong mind and a rested relaxed spirit.

Vulneraries

My story of Arnica and the contused thumb (page 92) illustrates the properties of vulnery herbs. The veins are involved here, and any broken veins after a bruising blow, a fall, a sudden sprain or crushing of any kind can leak slowly into surrounding tissues causing purpling. With the discolouration comes pain, swelling, throbbing and tenderness, maybe for days or even weeks or months. There is congestion and 'deadening' of the tissue area, and a great risk of clots or thromboses forming. These may remain for years, and may move dangerously much later. So a bruise is not to be taken lightly, nor a sprain. A vulnerary ointment like Arnica or Witch-hazel should be applied as soon as possible. Witch-hazel lotion is also obtainable from pharmacies and health stores, and it quickly absorbs through the skin, doing an even faster job.

Vulneraries seal off slow leaks in blood vessels, more though in veins than in arteries. Arteries need strongly astringent herbs like Yarrow to stop the much more powerful pressure of bleeding from this half of the circulation.

Vulneraries also stimulate lymphatic fluid drainage from a contused area. The 'eggs' which form on the forehead or the skull after a blow, and the hugely swollen sprained ankle or wrist, need a vulnerary applied every hour or so in the early stages, and less frequently as swelling subsides and healing begins.

Do *not* use vulneraries when the skin is broken as well as bruised. Use first the antiseptics, the astringents and the alteratives to minimise infection. However, a squeezed finger in the secateurs, a crushed toe, a blood-blister, or a swollen sprain or bruise *where the skin is not broken* will need a vulnerary herb applied.

See the individual herbs for specific instructions on when and how to apply each plant, and how often, but in general after any swelling disappears discontinue this type of treatment. It is not so effective for an *old* bruise area, and discolouration by blood and bile pigments may not respond well if the injury was received weeks earlier. Remember, the faster you apply a vulnerary after the trauma, the less will be the long and short-term damage. Within minutes is ideal; within an hour or two it's still possible to minimise damage, but after several days, and longer, vulneraries are progressively less effective.

Bitters

Many carminatives are also 'bitter tonics', or contain tannins and other principles which produce a tongue-twisting bitter flavour. Adding angostura bitters to make a pink gin can mitigate the sickly-sweet syrupy flavour of the juniper berries and sloe berries of the gin-base.

I remember an excellent dinner at a London club several years ago with an ex-Welsh Guards captain and his elegant lady-wife. The barman was new: he did not yet know the irascible temper of this long-time member. A pink gin was ordered. 'Yes, sir; "in" or "out"?' 'Out, you fool,' roared our host, 'do you want to ruin my dinner altogether?' There are two distinct classes of pink-gin drinkers: one just swirls the glass out with the bitters which are then discarded; the other leaves the bitters in the final drink. Like all British class-distinctions, one must not be confused with the other — especially in one's own club! The captain's stomach needed only a trace of the bitter tannins to stimulate the flow of saliva and gastric juices before the meal. More than a trace, and his particular upper digestive tract would feel the balance tipped too far, upsetting the processes of digestion.

Bitter herbs act as a tonic and stimulant to the mucosal linings of mouth, oesophagus and stomach. If you can't abide a bitter taste, there may be over-acid or irritated areas in this part of the digestive tract, and your instincts may be protecting you nicely. However, bitter flavours also stimulate the bile ducts, and the gall bladder may introduce too much bile through into the duodenum, causing ulcerated areas there. Ask your practitioner more about these diagnostic pointers. Iridology can be used with great effect in diagnosing digestive-tract conditions. If you love olives, crave bitter vegetables like artichokes and aubergines, cauliflower and cabbage, this may indicate an under-active upper digestive tract.

In herbal medicine, bitter tonics like yellow Gentian root (*Gentiana lutea*) and Aloes (*Aloe Vera*) may be prescribed when blocked or under-active gall and digestive organs are diagnosed. Whenever that bitter flavour occurs, the effect will be to stimulate production of enzymes, bile and stomach acids. Follow your taste buds here, and learn what they are telling you about yourself.

It is a sore trial to a herbalist when even the small dose of ten drops of mixture in a little water produces the patient comment, 'Oh, I don't like taking this medicine — it's so *bitter*.' Our pampered taste buds crave sweet foods and the sweet taste of fruits and other vegetables like potatoes and carrots: with a pout that would do credit to a three-year-old, I've seen mature adults refuse to experience a bitter taste, even though they may desperately need the tannins involved. I like the way of the Bedouin: for the stranger, a cup of bitter black coffee first, symbolic of life's trials and tribulations; then the sweeter sugary coffee and a broad smile, celebrating life's more pleasant experiences to follow. Don't be so spoiled that you demand sweet tastes all the time. Life doesn't work that way, and neither does your digestion!

Carminatives

Whereas rubefacients heat and cause redness externally, carminatives cause better blood supply and a feeling of warmth and comfort internally in the digestive tract. Think 'red' again; the artist's colour 'carmine' should help you remember this group. (Don't get your spelling wrong and think the word is '*calm*inative'! There is no sedative action at all from *carm*inatives, in fact quite the reverse.)

Although there is a very soothing and anti-flatulent effect in the stomach and intestines from carminatives, this is caused by *stimulating* the blood flow, increasing warmth and removing that 'cold-feeling' often described by patients with under-active stomachs that bloat and rumble uncomfortably when a meal heavy in protein or in stodgy carbohydrates or rich fats is consumed. If all three are over-indulged in at the same meal, interspersed with cold fluids like a milk-shake or icy mineral-water or fruit juice, the meal may sit undigested in a 'cold' stomach for hours, causing rumbling and burping and that lovely incomprehensible name for it all — borborygmus! 'Indigestion' covers many symptoms of this kind with a more ordinary general name.

There are many other ways of producing a carminative effect than by herbal teas or mixtures. A warm cup of almost any fluid will do the same thing, and so will a warm bath. Even alcohol of various specific kinds will warm and comfort a cold griping stomach. The spirits do it best, followed by aniseed and caraway liqueurs, *crème de menthe*, etc. In fact, stomachic 'cordials', originally alcohol and water extractions of carminative plants, were taken after a too-large meal as a medicine, not only as a special indulgence. You can still achieve the carminative effect from a herb tea, or even from plants eaten before or during the meal, without resorting to alcohol. Mint included anywhere in the meal or afterwards as peppermint tea or spearmint tea is a great carminative, and so is aniseed, caraway and thyme. The culinary herbs provide most of this group, so you should have little trouble incorporating them into food and liquids. They don't just add piquant flavours! Our ancestors added them for specific medicinal purposes, not only for ornament. Carminatives are a large class, and every French cook includes one or other of them in the meal. Scandinavians use fennel, dill and angelica; Arabs use mint and aniseed; Indians use cumin and cinnamon and mace; while the ancient Romans and present-day Italians use marjoram, oregano and basil. All are what Pliny called 'grateful to the stomach'. Reversed grammar notwithstanding, he was right!

Vermicides and vermifuges

I have often wondered whether ancient writers on things medical have been misconstrued by their translators on the word 'serpents'. It seems to me very strange that so much medical advice and herbal treatment was given for 'bites from serpents' in the British Isles especially where snakes are not only rare but in Ireland apparently non-existent! Did those earlier writers mean 'worms' of various kinds, and not 'serpents' at all? Egyptian writings understandably are full of antidotes and remedies for 'snake'-bite, and in a country where the snake population was high this undoubtedly referred to real snakes. As the Nile flooded each year after the rains in Africa built up the wall of water which flowed fast and predictably towards the Delta, snakes would have been a major problem all along the narrow fertile plain. It was, however, my late husband's theory, with his background of Egyptian archeology and hieroglyphic translation, that the Egyptian medicinal plants used for snake-bite were different from those used for 'the worm' intestinally. The glyphs were different: 'worm' and 'snake' were not the same medically, it appeared, nor were the plant-remedies interchangeable. There was clear difference expressed! A 'worm' inside, in a country where parasites of all kinds bred to a first or second stage in hot alluvial mud, was a serious matter too. How much this obvious division has been lost is a matter for my constant research, with accuracy in mind. Next time you read that Rue is used 'against the bites of serpents' see if the passage can hold more truth when 'against intestinal parasites of wormlike forms' is substituted. I wouldn't like to wave a branch of Rue, or Tansy, or even a clove of Garlic at a passing Australian Black, Brown or Tiger snake hoping the plants would protect me 'against the bites of serpents' as so many old writers claim. Nor would I take extracts of these plants correctively if actually bitten. They would do nothing constructive then! But I *would* take a mixture of extracts of Tansy, Garlic, Rue, etc., preventively each day when travelling in a country where intestinal parasites abound, and where food and water could contain them.

Vermicides kill parasitic 'worms' in the gut, or elsewhere, and vermifuges expel them from the body. Without exception, this category of herbs have bitter strong flavours, sometimes so bitter that dosing can be an unpleasant experience. The old-fashioned folk who don't mind a little wormwood and gall fare better than our current generation who often refuse to take medication because it doesn't taste 'nice'! Vermicides and vermifuges do an essential job with these bitter principles; worms don't like them either! The astringency and the tannins present cause contraction of intestinal mucosa and the bitterness also produces distaste in the parasite — which promptly falls off. The vermifuge effect then aids elimination through the bowels of the dead parasites and any debris around them. Luckily, most vermicides are so strongly astringent that there is little or no risk of blood loss as the little beastie lets go.

Aloe, bitter and oily, is another vermicide, but in a lesser degree. Malefern, perhaps the best and most strongly acting when tapeworm is the 'serpent' in residence, has been removed from availability to herbalists recently. In their wisdom, the powers-that-be have decreed that we are not to be trusted with this plant. Thousands of years of traditional use must bow again to the new God, science; that the scientists concerned are neither herbalists nor personally experienced in how and when it is prescribed and in what dosage seemed irrelevant to its banning!

Vermicides and vermifuges are prescribed in short sharp bursts, and at a comparatively high dose compared with usual herbal remedies. Doses of 40–50 drops of extract are not uncommon, followed at a later date by a second dose so that any hatching eggs or embryos present will also be stunned and removed. Anywhere from three days to three weeks, sometimes longer, can elapse between the first and second dose, depending on which parasite is present.

As world travel is now so fast and easy (if expensive), there exists greater danger than ever before that parasites may be transferred from a population which has developed a tolerance to them and moved in days by returning air-travellers, hosting them in the gut, to a population without any established tolerance. Maybe we've eradicated some infectious diseases, and even this remains to be seen, but a host of 'worm'-travellers and 'serpent'-parasites arrive on our shores and at our airports daily. Perhaps in the future, not only vermicides and vermifuges, but anti-parasitics, will become more and more essential in our health planning. Meantime, I'll do as the Egyptians have done ever since they recorded their daily routine on stone and papyrus: I'll eat my garlic and onions each day to *prevent* my intestines becoming parasite-attractive in the first place. Prevention is always better, and easier on the taste buds, than cure!

7 *Classification of activity and use*

*A*ll the preceding classifications are found in Materia Medica worldwide, both ancient and modern. Understanding their meanings can help to identify the body sites and body processes which a particular plant will affect. But they are *guides* only. With each plant that follows in the Materia Medica section, read carefully all the qualifications, the cautions and the contra-indications which elaborate on these simple terms. Nothing in nature stands alone; no quick short-cut exists in gaining the skills of prescribing, learned slowly and painfully over years of experience. *Don't* think it all sounds simple now. *Don't* think it's as easy as 'I have kidney problems, therefore I'll prescribe for myself one of those diuretics she's mentioned earlier'. *Don't* self-prescribe an alterative just to see whether you have a waste-removal problem. Herbal medicine prescribing is *not* simple, even for the trained professional. Many possibilities must be explored for ingredients to be accurate and effective with each different patient. The combinations possible are endless. Ancillary skills like Iridology can be of great help in separating the patient's story from the real story the body tells, especially when prime causes need to be identified and removed, not only the secondary blanket of symptoms they've produced later.

The professional herbalist studies for long hours the difficult Latin and worse Greek which produced anatomical names and titles for physiological processes, and for botany and chemistry. 'Homoeostasis' must be appreciated as an ideal state of healthy harmony of function, seldom achieved but always aimed for. Psychology, as well as physiology, is essential too. Classical herbal medicine evaluates not only a few symptoms but the season of the year in which they occur, the environment of city or country, the age, the sex, the attitudes of mind either inherited or taught, etc. — and not forgetting the stars in their courses! Culpeper postulated, and I agree with him, that it is a poor herbalist who is not also an astrologer! Certainly, a sore throat for a Taurean is much more significant than for a Scorpio, and a nutritional programme day by day is needed by a Virgo but not by an Aquarian! The greater energies of nature, those which affect plant growth, human behaviour, patterns of illness, and even threaten the earth's survival at times, cannot be ignored when deciding which plant is to be prescribed, picked at what season, for what illness. When sunspots flare, or a moon eclipse occurs, these greater energies of nature affect us all. In winter our moods are different; in spring our blood pounds a little more strongly. We may feel uncomfortably headachy before an approaching thunderstorm, or surprisingly happy in a spring garden. How can we confine our sore throat to a 'germ' only, when all the greater energies of nature set the stage for the birth and lifecycle of that 'germ' and whether it will affect a throat disadvantageously?

Part of the training of the classical herbalist is to *observe* nature's larger energies and how illness patterns occur in a rhythm and a flow. An experienced old grey-haired practitioner will observe the high humidity and expect all the skin diseases and respiratory problems, but when the first dry winds of winter blow, the skin-disease patients disappear and the respiratory dry asthmas change to bronchitis and wet asthma.

As the larger cycles change, so do the smaller ones. Every experienced herbalist knows that one week there'll be gall bladders predominating but the next week it's nothing but sprained ankles! Irrespective, almost, of different illnesses and the date the appointment was made, one week the Valerian is seldom reached for in the dispensary; the next week it's indicated for almost every second patient. It's astounding how many times a patient will return, years later perhaps, on the very same day they first consulted you. 'That's funny,' you'll say, 'it was the third of November six years ago for your first consultation. Today is also November the third.' What subtle energies, great or small, cause such rhythmical curves?

A traditional herbalist can only wonder, record and then hope humbly to find some reasons, some day, somewhere, so that we may plot our courses in even closer harmony with those energies of nature — the rules which exist already.

Materia
Medica

*Before attempting to use any of the herbs
in the Materia Medica,
read the section Prescribing
on pages 313–14.*

Agrimony

Agrimonia eupatorium

As a member of the major plant group Rosacea, Agrimony has little in common with the garden rose or indeed any other rose, except botanically. It is an erect plant growing from a single rosette whose leaves are cut and indented and are a pleasant shade of clear green. Its flowers are five-petalled and a brilliant yellow. As with much of nature, colour-coding exists here too to teach the keen observer some of the established rules of the game. Yellow-flowered plants are often found in practice to be efficacious for the body's 'yellow' systems: the liver, bile duct, gall bladder, pancreas and kidneys. Organs through which yellowish fluids pass are part of the elimination system too: if faeces are yellowish rather than brown, this may be a secondary indication for use of the plant.

Agrimony's seeds, hairy and hooked, cling to clothing or passing animals. To a classically trained herbalist, the hook shape in seed, thorn or leaf can indicate high levels of silica present in a plant.

Agrimony is not native to Australia, and you must live in cool, moist areas of this country to grow it well. Its growth habits vary enormously and all too often cause botanists headaches and internecine arguments when an Agrimony plant seems different enough from the norm to warrant re-naming it as a separate species. Like people, Agrimony plants are very different one from the other; some are shorter or taller, and the leaf shapes, like those of the dandelion, come with multiple variations. Its medicinal properties have been well documented over many centuries. Experienced manufacturers gather from as many different Agrimony plants as possible when making their extracts to ensure an average uniformity of contents.

All the great early herbalists mention this plant: all agree on its major uses. This in itself is rare, but the plant was mostly prescribed then on its own as a 'simple', so its usefulness is perhaps now better understood and more accurately documented (see page 314). It is prescribed for symptoms originating from the liver, from the kidneys and from any infection or irritation which causes either of these important organs to function poorly. From hepatitis to cirrhosis; from food poisoning to alcoholic excess: anything which causes poor liver function and uneven distribution of bile will go on to produce a difficulty with fat metabolism and consequent loose, fatty or floating stools, up to and including severe, watery diarrhoea. Any foods of a protein nature may then become more of a loading on kidneys and fluid excretion. Both liver and kidneys are areas in which Agrimony is effective, with secondary effects in the bowels. Blood supply to these organs is also improved by Agrimony through hepatic and renal arteries, and the portal vein.

The high silica in Agrimony stimulates excretion of irritating organisms or substances, and there is choline too to help balance the liver's partnership with cholesterol and lecithin. There is also carotene (the vegetable building block for Vitamin A production), and organic acids which quieten down an over-enthusiastic peristalsis. As well as volatile oil and some bitter principles, Agrimony is high in tannins so it has a strong astringent action, toning up relaxed bowels and moving fluids along well.

Agrimony
person-picture
This poor soul is really suffering! Nausea, even vomiting, at one end is matched by diarrhoea and gripes and spasmodic contractions at the other, with lower-back pain in between. If you've ever suffered from Delhi belly, the Cairo curse or the Honduras hop, you'll know how an Agrimony person views life! This is, of course, an extreme of the type, but most of us have had some Agrimony episode, even if it is only from the local Chinese restaurant's unusually spicy dishes or the Indian curry house's hottest combination. 'Intestinal hurry' is a polite term for the problem.

In accord with nature's three-way reasons for illness symptoms (the physical, the emotional and the circumstantial), the emotional nature of Agrimony is bright, cheerful and fun-loving on the surface, but *real* emotions may be hidden underneath and seldom honestly aired. Even when 'well', the 'Agrimony' person may edit their personality in order to be 'nice' and liked by others. In the process, the liver can become congested and so can the portal vein. There may be an explosive unburdening once or twice in a lifetime, or even once or twice a week, depending on the self-control of that person. Every barmaid and barman knows 'Agrimony' well.

Negative-chronic 'Agrimony'

If the above is the overall picture, can the negative or chronic story be much worse? Already this person is suffering from holding on to emotions and trying to hold on to their dinner and their excrement as well! If they fail in any aspect, the long-term prognosis deteriorates further. The enlarging and overburdened liver begins to crave increasing stimulus more often. Drugs of addiction may be next, or twenty cups of coffee a day hunting caffeine to kick along a few more sparks out of weary adrenal glands. Chronic alcoholism and chronic hepatitis together spell out a doom which also contains unexpressed emotions and unshed tears for many years previously.

When kidneys begin to labour and adrenal hormones cannot trigger off fluid excretion properly, this person is very sick indeed. As bowels continue to be loose and fast, absorption of various vitamins and other nutrients becomes harder and harder. Energy dwindles as a result and there is a renewed craving for stimulants, drugs, coffee, aspirin or any other crutch available. It is easily possible to die from negative chronic Agrimony symptoms! Gastro-enteritis can do it for a child; advanced symptoms of this type can finally bring the heroin addict a last sleep; and amoebic dysentery can cause the deaths of thousands. Irrespective of whatever causes the initial liver and bowel inflammation in either child or adult, Agrimony can relieve the symptoms of congestion, inflammation and excessive fluid loss: it does nothing whatsoever to kill off any invading organisms, nor to *prevent* symptoms occurring if you are going to Papua New Guinea, Brazil or Ethiopia. It is corrective of the *results*, not preventive against the causes. You'd need Garlic and several other plants to prevent the 'Agrimony' episode.

True negative 'Agrimony' is the clown laughing in public but crying or reaching for a bottle in private. Negative 'Agrimony' can have simple symptoms of bowels which are looser when worried or upset or apprehensive; or there can be constipation as they hold on and on and on, until the control slips and there is a series of explosive and runny motions in quick succession.

Positive 'Agrimony'

A *truly* cheerful person, who says it like it is, may lose some fair-weather friends, but the few close friends will be there until death. Positive 'Agrimony' is *emotionally honest*, telling all who are around what they're feeling at the time they're feeling it. It's warts and all! If you don't like it all open, honest and above board, go elsewhere for friendship, because positive 'Agrimony' will tell you, quite kindly, when your breath smells and how badly! At the same time, liver will function very well indeed, kidneys will too, and bowel motions will be medium-soft, well-formed and in a regular pattern daily.

But in those 'Agrimony' episodes of food poisoning, visiting foreign parts, or eating and drinking rather too well and too often, Agrimony may be prescribed professionally for you even if you are not normally of this nature.

Dosage

1   Agrimony is not used as a salad or household herb, nor as a daily tea, and is better left for professional prescribing.

2   It is often used with other related herbs like Garlic, Chinese Rhubarb, Tansy or Dandelion, which together cover other aspects of the same problems, and can be mixed with it in appropriate proportions by your herbalist. The plant parts above the ground are all used together medicinally.

> Agrimony's name *'eupatorium'* is perhaps better rendered as *'hepatorium'* in the opinion of one ancient writer, as referring to the liver; but there was also an ancient Persian king called Mithridates Eupator, who was a fabled concoctor of wildly exotic remedies and poison-antidotes. Whatever the origin, both claims carry some validity.

Alfalfa

Medicago sativa

*I*f you're American, it's 'Alfalfa';
if you're European or British, it
may be 'Lucerne', but it's the
identical leguminous Clover
family plant in both cultures. In
Australia we've grown accustomed to 'Alfalfa' in the cities but
many old Aussie bushwackers still call it 'Lucerne' and have baled it
for hay for their animals since Australia began. Well known as an
animal fodder, its therapeutic use for humans is more recent. Some
hard-working farmer or grazier may have been idly chewing a few
of the green three-leaved stems, or even a piece of the dried hay, and
observed a change in body processes. After all, the uses of plants
were first discovered and established by observation and deduction
not by government grants or spectro-analysis machines. Too many
of us won't believe the evidence of our own eyes.

Alfalfa is believed to be native to Greece originally, and may be
a plant which passed between Greece and Egypt, as did so much of
our early knowledge and experience. It is grown today in India and
Arabic countries, but still mostly for the beasts of burden and the
domesticated animals. Every Egyptian donkey driver, snarling up
the traffic in teeming Cairo today, carries under the cart a bundle of
Clover, or Alfalfa, as the animal's daily meal when away from other
pasture.

Humans have grown to appreciate its uses to them, as well as
to their animals. Most greengrocers sell little packs of Alfalfa
sprouts, with their two seed-leaves greening. Don't bother eating
the sprouts unless those *green* leaves are obviously present. If you
grow the sprouts at home, sow freshly every four or five days so

continuous supplies can be ready at this green, leafy stage. I put the Alfalfa sprouts containers on a sunny windowsill with the lid open for twenty-four hours so the green leaves can develop their full quota of chlorophyll, Vitamins C and B, and iron. While you may need to keep a partly used pack in the refrigerator, the sprouts will not develop their full potential there, especially if green-leaf stage is not yet evenly spread through the pack.

Many herbal writers ignore Alfalfa altogether. Mrs Grieve and Mrs Leyel, both academically trustworthy and accurate researchers, refer to it only for animals. Perhaps, like the Dandelion (which is also believed to be native originally to Greece), Alfalfa has saved itself for the more recent sins of the highly developed countries. Cultural sophistication always brings with it decadence from over-supply and over-indulgence in the good things of life at the table, far more than is needed for body maintenance and energy. Perhaps it's not coincidental that Alfalfa has become popular at the time it is most needed.

'The Remedy is always to be found close to the disease' is not perhaps a principle of established herbal medicine or an aphorism of Hippocrates, but I like to use it in the practice of herbal medicine — because it's true! Plants become popular and in the public eye when needed: plants which were useful and necessary in ages long gone are not necessarily useful today.

Alfalfa's properties show why it is so popular. First, for vegetarians, it is an essential dietary source of complete protein. Its 18.9 per cent average protein content is higher than beef and comparable with soy-beans. It also contains the nine essential amino acids needed to digest its own protein as well as any other protein consumed at the same time. As it is a legume, its effective buffering of too-acid conditions in the gastrointestinal tract reflects its alkalising properties. It contains pectin, a digestive enzyme which has also shown some protective qualities against harmful effects of radiation on healthy cells. It is high in iron, with the trace of copper needed to absorb the iron well. Its calcium is also above average in the plant world, and it contains useful levels of potassium, silica, phosphorus and magnesium for resilience and strength of the nervous system and its muscular controls. It contains Vitamins B_1, some B_2, A and C. Vitamin K is present as well, to create a balance between clotting and anti-clotting mechanisms in blood.

It's hard to find anyone who doesn't need Alfalfa in a general food sense, but a description of the more specific 'Alfalfa-type' will show when it is needed medicinally.

'Alfalfa'
person-picture

The 'Alfalfa' person is constantly on the go — and isn't that most of us in a 'civilised' mode of living? The classic Alfalfa type always has something on their minds to be done in the next few minutes or few hours, usually with one eye on the clock. They have multiple and different tasks, all of which demand constant nervous activity to complete. These people do not sit with empty minds looking at nothing, daydreaming on a river bank, or contemplating the sunset. A common phrase is 'I haven't got the time right now'.

This constant trickling away of nervous energy causes acid wastes to build up as end products on the physical nerve-fibre endings all over the body. You 'pickle' in your own brine! Without some rest, and elimination of these acid wastes, an otherwise healthy and busy person may become quite severely and chronically ill with symptoms which all reflect the irritating properties of constantly over-acid conditions in organs, in connective tissues, in the digestive tract, and on every physical nerve fibre from brain to toes.

Negative-chronic
'Alfalfa'

Think for a moment of all the diseases caused initially by irritation; followed by inflammation, congestion and impaired function. This person is irritable, swollen here and there, with itchy or even painful areas of congestion and soreness which may change locality from day to day or time to time.

From an itchy scalp, to the irritable eyes and sniffly nose of hayfever sufferers, or the chronic catarrh of the throat and the 'acid' taste on the tongue of older folk, you could class Alfalfa as a 'head' remedy. But it buffers and gently alkalises as it passes through stomach, small intestines and lower bowels. Even an itching anal area may not indicate a need for worm treatment, or monilia control, but only for an alkalising of a too-acid large bowel which is irritable and inflamed. In various hollow organs like lungs, bladder and uterus there can also be over-acid conditions present which cause the mucous linings to produce excess mucus as the irritation continues. So mucus, produced in greater quantities than those needed to protect and lubricate various organs and body apertures, indicates a need for Alfalfa.

So does any protein-digestion difficulty, especially of animal-protein origin. If an Aussie steak on the barbie gives you indigestion, add Alfalfa sprouts to the salad I hope you always eat with it. Protein-digestion is usually the hardest job, demanding the most energy, that the liver and digestive tract have to do. Incomplete protein-digestion is too common, overloading first the kidneys and next the bowels. Certainly vegetable protein is an easier alternative to eat for many of us, but even beans (and some dairy foods) can cause discomfort for the non-eaters of meat. Adding Alfalfa sprouts and Alfalfa tea to the diet, in general quantities as you would any other food, can help gradually, but seek professional herbalists' help when disease symptoms of this kind are present and you need faster, greater, and more accurate dosing than home-help can provide.

The negative 'Alfalfa' person reacts badly to insect stings and bites with swelling, red weals, itchiness and irritability. Even dabbing a used Alfalfa tea bag on such areas can alkalise quickly and relieve discomfort. To remove the tendency to such reactions Alfalfa taken internally in professionally prescribed accurate dosages appropriate to each individual's specific requirements is needed. The Vitamins B1 and some B2, as well as A and C, contained in Alfalfa produce its effective relationship with the liver, and its control of skin reactions, as well as giving the whole irritable nervous system a hefty dose of equanimity!

The negative 'Alfalfa' person-picture is one of nervous irritability and the consequent over-production of mucus, acid and inflammatory wastes; a person who may crave meat and other forms of protein but doesn't digest them well. Itching skin, eyes and nostrils, together with irritation internally, can produce an irritable nature. And don't forget the preoccupation with *time*!

Excessive consumption of acid-producing foods may turn you into negative 'Alfalfa' even if it is not truly your basic nature. Empty carbohydrates like white sugar and white bread, and overconsumption of alcohol, can also set up an over-acid residue to irritate tissues internally. If this diet also includes too much animal protein, the need for Alfalfa can become urgent indeed. A nation of tired, irritable clock-watchers may result if we commit all these acid-producing sins without an Alfalfa counter-attack.

Positive 'Alfalfa'

This person eats perhaps a *little* meat, but prefers vegetables, stone and melon fruits, and sea-foods. Dairy-food intake is medium to small. No difficulties are experienced with any part of digestion or excretion. The nose does not run, nor the early-morning throat-clearing begin. Insect bites and stings are just a momentary annoyance, then gone. In other words, those who eat Alfalfa as part of their general diet don't get to the point of needing it in therapeutic dosage. It is sad for me to comment that, until we all catch up with this dietary marvel, Alfalfa continues to be one of the most prescribed herbs by the professionals. Protein allergies are its main symptom indicators. If anyone in your household has allergies to milk, eggs, cheese, meat, mosquito-bites, prawns, or even oysters, digestion of protein may be the problem. Alfalfa will be part of the mixture prescribed for this patient.

Positive 'Alfalfa' people make time their servant not their master! These positive people crowd into their day all sorts of active tasks mentally and physically without sniffing and snorting and rubbing at itchy eyes or smarting skin. Of them you may say, 'They keep cool when the heat's on'. An excellent ancillary treatment is to immerse their bodies in cool or tepid water often. Showers, baths and swimming wash away the acid perspiration wastes that are also indicative of this type. They have a busy nervous system still, but not an irritable one!

Dosage

1   Include Alfalfa sprouts as a regular addition to meals, especially if the protein content of the meal is high.

2   Drink Alfalfa tea occasionally, especially after a heavy protein meal where there were no Alfalfa sprouts added.

3   The extract or tincture of Alfalfa may be added to an individual's mixture in appropriate dosages when any symptoms of the above kind need urgent or long-term correction.

4   Don't overdose yourself with Alfalfa to 'speed things up'! Remember that excess of this or any other plant can actually produce the *opposite* effect to that desired. If Alfalfa gives you a bloated distended abdomen, wind, and even pain, cut down on the amount and the frequency of its use as you're taking too much perhaps too often. It causes the same symptoms in farm animals which are too greedy and eat too much of it. Cut your intake down considerably, and gradually begin again with smaller amounts less frequently. Nature can't be forced, or she'll turn her other face to you and teach you once again the lesson of balance.

Aloe

Aloe vera, A. socotrina,
A. barbadensis, etc.

*A*loes, like all other plants, and most people, vary considerably when growing in different parts of the world. There is a basic difference between those Aloes native to the African continent and those indigenous to the Americas and islands of the West Indies, and over the centuries these varieties have been used a little differently too. Overall, Aloes are hardy, drought-resistant plants, the cuticle of their leaves absorbing any scarce moisture very well but losing this again much more slowly. In desert conditions, where night-time cold provides some condensation droplets after the searing heat of the days, Aloe grows and thrives. In neglected and deserted old gardens in Australia, any introduced Aloe may be the last plant to die, often growing in an increasing clump in conditions of desiccation and poor soil. There have been recent attempts to establish commercial plantations of it in Australia. It's a shame herbalists were not consulted beforehand as vast numbers of plants are simply not needed. The plant world yields bountifully from handfuls, not paddocks-full. Indeed, one plant, clumping naturally into more and more spiky cactus-like rosettes, is all a whole household will ever need, even perhaps a whole street.

Australia should be a willing host to this plant group. Unproductive desert areas may be greened with it, and we as a nation need its moisture-retaining properties for our bowels and our skins, as well as its protective role against intestinal parasites. A member of the Lily family, Aloe's tenacious root system also holds soil together against strong winds or water erosion.

Before you rush out and pick Cactus, Agave or Bromeliad by mistake, thinking these plants fit the description, take a good-sized piece of your supposed Aloe leaf (and flower if possible) to your local nursery or Department of Agriculture office. More harm has been done by people using the *wrong* plants than has ever been done using any of the herbalists' range of remedies! The Aloe family has pointed thick leaves growing in a rosette, covered with a smooth, hard and often shiny cuticle inside which is a soft sticky mucillaginous jelly in which the leaf's moisture is retained. I take an Aloe leaf into class for my herbal medicine students, and run a thumbnail down it to break through the cuticle so the sticky juice and the yellowish droplets begin to ooze out. The leaf is left there, unwatered, for weeks. Each week, I repeat the performance, and a little more juice oozes through the protective outer skin. My students get the picture: Aloe *retains* moisture, even in the most extreme conditions!

At the Aswan airport in Egypt I spotted two thriving Aloe plants on either side of a pedestrian walkway, happy in the searing heat and dry desert wind. As I bent to look closer, a local man in his faded indigo *gelabiah* smiled and made the gestures of picking a leaf, cutting it with the thumbnail, pointing to the white-hot sun above and then to my face which was somewhat red from yesterday's desert walking. We spanned several thousand years of use in a few minutes. I regretted that I did not have enough of the language to explain that I too knew and used the ancient ways, and found them just as effective now as then.

There are not only mucillaginous soothing demulcents and emollients in the Aloe leaf, but there is a substance now called Barbaloin which promotes the speed of healing reddened or irritated areas inside and outside the body. Vitamin B12 has been found as well. The bitterness of Aloes is legendary. These bitter-principles, aloin and others, are what upset all sorts of intestinal parasites so much that they lose their grip, so to speak, and leave you. As Aloes grow naturally in countries where parasitic infestation is a common hazard, we see again a little portion of that 'divine plan' my grandmother saw so clearly.

Aloes are mineral-rich plants, too, with potassium, magnesium and iron. These minerals aid muscular and peristaltic movements of the lower-bowel areas, so Aloe is laxative, tonic, demulcent and healing. Not a bad combination against our newer 'civilised' parasites like Guiardia Ilamblia, monilia, candida, etc., as well as against the older-known amoebas; even against bilharzia. Any ancient Egyptian farmer who ate garlic and onions, and drank the juice of diluted Aloe concentrate had little to fear from Nile water except crocodiles!

'Aloe'
person-picture

The 'Aloe' person lives in a dry climate, or has dry bowels where movement can cause straining, even haemorrhoids. Faeces can be like bullets, and there can be some blood occasionally passed as this hard dry matter rubs against bowel walls and causes any haemorrhoids present to leak slightly. Any episode of prolonged constipation may need Aloes as one of the ingredients prescribed. It should *not*, however, be given for constipation during pregnancy as the stronger bowel movements which follow may cause the uterus to move strongly too and to interpret this as the signal to begin contractions. Aloe is not an abortive agent as such, but its powerful stimulus to the lower abdominal organs should be avoided in pregnancy.

The 'Aloe' type may also be rather bloated abdominally, without obvious cause. This won't be a beer-belly, or from eating too much or too quickly. It will be from intestinal irritation, either by parasites or from unusual food which is not sitting comfortably in the digestive tract.

There can also be skin reactions to excess sunlight. Everything from a painful sunburn to a dermatitis-like rash after sun-exposure needs Aloes applied externally in one of the dozens of different creams, lotions or gells now on the market. These emollient uses of Aloe are excellent too for insect bites and stings and for itchy, rough or reddened spots and blemishes.

The 'Aloe' person is *dry*. Dry inside and out, with need for lubrication and softening.

Negative-chronic
'Aloes'

Children with bloated abdomens and sad eyes in news films about starvation in Africa may need Aloes as well as food. When the abdomen becomes grossly distended, faeces can begin drying and become impacted. Any parasites present, either micro-size or larger — like tapeworm, roundworm, hookworm, etc. — will also irritate the bowel walls when protein food is not forthcoming for them. The extreme of negative 'Aloes' is that starving bloated child with the wrinkled skin of a seventy-year-old.

In our affluent societies negative 'Aloes' may still show the abdominal bloat which appears to have no real cause in diet or alcohol intake, but which comes and goes in size as well as in discomfort. The micro-parasites spoken of by so many homoeo-pathic researchers since mid-last century have escaped the notice of orthodox medicine until quite recently. If you have a 'tummy' that wobbles out in front of you, and your diet is small and good, there may be reason to consult with your professional herbalist as to how Aloes can best be prescribed for you.

After years of intestinal irritation, ulceration may result, caus-ing even more bloat and real pain. Aloe is needed even more now. Ulcerative colitis, diverticulitis, even spastic-colon problems may be diagnosed, as the bowel refuses to move well, becoming more and more full of dried-out faeces and sore places. Not a pretty picture! Severe symptoms of this kind may need hospitalisation, even sur-gery, so preventive care with Aloes should be undertaken early if the above general picture fits you.

Negative 'Aloes' has skin which wrinkles too early. The *dry-ness* again is the cause. Surface applications of Aloes would have helped to retain moisture over the years. Many cosmetic prepara-tions now contain it for this reason. So if you're wrinkled, bloated, constipated and sunburned, Aloes should fit you perfectly!

Positive 'Aloes'

Smooth, supple, unwrinkled skin at seventy is every woman's dream, but the process of wrinkling may begin twenty-five years earlier — and this is when moisture retention should be addressed. Regular applications of Aloe-rich cosmetics can fool Father Time into passing you by because you look twenty years younger than your age!

Positive 'Aloes' has regular, soft, easy bowel movements, and a stomach without microscopic or other fellow-travellers. Positive 'Aloes' usually prefers a vegetable and fruit-based diet with whole carbohydrates for energy: typically, there is no craving for protein.

If you have had an overseas trip to countries where parasitic infestation may occur more readily in less hygienic conditions of living than we have in Australia today, you may return with a poddy tummy, changed elimination patterns and sagging skin. An episode of the 'Aloes' type can be treated promptly on your return.

Every desert dweller needs *some* moisture to survive. In the Australian outback, diluted Aloe juice should be as regularly taken as billy-tea. Luckily, commerce has taken a hand with the Aloe, and there are now various brands of Aloe juice available. These are concentrated and should be diluted for general use as a household remedy. Even a tablespoon of the juice added to a cool drink can be enough, each day, to give a general effect in bowels and in a sore or irritated intestinal tract. Don't overuse Aloes! Its use is probably self-limiting because of its bitterness, but some folk will do amazingly unreasonable things in a search for good health. Remember, too much will produce an *opposite* effect — griping and spasmodic intestinal pain as bowels growl and grumble and move *too* quickly.

Dosage

1 Although Aloe *juice* straight from the plant may cause irritation on healthy skin, it will relieve irritation, itching, etc., if these symptoms are present in an emergency situation. Irritations from insect bites and stings, from sunburn, even from blisters on the heel or a burn from a hot iron or saucepan, can respond well to the plant juice applied direct. But make absolutely sure it's the right plant! And *don't* apply the fresh juice to *healthy* skin areas.

2 There is no such thing as Aloe tea! Apart from its bitterness and strong unpleasant taste, its properties need alcohol as well as water to extract some of its most useful active ingredients.

3 Professionally, dosing will be gradually and carefully adjusted to suit each individual's symptoms and the length of time they've been presenting. For children (and animals) the dose need only be, and should only be, small. It is necessary to avoid large isolated doses, as the sudden griping peristalsis so caused may be not only unpleasant but even dangerous.
Leave this herb to those professionally trained, possessed of all the cautionary education that you yourself may not have received.

Arnica

Arnica montana

'*A* blow with a blunt instrument' indicates a need for Arnica applied as a tincture or as an ointment. It doesn't matter whether it hits *you* (a cricket bat or a flying cricket ball) or you hit *it* (a chair leg or a slippery back step), the effect is of a *contusion*, not a cut. Arnica is a great vulnerary applied externally. It is almost never used internally by herbalists and only in minute doses by homoeopaths.

Nature gives you clues here, as always. The plant grows in lower mountain areas around Europe and was probably also taken to the United Kingdom where it is not a native. It grows naturally in relatively high mountain-meadows around the 1,000-metre mark and right where climbing accidents and falls can occur either in summer or in cooler weather when light snow and misty conditions may cause half-visible rocks and other obstructions to be bumped into or tripped over by the hasty climber.

The flowers of Arnica are just the yellow of the yellow stage of bruising. After the broken blood vessels cause the first purpling, bile-pigments are broken down next and cause the yellow stage; a greenish tinge may also be present then too as the leaked blood is changed and eliminated through lymphatic drainage away from the affected area.

As you would expect by now, any plant that halts bleeding will have an astringent effect, and Arnica's action is quick indeed, even when only absorbed locally through the skin at the injury site. In fact, if it is applied either as a lotion or an ointment immediately after a blow or a contusion, you may avoid the entire process called 'bruising' altogether. Crushed small blood vessels seal off very quickly when Arnica is applied, so swelling and pain is minimised, and discolouration from subcutaneous leaking blood, and its slow breakdown and elimination, is not experienced.

Mallic and gallic acids are also present in Arnica and act as oxidising agents, cleaning up the area and reducing the likelihood of any thrombus to give trouble maybe years later. Arnicin, the major active principle, brings better energy to the broken or strained or sprained tissues, and hastens repair work. All in all, a great herb for the intrepid — but hasty or clumsy! — mountain climber. After a fall, flowers straight from the plant can be laid on the sore spots with a little mountain-stream water on a clean handkerchief to keep them in place for 15 minutes or so. The root, or more correctly the rhizome, of Arnica is also used in extraction of its properties for professional medicinal use.

'Arnica' person-picture

Either a clumsy oaf, or a person always rushing about and leaping up when their body quickly responds to a head-instruction to get moving, may need Arnica too often. Such haste can result in bruises on knees, ankles, arms, even head. Walking into a low branch while talking animatedly can be a common Arnica episode for gardeners and farmers. Carpenters bang into timber, plumbers into pipes, and brickies into scaffolding. All physical workers may need it occasionally, but so do office people when they crash knees into desk corners, or swivel-chair themselves carelessly. Home handymen and women need it in reserve in the bathroom cupboard, and so do the children of the household. There can hardly be a person who won't occasionally need embrocation from this small untidy alpine plant.

My own best — or worst — experience of an Arnica-episode was when I shut my heavy frontdoor firmly over my thumbnail as I rushed out to the clinic for an early consultation. I could not release the thumb immediately as the door was self-locking and I had to rummage for keys in my handbag. Not a pleasant few seconds!

Negative-chronic 'Arnica'

One of the main dangers from an untreated bruise is the leaked blood internally. Unless quickly broken down and moved out, a clot or a thrombus (a clump of broken, dead tissue) may remain for years, only to move at some later date and obstruct some more vital areas of circulation, even the heart itself. 'Oh, there's no bones broken, and no open cut, so there's no damage done' can be a very wrong statement — and a dangerous one. Bruising, like any other damage, must be cleaned out and repaired, as the body doesn't forget the damage as easily as the head may. Twenty years later the weakened area, still a bit puffy and obstructed ever since, may become prime real-estate for random cells to set up as their territory and a cyst, a tumour, even a malignancy, may occur with congestion, dead tissues and dried-out old blood as fertile soil. That old-time medical advice, 'always treat every bruise or contusion to avoid a cancer years later at the same site' makes naturopathic sense. Bodies *don't* forget and forgive unless the site is cleared of debris first.

People who bruise far too easily are also people who may feel life's assaults like physical blows. The growing numbers of leukaemic children and adults record natures where sensitivity to life is recorded as a 'blow' or a 'buffeting': 'I've been kicked around by life', say these people. Or, 'Life has bruised me badly'. 'Bruised' emotions may not be able to have Arnica dabbed on them, but the physical evidence on the skin certainly can — and as soon afterwards as possible.

Strains and sprains that tear and stretch internally but don't break the skin are also typical of an 'Arnica' episode which, incompletely treated at the time, may leave a permanent weakness to degenerate further later. Add a few drops of Arnica tincture to a deep basin of cool water and put the wrist or ankle in it for 15–20 minutes as soon as possible after the injury.

Positive 'Arnica'

Let me return to that Arnica episode I described earlier. I was left dangling painfully by a squashed thumbnail! When I had stopped squawking and unlocked the door, I headed for the bathroom cabinet and put a good dollop of Arnica ointment all over the nail and first thumb-joint, then a quick dressing to cover it all. The pain stopped first, then the throbbing, then the swelling and, after driving the seven kilometres to my clinic, I removed the dressing and began work. Even I was astounded that by nightfall there was *no* evidence at all of a bruise, nor a discoloured fingernail likely to remain for months and turn black, nor any pain! It was as if my hasty exit had never occurred; there were no further symptoms of any kind at all at that fingernail, and never have been. Perhaps one of the beauties of using plants applied quickly as medicines is the assured *completion* of an illness or trauma so that there is no area of damage or weakness left to cause later symptoms.

Dosage

1 Arnica tea doesn't exist! The plant is *not* taken internally at all in the household sense.

2 A jar of Arnica ointment or lotion is a useful addition to the family medicine cabinet to keep on hand against bruises, bumps and accidental trauma *where the skin is not broken*. Do *not* apply the ointment if there are cuts or bleeding at the wound site. (See Castor oil, pages 123–5, and Calendula, page 116–19.)

3 Homoeopaths may prescribe 'Arnica 6C' or 'Arnica 30x' to be taken internally for shock symptoms, but leave this form of Arnica's use to the professionals. Trained and experienced herbalists *may* occasionally judge a need for a few internal doses of the tincture, but this is rarely done and only with very particular symptoms.

Blue flag

Iris versicolor

*H*ere I go, leaving myself wide open to those critics who rail against herbalists for the 'dangerous' plants they use. Blue flag must only be prescribed by competent and well-trained professional practitioners: it contains at least one, and possibly several, alkaloids, one of which seems identical with myristin. As you read in the first section of this book, alkaloids may disturb body functions when taken in isolation; when *whole* plant parts are used, however, there can be a synergistic effect on the alkaloid from the other ingredients present.

Any 'stirring' effect of Blue flag is due to its high content of iron, copper and cobalt compounds. As copper and cobalt traces are needed in order to absorb iron well, the iron in the Blue flag rhizome (the medicinal part) is quickly and easily available. Added to the alkaloid(s) and the alterative effect of the iron, etc., is oleic acid which stimulates liver function.

Blue flag was listed in the American Pharmacopoea as source material for a compound called Iridin which for many years was used to treat glandular enlargements, especially hypo-function of the glands of the stomach. King's *Dispensatory* (the 'Martindale' of the Americas) lists Blue flag fully.

While North American Indians knew well the specific uses of Blue flag, especially in treating glandular disorders which resulted long after venereal infections (perhaps even in the later children of venereally infected parentage), it is not a favoured plant amongst professionals today. This is a great pity, as its indications are specific, and are not well covered by any other herb as a possible substitute.

'Blue flag'
person-picture

'Blue flag' presents a picture of emotional ups-and-downs, hormonal imbalances, glandular disorders and even hysterical outbursts of an irrational kind. The cause for such difficult-to-assess, and even more difficult-to-treat, symptoms often lies in genetic influences. This patient finds these emotional and physical disturbances in function even more distressing as there may seem to be no traceable reasons for the hormonal imbalances and the emotional roller-coaster ride they produce. They are a puzzle to themselves, let alone to the struggling diagnostician! Many of these patients try very hard indeed to clear up their own health, to control emotional sensitivity and to eat right and think positive — often to no avail. It doesn't help to question them about a possible 'dose' in parent or grandparent before they were born, nor does it mean treatment is easier even if corroboration is possible. What is needed is deep-seated re-balancing and readjustment of glandular function, especially that of the adrenal glands, the thyroid and that most difficult gland to balance, the pancreas. While orthodox medicine does not assign much anatomical or physiological relationship between pancreas, adrenals, thyroid and *bowels*, classical herbalists, with iridology to back up their diagnoses, know that inherited tendencies are often responsible for these interdependent effects.

Negative-chronic
'Blue flag'

Our recent world-wide panic over acquired immune deficiency syndrome (AIDS) has brought to light again for orthodox medicine a basic law of nature which had for years been overlooked: humans cannot easily cope with multiple exchanges of sexual chemistry and the various associated secretions. Some animals, birds, even insects, are weakened so much by multiple sexual frenzy that they *expect* death as a natural result! We humans, in our arrogance, try to create new rules, and believe that we will not suffer at all from their consequences! There is a vast body of written data available to show that syphilis, gonorrhoea, herpes, etc., have been known for centuries as causing various predictable weaknesses and tendencies in descendants. We cannot escape the biblical 'sins of the fathers visited upon the children unto the third and fourth generation'. Every animal geneticist knows this truth and abides by it. The world around us is often much more sensibly regulated than we are.

How to begin listing the multiple and varied symptoms of long-term 'Blue flag' kind? Almost every body zone may be affected from time to time, but the overall negative areas are *glandular* as their originating causes. Whether it's thyroid or pancreas, genitals and adrenals, or the related lymphatic glands which have to 'clean up' after the glandular balances have broken down, this picture is one of waste removal become inefficient because the body's regulating systems have slipped right off the balance-arm altogether. Without good hormone production, secretion and control, the body is a wildly erratic organism where even great will-power and loads of positive thinking will slide off ineffectively. Think for a moment of the terminal symptoms of AIDS: the major glands enlarged or with hypo-function; the lymphatic nodules, lumps and tumours; the sexual and reproductive areas worn down by excesses; and the liver often grossly overloaded by alcohol, marihuana, tobacco, heroin, etc.

Blue flag was extensively used in the American Indian traditions, and in South America amongst the ancient civilisations — and for the same reasons. For syphilis in its secondary or tertiary stages; for gonorrhea at any time but particularly in gonorrheal 'arthritis' and gonorrheal 'rheumatism'; for blood-'cleaning' during glandular enlargements and swellings; for removal of wastes via lymphatics and bowels after venereal infections; the dried powdered aged rhizomes of the mauve-flowered Blue flag were prized by all. As the syphilis spirochete lives in the bowel areas of the shaggy llamas of South America, it is quite probable that this most primary of primitive warnings for our species was transferred to humans there. Nature is clear in her rules; a species is at risk if sexual and reproductive practices threaten its survival. Either one or the other must change.

So how does the herbalist judge that Blue flag is an ingredient needed in a patient's mixture, especially if the family medical history is unsure? With great deliberation, and using all the training and experience possible. Any conscientious herbalist approaches this plant's use with great care. Thorough training in the delicate balances of the endocrine and lymphatic systems is essential before any dosage can be worked out, and monitoring of each patient also needs supervision of the professionally trained practitioner. This is *not* a do-it-yourself herb! It would be thoroughly irresponsible, even downright stupid, to self-treat with Blue flag. Even I approach its use with respect for its deep-seated action and its ability to dig up past 'sins' preparatory to throwing their results away via the bowels.

All endocrine and lymphatic glands are stimulated to better secretion and discharge of their hormones into blood stream and tissue fluids by this herb. Liver is also stimulated in function. The effect is not a quiet one! Leave your professional practitioner to decide if it is needed — and if so, in what dose.

Positive 'Blue flag'

It is hard to find a group of humans with excellent genetics for hundreds of years past. Humans fall from grace all too often but, with a knowledge of natural remedies and an understanding of the reversal processes nature requires before final disease removal can be expected, there can be help available for our grandfathers' or great-grandmothers' sins now dormant in us. The positive removal of ancestral effects on today's endocrine and lymphatic systems is possible — if slow.

Positive 'Blue flag' from birth, with endocrine harmony and active lymph flow, is the child of clear genetic background. There will be a family history of simple living, good food grown at home, strong physical energy output and healthy old age. We should all be so lucky!

Dosage

For the consulting room and the dispensary, not for the kitchen or the garden. Don't ever ask for it as a 'tea' either: such a variable dose is not indicated. It is prescribed in tincture or extract only, and is often added first in a minute quantity to other ingredients in a 'conditioning' mixture when indicated.

A botanical relative from the Mediterranean to Asia and Africa is another Iris. *Iris germanica* or *Iris florentina* don't show from their later naming their earlier origins. The three fall-petals of this Iris were represented on the royal tombs of the ancient world as an emblem of beauty, majesty and regal splendour. The water gardens of Babylon, Heliopolis in Egypt, the fertile soils between the Tigris and Euphrates rivers, included white and gold-flowered scented irises as well as the lilac and soft mauves of the common kind. The drying rhizomes give off a beautiful delicate perfume as they change chemically. As orris root, it was, and still is, used worldwide as a preservative, a cosmetic and a tooth-cleaning ingredient.

Broom

Spartium scoparium,
Genista scoparius,
Cytisus scoparius

A plant which has decreased in favour since its golden years of use between the fifteenth and seventeenth centuries, Broom is no longer a household name, nor even popularly used by herbalists today as often as it was then. Not only was it found in official medical Pharmacopoeas until comparatively recently, but it lent its name to chivalry as well. It is the heraldic plant of the Scots Forbes family, and indeed gave its apothecary-name, *Planta genista*, to a line of English kings — the Plantagenets! A common native of the British Isles, France and indeed all of Europe, its bright yellow fragrant flowers and woody branches of almost leafless green 'stems' were often seized in the battlefield to identify a leader to follow into the battle, almost like a floral flag. There are records of kings, generals and European nobles using a torn branch of Broom as a helmet-crest or an identifying rallying symbol for troops in the field. Richard II of England adopted it in his Great Seal, and its facsimile adorns his tomb. A noble, popular and traditional herb!

In those early days, one of the most commonly presenting diseases was dropsy. Huge bulky figures of those earlier kings (and a few queens too!) remain in stone, metal and marble for us today to identify the dropsical diathesis. Perhaps Henry VIII of England would be the best-known example.

The name 'Broom' is duplicated in many other languages when describing this plant. Its tough needle-stems were always used bound together to form brooms for sweeping up in the peasant's hut or the castle, much as Willow was used.

The flowering tops of Broom are used for the extraction of its medicinal properties, some of which are given up to water but others need alcoholic or ether extraction from the dried plant. Too

99

long a drying period will weaken all the plant's properties, while the fresh plant tops may conversely be *too* active. You can see how traditional and careful botanical extraction must be blended with the skills of a gardener in order to pick and use plants which are at the peak of their medicinal qualities. Pharmacognosy alone is never enough!

Its beautiful yellow perfumed pea-flowers proclaim this plant a legume, a relative of peas and beans, although it has never been used as a vegetable and would, indeed, be a very bitter and unpleasant one! Its medicinal properties include sparteine, discovered and named as late as 1851; and scoparin, a glycoside, where most of its diuretic properties originate. There is volatile oil, and fatty and waxy substances in the flowers, and tannins, mucillage and albumen for kidneys; lignin, a resinous material found in other medicinal plants like Guaiacum, has a strongly stimulant and laxative effect on bowels, aiding general solid and fluid excretion.

Sparteine, the alkaloid, has attributed to it quite *opposite* effects on the heart and circulation, and the nervous system. Some writers and clinicians say it stimulates: others say it sedates. Nature's rule never varies. 'A small amount of any substance gives one predictable effect; a large amount of the same substance produces the opposite effect in the same body areas.' *Both* seemingly-opposite activities of Broom are possible: dosage, therefore, is all-important. Don't self-medicate on this one!

The action of scoparin is on the renal mucous-membrane, stimulating uric-acid elimination as well from the blood, and thereby taking a load off the heart. In the centuries where gout was common and uraemia too, Broom was quite justifiably popular in treatments.

'Broom' person-picture

The 'Broom' person is often large, and can retain much abdominal fluid. General fluid secretion and excretion will be unbalanced, and there will be a danger of uric-acid-related symptoms. Today's 'Broom' may have these symptoms originating from either the spleen, or the blood-related processes the spleen manages. Anaemia in varying degrees may be present, and may be intermittently present together with disordered iron-absorption and metabolism. In acupuncture terminology, this is a 'wet-spleen' person.

Emotionally, 'Broom' can be loud and brash, but sometimes quite the opposite. There can be self-effacing and self-critical depressed periods, alternating with what may appear to be a Walter Mitty-like exaggeration and some strange fantasies and dreams. George III of England showed all aspects of 'Broom', and his personal life-story is a classic of this type.

Negative-chronic 'Broom'

These people can strut about, acting and declaiming. They can be headstrong, verging on manic behaviour in extreme cases; the depression which follows can be typical too. As well as the tender spleen and consequent blood-quality problems, there can be adrenal incompetence and massive fluid secretion-excretion imbalances. 'Volatile', 'unpredictable', 'geniuses', 'mad-professors', even 'mentally unstable'; all are valid comments on their natures. Creatures of *extremes* of feeling, these may cause massive surges in blood pressure, a source of many problems in treatment.

From great (and perhaps even inappropriate!) self-confidence to abysmal self-criticism can be a daily journey. Keeping many body processes *stable* can be a difficult job for the therapist. It's either right 'on' or right 'off' for these people; compromise and halfway marks are unknown to them.

It's quite difficult to describe them more accurately than above, because of their inherent unpredictability. Whatever course of action you think they'll adopt, a last-minute change may throw all plans and arrangements out the window. Other people often dread this unpredictability, and either leave them, or live on a roller-coaster of ups and downs, never able to plan ahead.

Severe cardiac symptoms may eventually present. The heart grows tired of these surges in blood pressure, and failing kidneys put an even more uneven load on the major circulation. The spleen may become grossly enlarged, and very tender even to the touch. If an over-large meal is taken, heavy in protein, there can be a real risk of cardiac distress later. Not a pretty picture!

Positive 'Broom'

Heart is beating strongly and without extra or dysrhythmic pulses. Spleen begins to reduce in size, and more stable diuretic-hormone production and distribution is the improvement in adrenal glands and through kidneys. Fluid excretion is better managed. Emotionally, this person remains subject still to *extremes*. Be prepared for a 'door-mat' attitude in the morning and a 'dictator' in the afternoon, followed by a dissertation on abstract mathematics after dinner. 'A genius!' friends may exclaim, followed by, 'but I'm glad I don't have to live with him or her!'

Although treatment with Broom and other herbs will reduce the peaks and raise the valleys of these emotional zigzaggers, giving them (and you!) a relatively calmer ride through life, their tendencies are always to exaggerated emotional and physical responses to stimuli. Adrenaline pumps, the heart flutters, and strong secondary pulses may be found at the abdominal aorta, the temples or neck, even around the groin. Those around them often spend much of their nervous energy trying to placate and stabilise them in order to avoid another 'up' and another 'down'.

Physically, other herbs like Buchu, Uva-ursi, and perhaps Fenugreek, Dandelion or Hawthorn, may be added to Broom for secondary symptoms and circulatory protection in a therapeutic mixture.

Dosage

1 Broom tops are not drunk as a tea, although they have been added to beers and ales in Europe in earlier times. The bitter taste alone is enough to deter you!

2 In extract or tincture, Broom, although less used nowadays, was one of the last plants to be expunged from Pharmacopoeas world-wide when pharmaceuticals of man-made origin replaced most of the herbs formerly accepted by orthodoxy. It is still best prescribed for you by a professional herbalist only after careful assessment and diagnosis.

> Broom grows very well indeed in Australia. It requires only poor, sandy or rocky soil, and its strong root system binds the soil and prevents erosion. It needs little watering, remaining woody in times of drought, but breaking into fast green again after wet weather. It will cling to rocky cliffs and actually relishes salt-laden winds on exposed sea-fronts or on sand-dunes. Even if it is not needed for medicine, you may care to make a besom broom or two in memory of your ancestors!

Buchu

Barosma betulina,
Diosma betulina

This native of the southern-most
tip of the African continent was not only unheard of in mediaeval
usage, but only recently introduced into the repertoire of today's
herbalists. Its uses by the Hottentots were observed by the early
Dutch colonists there, and quantities of the dried plant were then
shipped through London to Dutch relatives and friends in America
for inclusion in proprietary medicines. (It always baffles me how
some of today's pharmacists can vilify herbal medicine when it has
been used effectively by their own trained graduates for hundreds
of years!)

The African name *Bucku* covered several different species of
this plant, but the 'official' variety now is only *B. betulina*, as it
contains several principles which the others do not.

The contents of Buchu, after drying, are rich in principles
which are effective at the kidneys and bladder, promoting diuresis
and washing out gravel and irritating substances. There is a volatile
oil, and much mucillage to soothe any irritated mucous linings and
an antiseptic called diasphenol which helps remove infective debris
— perhaps the cause of the irritation initially.

The plant is shrubby with five-petalled white flowers, and
fairly nondescript brownish fruits. The thick, shiny leaves are the
parts used medicinally, with some flowers added occasionally. It
grows in fairly dry and poor hilly conditions, and in roughly similar
latitudes to the southern parts of the Australian continent. Perhaps
some enterprising nursery may look into growing it commercially
here, so we can become independent of import difficulties.

'Buchu'
person-picture

I believe there to be more to the
Hottentot uses of Buchu than was observed by the first Dutch

colonists. Or perhaps they *knew* more, but decided to keep this extra information close to their chests! Much of what irritates bladder and kidneys may be from infections of the venereal kind. Chronic cystitis or urethritis may often result from sexual over-activity or multiple sexual partners. I believe Buchu to have been locally used when discharges of the venereally-communicated diseases were present. This person-type may have intermittent malodorous discharge from vagina or penis, and be given a diagnosis today of 'non-specific urethritis' or 'cystitis' when there are other organisms present which are potentially much more severe.

As well as irritation in bladder, kidneys and urethral tracts, there may be symptoms of abnormal periods in the female and inflamed or painful prostate in the male, showing the observant diagnostician that reproductive system symptoms may reflect long-term low grade infection here too.

In practice, Buchu produces a marked improvement in adrenal-cortex function and adrenal-hormone stimulus too. I think those Hottentots knew a thing or two!

Negative-chronic 'Buchu'

As our ancestors knew well, unrecognised or untreated infections in kidneys and bladder may go on to infect reproductive organs as well, and *vice versa*. The urogenital tract is the site of symptoms when long-term or recurring exposure to such infections is not recognised for what it is, and this is where Buchu can be more effective than other remedies used singly for either the genital areas or the urinary organs.

Homoeopathy, one of the sister-modalities to herbal medicine, recognises and uses some treatments which effectively belong more to your ancestors than to you, but Buchu, for the herbalist, digs back into inherited predispositions towards urogenital irritation because somewhere in your family tree, long before you were conceived, there could have been either unadmitted or untreated discharges which were venereal in origin. Grandfather or grandmother could have had a brief lapse from Victorian rectitude, and any following discomfort may have been ignored with straitlaced short-sightedness. Ensuing children and grandchildren, however, may suffer now from otherwise unexplainable symptoms of urogenital sensitivity disproportionate to any other infection or irritation source. At times when adrenal-glands and other hormones are under great change (that is, puberty, pregnancy, menopause) otherwise unexplainable urogenital irritation may surface and, what's worse, so may symptoms of pseudo-rheumatoid aches and pains in limbs and lower back. What a herbalist would call the 'urogenital-rheumatoid-diathesis' springs apparently from nowhere.

I would prescribe Buchu when this person-picture presents itself, and over the years I have found it to be astonishingly effective. Many indigenous remedies from small localities are 'well-researched' by that great experience-teacher, Time. Native peoples don't keep on using a plant which is ineffective!

Positive 'Buchu'

Not only free of irritation in bladder, kidneys and genital tracts, but also free of the 'aches and pains' found with infections in these zones, the positive 'Buchu' person had righteous ancestors at best, or forebears who had any infections and discharges treated to completion, not suppressed or ignored. A good douche, with the juice of a lemon in a cup of water, could have cleaned out recent infection for the female, and various other herbs like Cleavers, taken internally, could have treated the male.

Giving Buchu as a remedy will produce fairly obvious comfort quite quickly, as its mucillage soothes and lines, and reduces irritation quickly. Symptoms can sometimes be slow to diminish when some herbal combinations are given, but Buchu is a speedy actor, and therefore a boon to add when long-term causes must also be treated more slowly with other plants.

Dosage

1   Buchu tea *may* be available from a herbal pharmacy specialising in plant preparations, and this is certainly how it was used in Africa — as a decoction, and drunk cool; or as a handful of the fresh leaves steeped in cold water and the strained liquid drunk. However, bear in mind that home use may not be accurate and effective unless you're a Hottentot with tribal experience.

2   Extract or tincture of the plant may be a constituent of a composite herbal mixture obtained from a practitioner. The strong combination taste of peppermint-aniseed type, mixed with a rich, sweetly-bushy aroma, make this a pleasant herb for the patient to take. When freshly prepared, the tincture is a beautiful and unusual indigo-blue, oxidising to the usual uniform brown as it ages or is exposed to the air. Like that well-known Southern American spirit, it has a flavour like '. . . Ummh?'

Burdock

Arctium lappa

It is a good thing that Burdock does *not* grow in the wild in Australia for in countries where it does grow naturally, it can reduce the price of wool fleece as its sticky and hooked 'burrs' catch in the hair of passing animals, causing tangling and matting around each sharp barb. The high price of our wool reflects its freedom from burrs, as well as its other qualities. Accordingly, Burdock is a declared noxious weed in Australia, and rightly so.

In countries where its use is long and traditional, Burdock is revered, almost, as one of the most powerful blood cleansers available to the herbalist. It has also been used as a pot-herb or vegetable, and in Japan the young stems, stripped of their leaves, are steamed like asparagus and eaten as a delicacy. I once bought a tin of 'Burdocks' from a Japanese food store in Sydney, and I found them delicious.

The plant's leaves are somewhat similar to those of the common Dock — hence its popular name. Its generic surname and species name indicate its character more accurately: 'clutched by a bear' is a loose translation. The embrace of Burdock seeds on the clothing, on animal-hair, even on birds' feathers, is a very tight one! Strictly speaking, the word 'seeds' is inaccurate; 'fruits' is more correct botanically. The flower is thistle-like, the pinkish-red flower-head clustered with sharply hooked barbs which can explode from the ripe seed-head and land some distance away. It is actually a 'Daisy' family member, from the large Compositae classification. Its growth is strong and erect, to 1.5 metres in good conditions. It is an accommodating weed, finding sandy gritty soils comfortable, but growing in richer loams too.

As a medicinal plant, it figures in the major herbals of many European countries. It is unfortunately true that common names of plants can be wrongly applied to several similar plants and, through later translations (by people who are skilled translators but *not* herbalists), the same name has been applied incorrectly to several closely related plants. Burdock is a good example of this. Mrs M. Grieve, otherwise an excellent and accurate researcher and writer, has listed 'Personata' amongst the common names for Burdock, but there seems to be confusion here between the Latin and the Greek. 'Personata' is described by Dioscorides as 'a whitish stalk, and sometime also ye herb is without': 'leaves like to those of Colocynthis' (the Bitter Cucumber of Egypt). Neither of these descriptions fits the Burdock plant! Dioscorides describes Burdock — and its medicinal uses — accurately under the name 'Arktion', or 'Arcturum'. He mentions its use for sciatica and for kidney stimulation exactly as I prescribe it today. It is an eerie feeling to share herbal medicine practices with a Greek travelling with the Roman armies during the first century AD! The illustrations in the 1650s translation by John Goodyer were added to the first-century manuscript of Dioscorides by an unknown Byzantine artist in 512 AD. His drawing of the plant 'Arktion' shows the typical Burdock growth and thistle-like flowerheads. So for me, 'Arktion' it remains.

The dried roots of the plant are used as the main medicinal parts, but seeds and leaves have their uses too. Some herbalists prefer the seeds alone, but as the greater medicinal concentrations are found here, a lively elimination through the kidneys may even reach the uncomfortable stage if seeds are used alone. Seeds and roots together are certainly easier on the patient.

'Burdock' person-picture

All the symptoms of Burdock point *downwards*. Pain over the kidney zones, often wrongly self-diagnosed as a 'bad back', can radiate down to the legs, knees, ankles and feet. There may be a 'hot' quality to this aching or pain, the limbs being inflamed or overheated, and maybe swollen as well. Hips, too, may feel sore or bruised, aching when the full body weight is on them in long periods of standing.

I often think of Burdock as the shop-assistants' and hairdressers' herb. Long hours of standing in the one spot, without opportunity to walk briskly and stretch out the legs, can put severe gravity loadings on the hips, and from there to the lower limbs. It could also be called the 'art gallery and museum' herb. Hour after hour you stand and admire, stand and learn, stand and evaluate, emerging exhausted and really needing to lie down flat for an hour to 'get the weight off your feet'. When you've been upright too long in the one spot, muscular slumping may put added gravity loadings on the lower-body areas, even causing a pelvic misalignment which can quickly lead to sciatica. One definitive indication for a herbalist to prescribe Burdock in your mixture is when *all* symptoms of this kind improve and decrease on brisk *movement* of the legs and lower body.

In advanced pregnancy, there are often symptoms of the Burdock kind, where sciatica, aching legs and slow kidneys can make the last few months before the birth a misery. It is, of course, the increase in weight and the change of posture in the lower spine that produces a pseudo-Burdock episode. *Do not* attempt to self-medicate with Burdock in any form during the latter stages of a pregnancy! The powerful action of the plant, stirring kidneys and lower abdomen, could bring on enough 'movement' to trigger uterine contractions. It is most certainly *not* an abortive agent in any way but, like any other care taken during late pregnancy, stay right away from Burdock then.

Burdock is not an especially mineral-rich plant, with only 3–4 per cent of mineral ash residue if burned. However, what minerals it does contain are all effective at the kidneys and the sciatic nerves: sodium and potassium begin to balance fluid excretion again, and a muscle-sugar, inulin, effective through kidneys, stimulates kidney function too as well as improving muscular tone in the lower body. A glycoside, Lappin, adds further energy to kidney excretion.

Another of Burdock's minerals is silica. This powerful excretory mineral helps to break up any calcium stones in kidneys, and also improves the nerve-sheath of the large sciatic nerve, a vulnerable nerve when there is any 'dropping' of body weight towards the hips, pelvis and legs, Vitamins B_3 and C are found respectively in the seeds and leaves/stems of the plant. There is good iron available from the root, and many plants will indicate iron-richness, like Burdock, by a pinkish-crimson tinge in the flowers, stems or leaves. Mucillage is high in the root, soothing and taking the rough edge off this plant's alterative properties. Any kidney stone or gravel will be soothed down as well as chemically changed gradually by Burdock root-and-seed extract or tincture.

Negative-chronic 'Burdock'

There are many other causes of 'aches and pains', too often loosely labelled as 'arthritis' or 'rheumatism'. Chiropractors and osteopaths can tell thousands of stories of patients whose 'rheumatism' went on adjustment of the spinal-segments relating to kidneys, hips, pelvis and lower-limbs. It wasn't 'rheumatism' at all, but a badly aligned lumbar-spine with consequent pelvic, hip and leg interference with blood flow and nerve supply. Burdock can be an excellent ancillary treatment in an individual's herbal mixture when such manipulative work is required.

Chronic 'Burdock' can't sit in a chair for long without hot red pain in lower limbs and sacroiliac joint. A long air flight, with the too-broad seats the designers inflict on us all, can be misery. Legs ache and *must be moved* to gain relief. It can be Heaven to 'stretch the legs' at every touch-down, walking briskly round and round the airport to relieve the pain which is *worse when immobilised*. Negative 'Burdock' is always worse when still, and better for exercise and fresh air. A too-warm room, and too long in the one position, and the 'rheumatics' can become fierce in the lower body.

Professional herbalists prescribe for this person with care and caution if Burdock is selected as one of a remedy mixture of herbs. Its action, like that of all plants rich in silica and iron, is powerfully eliminative. As a strong, fast alterative, it should be prescribed only in small doses over a period of time, but never permanently and *never* in large doses close together. For this reason, I do *not* recommend its use as a medicinal tea, the strength being hard to regulate accurately on a home-use basis. Although an occasional cup once in a while shouldn't cause discomfort, individuals vary in their reactions to this plant, and accurate dosage can be critical. Always consult your trained herbalist *first*. This way your own needs can be diagnosed and prescribed for with the necessary safety instructions given on frequency and strength of dosing.

Negative-chronic 'Burdock' needs to walk every day, but can't find the time! Negative 'Burdock' is by nature phlegmatic about pain, often brushing it away with 'I'm used to it, don't fuss.' It can come as a surprise to find such martyrdom may be relievable! At night, sciatic pain may be unbearable. No matter in which position the legs and hips are arranged, pain can stop sleep descending. Movement brings the only short relief available until the new position also becomes painful. In desperation, many negative

'Burdocks' take pain-relievers constantly, especially before bed. Kidneys can become even more overloaded by over-consumption of aspirin or related pain-killers, and chronic 'Burdock', set on a path of kidney stones, back aches, sciatica and swollen painful legs for life, grits the teeth and lives in unnecessary purgatory. Combining manipulation, massage and herbal medicine in which Burdock will be included can open the door on a pain-reduced existence otherwise never imagined possible. The emotional stoicism of 'Burdock' may put off seeking such treatment themselves; it's more often a relative or friend who insists on an appointment, and brings in suffering negative 'Burdock', who sits painfully still for the hour of consultation, without complaint.

Positive 'Burdock'

Positive 'Burdock' *walks*! They love to stretch out and go for kilometres, hips rhythmically alternating and arms swinging. I see the positive characteristics of this sign in the Britisher walking the dog. Twice a day, round London squares and in countryside villages, there are the English, striding out briskly. Australians tend to drive or ride everywhere, even a couple of blocks. As a nation, we are lazy with our legs, and our poor spinal posture reflects this. Jogging never was, in my opinion, any sort of an answer for lower-body exercising, as it *crashes* the spine down hard on hips, knees and feet as you pound the pavements. Many former joggers may need Burdock later on to repair the damage!

As always, nature insists on balance. Positive 'Burdock' exercises briskly, moving the lower body especially, then relaxes again, content to sit and read or sit and talk, with no red pain stabs in lower limbs. Golf is a positive 'Burdock' exercise: kilometres of walking, with an occasional upper-torso swing at the ball to break the emphasis and balance top and bottom energies, is ideal. Most golfers don't get 'rheumatism' either! I know a lean, fit man who has just celebrated his sixtieth birthday and who walks four kilometres to and four kilometres home from his city office each day. He'll live a long and pain-free life, with kidneys pumping well and back remaining straight as it always has been.

Dosage

1   Although Burdock tea may be taken, read again the above contra-indications restricting its too-enthusiastic use. Better by far

to seek a professional herbalist's assessment of whether you do need this plant medicinally or not and, if needed, in what quantity.

2   Burdock is included in many proprietary formulas for the treatment of 'rheumatism', sciatica, kidney stones, etc., but I prefer to see it carefully added to any prescribed mixture so that its dosage may be more accurate and more comfortable for each individual. Burdock often receives 'bad press' unless its application is well understood. You may have kidney stones and not know it, take too much Burdock for your personal reaction requirements, and flee to your medical practitioner who reinforces your growing apprehensions about the 'dangers' of herbal medicine. Consult a herbalist about herbs and a medical practitioner about orthodox drugs: each may not necessarily be well trained in the other's skills.

Burdock has often been prescribed internally and externally for relief of eczema. If the kidneys are functioning less than well, the skin (often called the 'third kidney') may weep with irritable wet eczematous disfigurement. The leaves of Burdock, well-pounded, are an old poultice treatment for weeping eczema. I have also sometimes prescribed Burdock tincture internally for eczema externally, but only when specific hereditary factors crop up of the 'Burdock' kind in parents, grandparents, etc.

Burdock is not a general or specific treatment alone for eczema; this distressing skin disease should be well diagnosed and fully evaluated by your practitioner. Don't ever be tempted to rush out to the nature strip, pick any old weed, and lay it on the red wet eczematous areas of skin on your child. This sort of careless haphazard use of plants, in the childlike faith that all things of nature are 'good', is responsible for much of the bad press mentioned above.

Cajeput

Melaleuca leucodendron

*A*ustralian plants are rare in world-wide herbal medicine history. Eucalyptus oil is a comparative newcomer and Ti-tree oil is even more recently becoming known. However, Cajeput, or Cajuput, a variety of Ti-tree, has been known to East Indiamen and spice traders from China and the Malaysian states for several hundred years.

The Australian varieties (*M. decussata*, *M. ericifolia*, and others) are now called 'Ti-tree', the name 'Cajeput' not being applied to them today.

Long used as an internal remedy for parasitic worms, and as a stimulant and diaphoretic, increasing perspiration and therefore cooling the body, Cajeput oil should only be taken with the greatest of care and in very tiny doses. Its properties as a *counter*-irritant may actually cause irritation if the dose is too high. I would only advise its internal use diluted down considerably with a water-based drink. (See Dosage.)

In many medicinal plants cineol and terpenes are amongst the aromatic ingredients, and they are obviously present in the resinous strong-smelling Cajeput oil. Butyric and benzoic acids are also present, and valerianic acid can be smelled too, with its characteristic musty odour.

'Cajeput' person-picture

*P*arasitic infestation of many kinds indicates a possible need for small, carefully spaced doses of Cajeput oil. For roundworm, threadworm and other many and varied infestations in tropical countries, a few drops of the oil mixed with fruit juice can begin to make an uncomfortable climate for possible parasitic invasion.

Today's changing parasitic colonies may not in this country include some of the deadly ones like hookworm and heartworm in humans, but our domestic animals and household pets may need Cajeput oil from time to time when such complaints are diagnosed, or even preventively. Mind you, your cat may never purr happily for you again after its first dose of this bitter musty oil! Cats may be caught once, but at the very faintest whiff of the oil the second time, that cat will be streaking through the nearest window and off over the rooftops. Entrapment of some kind, and great guile, will be needed a week to three weeks later when the second dose is due!

External parasitic infestations, like ringworm, also respond to Cajeput oil applied locally, and the Australian Ti-tree oil does a similar job. I advise dilution again; a few drops of the oil being diluted further with Safflower or Almond oils, or even with an Aloe-based cosmetic cream, gell or lotion. Avoid direct and concentrated applications, especially if the skin is open. Cuts, weeping sores, ulcers, etc. may attract secondary parasitic invasions especially in humid tropical climates, but on persons with sensitive or open skin there can be almost a cauterising effect from these oils. The surface may be germ and parasite-free, but it may also be almost 'burned' by the pure concentrated oil.

Negative-chronic 'Cajeput'

The long-term effect of chronic parasitic infestation is general weakening and debilitation. If blood-suckers or cell-robbers are in residence, *they* are receiving much of your nutritional intake, leaving you competing for the nutritional leftovers. Obviously, it is preferable to remove all pathogenic organisms, and leave only the 'friendly' bacteria and minute body-cleaning populations that act as scavengers for wastes and debris. Unfortunately, Cajeput oil may also temporarily reduce the numbers of body-friendly 'parasites'. Be aware of this, and use it only when positively indicated.

Another sideline of Cajeput and Ti-tree oils is the stimulation of circulatory slowdown-zones when they are applied externally. Chilblains need these oils, and regular rubbing in of them will irritate the small peripheral blood vessels, reducing the itching and soreness by stimulating better blood flow.

Some fungal 'parasites' may also leave when Cajeput oil is in contact with the fungus-affected part. Fungus in the ear, often contracted by swimmers in less-than-clean waters, can be treated by mixing a few drops of the Cajeput or Ti-tree oil with a few drops of Olive oil, and dropping this mixture into the ear cavity each night, to be gently wiped out with a cotton bud the next morning.

Ringworm on the skin, even tinea between the toes, can also respond well to the same nightly application of these oils diluted with Olive oil as above, or with an Aloe-based cosmetic cream or lotion.

Chronic parasitic infestation can also lead to specific organ invasion and possibly severe blockages if left untreated. It may take professional diagnosis to evaluate the need and the dosage rate, but the treatment can then be done by the patient at home.

The negative-chronic picture is one of carrying too many freeloaders which are sapping energy and vitality, or invading and taking over major organs and functions at your expense. Tiredness, bad breath, wind and discomfort may herald their presence internally, or *itching* of various kinds, with discolouration, irritation and tissue breakdown, could signify skin or body-cavity infestation.

Dosage

1   For chilblains, daily applications as described above.

2   Internally, dilute several drops, to a flat teaspoonful (maximum!) of the oil with a water-based drink like mineral water, or fruit juice, and stir well to mix.

While this may need to be taken once a day when acutely under parasitic attack (amoebic dysentery, candida albicans infestations, etc.), it can be dropped to occasional or preventive intake as the attack eases. Consult your herbalist for accuracy here.

3   Local applications may be made to the skin, added to cosmetic or other therapeutic ointment bases, when topical infestation occurs, or introduced into ears, throat, etc., when fungus irritation and itching is present. Again, duration of this method of treatment will need monitoring and professional assessment.

4   And don't forget the dogs, cats and farmyard animals! Your naturopathic or homoeopathic veterinarian will be of assistance in a treatment programme, but don't neglect to tell your orthodox vet too what good results you've had with the simple diluted-oil dose outlined above. An eyedropper may be needed to measure out and

squirt in a dose of a few drops of Cajeput oil, plus whichever dilutant you choose.

5 *All* methods of internal dosing should have a repeat-dose after a week to three weeks, depending on the parasite. Eggs present may hatch after the original adults are killed off. Follow the 'few drops' initially with a second few drops a week to three weeks later to complete the elimination of all the parasites' families and children too. Preventively, this makes sure the whole parasitic invasion is limited and controlled.

Calendula

Calendula officinalis

The English Pot-marigold is this plant's common name, although it is native to China and the southern parts of Europe, the Mediterranean and India. This common Marigold, growing and blooming well in difficult between-season planting gaps, is a favourite of park gardeners. Even in mid-winter, its bright orange open-faced flowers, unfolding as soon as the sun is well-risen, can cheer an otherwise dormant and resting garden.

*Don't confuse this plant with the African Marigold, a tall, rank grower with orange-crinkled multiple petals like a crazy pompom dahlia! The African Marigold (*Tagetes *sp.) is also a winter bloomer, but its feathery fernlike 'cut' leaves cannot be confused with the pale-green, hairy, simple leaves growing from a basal rosette, of the medicinal Calendula. If confused between the two, check with your local nursery, or seedsman.*

Although as a garden flower Calendula has now been hybridised into every shade of orange, cream and yellow flowers, with huge heads and multiple re-curving petals, the medicinal properties are only available from the simple ancestor of all these hothouse beauties — the single, open, daisy-like orange-petalled and smaller flowers. In classic herbal use, only the petals are harvested, dried and used as a tea, or mixed well into an ointment-base for home use externally. By the professional, Calendula tincture or extract *may* be prescribed internally, but its dose must be carefully regulated and monitored for each individual. It is traditionally used internally for viral infections of the liver, and for varicose veins — but with great caution as its liver-stimulant effect may stir up a slow liver a little too fast and produce a 'bilious' nausea. Also, due to its high carotene content (the orange-coloured building-block for Vitamin A production), it *is* possible to overdose internally and upset the liver, gall bladder and pancreas. Slow, steady and gradually are the ways to introduce a carotene-rich plant internally.

Although it is unusual for this internal dose to be given often, its effectiveness is based on salts of potassium, calcium and sulphur. The potassium is especially high. As this most necessary mineral is used to make glycogen, a muscle-sugar, as well as to regulate fluid excretion and general fluid movement, the internal effect of Calendula can be tonic indeed to the liver, the kidneys, the muscles, and indirectly to the blood-flow rates and the heart. You can see why there is always a need for *care* in its internal prescribing.

Externally, it is one of the chief antiseptics used by herbalists world-wide. As a tincture or as an ointment, it should have pride of place in the family medicine cabinet, on a boat, in a bushwalker's pack, in the workplace for minor accidents, and in the schools. For the herbalist, it replaces iodine tincture and those proprietary antiseptics which can be harsh to skin and even harsher to eyes, nostrils, vaginal areas, etc. Calendula ointment may be quite safely applied to the most delicate body areas, to nappy-rashed babies' bottoms, and to the ulcers and bed-sores of the aged. As an ointment it is used wherever there is *cut* or *open* skin, where there is *crushed* tissue internally or externally, or when a *burn* or a *scald* causes 'weeping' of plasma. It appears at times to be miraculous in its *speed* of healing; almost the next day, even with severe trauma, there should be no sign of inflammation, throbbing, infection, or scar tissue to form later. It promotes granulation in open wounds, and its great antiseptic properties make it the *first* first-aid to reach for. The carotene, the potassium, and its oxygenating properties reduce local swelling too. It has to be experienced to be believed!

I have used it many times for others. On a bushwalking holiday in the high Snowy Mountains of NSW we were camped next to a young motor-bike rider and his inexperienced pillion-riding girlfriend. On each journey, she burned red weals across her inside ankle as her foot found the hot-metal exhaust, not the footrest. I applied my Calendula ointment to the latest one in a ladder of angry burns up the leg. By the next morning, there was no trace at all of where the injury had been! I bequeathed her my Calendula when I left for home: she begged me! Almost as astounding as its ability to heal *open* wounds fast and safely is the way a blister appears to reduce its fluid and act like normal skin again when Calendula ointment is applied. The blister doesn't 'shed'; it just flattens and reduces back into healthy tissue.

A compromise way to treat varicosity in legs, ankles, around knees, etc., is to rub Calendula ointment *gently* around (above and below) the affected zones. Better yet, use one of the cosmetic Calendula creams which absorb well into the skin and leave no sticky residue.

I am writing this with two badly crushed and torn fingers (on my left hand, luckily). While 'acquiring' some free rocks for a new garden rock-pool several days ago, I slipped with the heavy weight of one and jammed two fingers between it and another one. To remove the fingers meant laceration as well. While the air thickened and I meditated on nature's punishment for rock-stealers, I reached into my backpack for the Calendula. By the time I had reached the car several minutes away (with the rocks still clutched!) the throbbing had eased already. Today the wound is clean and clear, and both fingers are easily bendable and almost healed. And I know there'll be *no* scarring at all!

So although a person-picture for Calendula is not specific, all of us will have need of its antiseptic and quick healing properties at some time in our lives. Far better to apply the ointment immediately to an open wound than to risk infection, poor healing, and perhaps even restricted use eventually of the part damaged.

Although not strictly an 'external' use, a vaginal douche may be made from Calendula and other ingredients like Lemon-juice, Golden Seal root, etc. Even a tea made from dried Calendula petals has been used alone, and effectively, for vaginal warts, for irritated or dry vaginal walls, and as a gentle internal 'wash' after a period. Vaginal hygiene, more essential than ever today, is gently improved by such a douche. Even when there may be bleeding or tearing of the vaginal walls, with fibroids at menopause, or even after child-birth, a Calendula douche, as below, is a great insurance against infection and irritation.

Dosage

1   As an ointment, apply immediately to open wounds and cover with a dressing. Re-apply each day for at least three days.

2   As a cosmetic cream apply liberally to face, neck, hands, etc., either day or night, and as a protective cream in cold, windy and harsh weather conditions, or after sunburn.

3   Make a douche from one cup of warm boiled water, juice of a lemon, and 1–2 teaspoons *only* of Calendula extract. Use every few

days if discomfort is present, or occasionally (weekly or fortnightly, say,) as a preventive cleanser and antiseptic wash.

4   Herbalists do sometimes prescribe Calendula as a mixture-ingredient for various liver and other symptoms, but its dose must be carefully assessed.

5   Gently apply the ointment *above and below* varicose-vein sites each day.

Camphor

Cinnamomum camphora

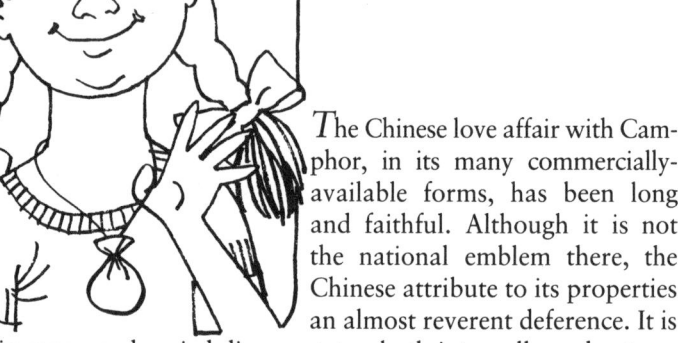

The Chinese love affair with Camphor, in its many commercially-available forms, has been long and faithful. Although it is not the national emblem there, the Chinese attribute to its properties an almost reverent deference. It is used in many and varied disease states, both internally and externally. 'Tiger Balm' contains it, and its strangely penetrating odour can be identified in other proprietary medications too. Its fame spread to Japan, and to other parts of Asia and India. Like Ginseng, it has had semi-miraculous 'cures' attributed to it. A closer look at the story, and the legend, can elucidate for us its great claims to fame.

The Camphor laurel tree grows well in temperate climates, but will also withstand extremes of heat and dryness in Egypt as well as frosts in inland Australia. It seems comfortable too in high humidity, strong salt winds, even the harshest environments of poor rocky soil and no attention whatsoever. It is next to impossible to kill it off once established. A nextdoor neighbour, who didn't appreciate its shade, its smell, or its prolific growth, used to drive my poor mother wild: that neighbour tried poison, tree-killing sprays on leaves, hormones injected into roots (on her side of the fence!), and every Australian epithet known to him, but that old tree refused to notice anything untoward. Every few years, my mother would feel a little guilty, and would have the tree lopped almost to stump-size; but the vigorous new growth would appear within days, almost, and once again the smell of Camphor would fill that garden corner as soon as the sun's heat warmed the new sprouting leaves.

Gardeners often curse the Camphor laurel, calling it 'poison-ous' to other plants within the diameter of its canopy. It is true that it's next to impossible to grow other plants within its orbit, but what's wrong with a wooden bench surrounding its strong trunk, where you can sit and inhale, and contemplate? Perhaps its worst feature, in suburban areas, is its crushing root pressure against drains. Give it a wide open space! If you've ever added Camphor leaves to a compost-bin and wondered why they didn't rot away, and even prevented other rubbish rotting down too, it's the aromatic oily resins that preserve so well as to inhibit decay and putrefaction. It is easy to see why ancient Chinese dynasties recom-mended its use for embalming, for lacquer-ware, for inks which would not fade and pigments which would last bright and true for centuries on the walls and ceilings of royal palaces. 'Everlasting' is a quality of Camphor.

Mature trees store longitudinal 'lumps' or 'veins' of Camphor solids in trunks and branches, and the tree must be sacrificed to extract these. As it may take twenty to fifty years to complete this process, the cost of such premium-quality camphor can be high indeed. Today's commercial extraction from 'coppiced' new growth of leaves from old trunk bases is less costly, but the quality suffers.

If you're as old as I am, you may have spent your childhood with a small block of solid Camphor suspended in a red-flannel bag around your neck and against the skin under clothing. No one in our family ever had a chesty cold or bronchitis or asthma or pneu-monia, and certainly never a viral 'flu! Over the winter the solid Camphor would slowly vaporise with body heat, the block shrink-ing in size, absorbed through the red flannel into the skin, and penetrating deeper and deeper into tissues of respiratory organs. It's a strange peculiarity of Camphor that it will absorb better through skin (via the fatty layers) than it will when taken in small doses internally, as the Chinese have always done. It's better for Australians to rub it in only as our digestive tracts are not appar-ently as acclimatised to it as are the Oriental variety! Camphor doesn't mix well with water. Accordingly, it is a difficult substance to blend with body fluids which are mainly water-based. It works best when fatty tissues are its absorption areas.

Camphor has long been used for inflammatory disease processes and as a primary treatment against viral and bacterial infections in respiratory and other organs. Rubbing it on the skin over the organ area is surprisingly effective, and fast!

There is not really a 'person-picture', for either negative or positive Camphor states. This aromatic resinous substance may be needed by all of us from time to time if its penetrating heat and its isolating properties against infection are called for.

Don't overlook its *preventive* virtues. A little red-flannel-bag factory could be a good cottage industry!

Castor oil

Ricinus communis

Don't wince yet! Herbalists don't prescribe Castor oil internally. I remember the cobalt-blue glass pharmaceutical bottle in the medicine cabinet when I was a child; even the threat of a teaspoonful was enough to make anyone's bowels move — without even taking it!

I saw the plant growing as a hedge round the small hard-won family fields of the no-man's-land between Jordan and Israel. It also grows as a shrubby weed of waste lands all over the world. Its original handsome reddish stems, hollow like bamboo, become straggly, leggy and greener and more nondescript as the one original parent tree throws out its seeds explosively to produce a paddockful of unwanted growth. It grows best in poor sandy soils full of stones and rubbish, amongst ruined fallen-down buildings and around overgrown fences. Everything about it shrieks 'decay'.

Nature often gives clear and unmistakable indications if the observer is trained to see. Castor oil has long been used medically for the fast and complete emptying of whatever intestinal rubbish has been slow in leaving the small and large bowel. But herbalists prefer to use milder plants like Senna or Cascara when a bowel movement is due, or overdue. Herbalists do use it *externally*, however. Here its reference to processes of decay and putrefaction indicate its use in drawing to the surface any 'foreign bodies' which have penetrated skin, eye tissue, ear, etc., and around which infection and inflammation can occur. Even deep cuts and wounds, trodden-on nails, thorns from the roses or sharp coral at the beach can need Castor oil applied externally overnight as a poultice on a dressing. Whenever an anti-tetanus shot might be indicated medically, a herbalist could suggest Castor oil applied on a dressing over the wound, for at least ten hours and preferably for twenty-four.

The main property of Castor oil is its lubricant effect. The oil is carefully extracted by rolling and pressing of the tick-like seed, without undue heat applied. Castor oil is added to the finest of machine-oils, as well as to aircraft-engine lubricants. It is an ingredient in washing powders and detergents, loosening the dirt and the biological debris from dishes and from clothing. It 'draws' splinters from skin, metal or glass fragments from eye tissues, and even bacterial and viral 'rubbish' from boils, carbuncles, infected fingernails and festering sores. Its lubricants surround and isolate the putrid matter, which then 'floats' on the tissue fluids and is quickly expelled through the skin.

When splinters of glass or metal penetrate eye tissues, there may only be recourse to surgery in the medical world. The herbalist prefers the gentle but powerful drawing and lubrication of Castor oil; a few drops in each eye immediately after such an accident, followed by closed eyes and rest, will minimise the damage first, then lubricate and remove overnight the offending 'foreign body', which can actually be shed from the tissues and just fall out the next morning. Students, patients and practitioners have proved Castor oil's effectiveness in these circumstances, and have avoided painful and traumatic surgical extraction from eye tissues. Paronychia, a fungal condition of the fingernail edges, can also be poulticed with Castor oil nightly until the redness eases and the nail-bed clears of the infection.

Corns are more rare today with our freer life style and open-style shoes or bare feet that go with it. But if plastic or synthetic shoes are worn, corns are much more likely. Leather breathes with the feet; synthetics hold in the perspiration and stick tightly to skin, causing ideal conditions for fungus and viral population explosions. Rub a little Castor oil into roughened or calloused areas, into corns, around plantar warts, even into bunions, to ease and draw, soften and lubricate.

There is no person-picture for Castor oil. It should be a stand-by always in the family medicine cupboard for wounds and punctures where it is possible that particles have entered the wound or that bacteria or viruses have gained admission. Just a few drops only are needed on a dressing for a small wound or puncture, slightly more to draw out more deep-seated foreign material over-night. If *throbbing* occurs after a puncture-wound of any kind, apply the Castor oil dressing as soon as possible.

There are tantalising quick references in old texts to other uses for Castor oil. As well as being used in oil-lamps in Asia (it's a native of India where it grows into a

large tree), there are several oblique references to its use in *cooking* in ancient China and in Egypt. Saints preserve us! Even with an allowance for poor translation, such a prospect is not a pleasant one for the gastric mucosa to contemplate! I don't fancy stir-fried vegies in Castor oil, nor flat bread cooked in it either. Are the old texts to be believed?

It is my opinion that again those highly qualified translators may have been inexperienced in the subject they translated. By no stretch of the imagination could the bitter tasting heavy oil from Castor seeds be used in that form in cooking without all the population dying unpleasantly from ruptured bowel walls and intestinal haemorrhages! One clue only is found in Chinese antiquity: there was apparently a way to remove from Castor oil its purgative substances (now Ricin and Riccinin), and then to use the oil in cooking. I am more tempted to believe one or the other of the alternative translations: either 'in cooking' meant as a fuel oil in an oven or stove, or an entirely *different* oil, Linseed, also prepared from plants which grew then in both Egypt and China, was the oil referred to in the original text.

Nursing mothers having problems maintaining good milk supply and flow have for hundreds of years, and in widely different cultures, used the drawing power of Castor oil rubbed gently into breast areas to 'pull' the ducted milk towards the nipple.

Apply just a few drops to each breast *after* feeding the child. (Keep away from the actual nipple area though, or you may 'leak' uncomfortably between feeds.)

And to help *reduce* milk production when weaning the child, have a few drops of Castor oil rubbed into your upper *back* morning and night to draw fluids *away* from the breasts. True! It works!

Use only old bed-linen or clothing when Castor oil is applied to the skin or on a poultice dressing. It will stick to any other surface it touches, and may be difficult to sponge out or wash. Castile soap, a pure liquid soap available from health stores, removes it best.

Celery

Apium graveolens

Any discussion about Celery assumes it to be a vegetable, commonly known and ordinarily eaten in a general diet. The borderline between food and medicine is hazy and nebulous. When does Celery stop being a food and begin to be a deliberately-chosen therapeutic substance? Years ago a rather strict natural health body requested from me a lecture on herbs, 'but only as *foods*, not as medicines'. I had to decline their invitation as the task was impossible. Once any food is ingested, there is a predictable body-effect depending upon the nutrients in that food. The carrot will affect liver and pancreas; the asparagus-spear will affect kidneys and bladder; while Celery, with its alkaline digestive residue, will do its own particular job of acid–alkaline re-balancing, and liver and excretory organs of kidneys, bowels, even skin, will be stimulated by the sodium–potassium balance in this vegetable–herb. Its magnesium, also alkaline-reacting, will calm nerve signals irritated by their own acid wastes from high activity, pain, over-anxiety, etc. Its silica will also give resilience to the physical nerve-sheaths, and an added zip to excretion, especially of *acid* wastes. It's hard to eat a few lengths of Celery without a 'medicinal' effect!

Celery seeds condense all of Celery's virtues into even greater concentration, and add the B-Vitamins and phosphorus found in seeds. These are mostly used to make herbalists' tinctures and extracts. They can also be used as a tea — but with caution and very gradually introduced. A *level* teaspoon of the seed can be crushed a little with a kitchen mallet or pre-soaked in a little cold water, before adding the boiling water to make a tea. Celery's stimulus to excretory organs necessitates restraint! A cup of this tea every few days is the absolute maximum needed, even when the person-picture below fits closely. Don't go overboard — especially all you osteo-arthritics! The silica and the sodium–potassium partnership in Celery seeds are ideal for gradually changing insoluble calcium build-ups in osteo-arthritis. Too much Celery seed tea and you'll feel that jack hammers are at work in the arthritic concretions! Nature won't be rushed!

'Celery'
person-picture

This is a busy and conscientious person. Every part of the nervous system is in action, but too often this constant over-stimulation leads to irritation of mucous-lined areas of the body, and what some naturopaths too loosely call 'excess acid'. An iridologist will see at first glance the very white fibres over the whole iris, and the stomach area inside the nerve-wreath itself. There will be jagged and irregular peaks around this automatic nerve-wreath circle, and they will be glaringly-white. (See *Iridology*, Nelson, 1980, page 61.) The whole iris will appear to be recording at 'white heat'. Such people will often feel 'hot and bothered' too. As the pace of their living remains high, adrenal glands will be called upon for constant output. Fluids may then become difficult to regulate, and 'weight' may increase. It would be truer to say that *size* increases, as most of the excess is in tissues which are waterlogged, not fat. Emotionally, these people find it unpleasant to be idle, and often take on responsibilities and extra duties to avoid boredom and an 'empty' space about their lives. But as their daily load increases, so may their size! In this category fall those people who put on 'weight' as they become more and more constantly stressed — and it has nothing whatsoever to do with food!

Negative-chronic
'Celery'

This person has been so busy and conscientious for so long that adrenal output is failing, and fluid regulation becomes difficult indeed. As a result, kidneys begin to labour, and there may also be irritation and over-acid conditions around joints and large-bone ends. All the physical activity that 'Celery' people are capable of will not be harmful if there is an absence of worry and emotional irritation. Physical activity helps to pump out their excess acids through kidneys, skin and lungs; but if anxiety and over-concern also are present, the extra nervous activity will be too much for those tired adrenal glands to cope with.

These people 'fear' for others: much of their labour is protective and defensive, they will exhaust themselves for a family wedding or a business crisis; then up will swell the fingers, and the waistline or neck will feel pressured by clothing. They *swell* with acid fluids under pressure.

Many of them crave water around them and over them: they love a shower or warm bath, and any aches and pains improve with *warm* water but worsen with cold plunges. They should *never* do the great Australian sunbake and then dive straight into the cold waves or the icy swimming pool. If they do, there will be a little heart-thumping or pounding. Enter water gradually should be their rule.

Not all the chronic Celery-needers are nice people, concerned about those around them and exhausted with their efforts for others. Some are downright selfish in their demands that others stop 'being a terrible worry' to them. They can rule a household by threatening 'Don't do that or you'll worry Mother', or 'You know how I worry when you're away for the weekend', or other such emotional blackmail. These people can be 'martyrs' to arthritis — and how everyone around them pays for it by feeling guilty somehow of causing their pain and distress. The most negative of chronic 'Celery'-types, although being the cause of their own misery, puts a burden of guilt on all and sundry — 'because I was so *worried* about you'. You feel that their every ache and pain is your fault!

It is not coincidental that Celery is prescribed by professional herbalists in a support mixture for those medically diagnosed as diabetic. Its beneficial action on liver and adrenal glands is a boon, and many diabetics find a reduction in fluid retention and better digestive competence when it is included in a general tonic mixture with other herbs. For the fluid-engorged diabetic, Celery's gentle but balanced persistence in stimulating liver, adrenals and kidneys can be beneficial indeed.

Positive 'Celery'

Still enjoying water as an anti-stress mechanism, positive 'Celery' doesn't worry much, having learned that such stresses may be destructive to essential defence-glands, the adrenals. Such people really leap into the active mode physically, mentally and emotionally when real defence is necessary for themselves or others, as life's challenges and shocks affect them or those they love and care for. But they don't exhaust their defence fight-or-flight apparatus by constantly firing at shadows. Able to turn off their minds and think of other things, they often put a problem aside for a while and when they return to it a solution may be easier. They refuse to concern themselves with tomorrow or ten years hence, and they never say 'what if . . .?' or 'I'm worried about . . .' When there is a real emergency, their well-rested adrenal-glands jump into necessary action and deal with it effectively and strongly. Then they say 'I'm hungry', enjoy a good meal and fall asleep.

Dosage

1   As a tea, a *flat* teaspoon of dried Celery Seeds, soaked or crushed a little (as above), every few days or as prescribed.

2   Celery extract or tincture prescribed with other similar herbs may be taken three times daily, or as prescribed.

3   Don't forget to *eat* Celery! Inclusion in the diet can begin in childhood to avoid a hereditary tendency towards arthritis, or diabetes, developing much later.

> Celery is always an ingredient in any vegetable salt. Not only is the flavour improved and sharpened, but this *vegetable* form of sodium chloride doesn't cause fluid retention as does mineral 'salt'. Its sodium chloride stimulates digestive enzymes, and its pectin and apiol are also digestion-improvers.
>
> A few years ago a Scandinavian 'breakthrough' was put on the market there — a 'salt' which didn't cause fluid retention or arterial hardening, containing potassium chloride, sodium chloride and magnesium chloride. Its formulation was almost identical with the balance of these compounds in Celery!

Chamomile

Matricaria chamomilla
Anthemis nobilis

The German Chamomile (*Matricaria chamomilla*) is an upright-growing annual, with ferny grey-green leaves and white daisy-like flowers with definitive yellow cone-shaped centres. The English Chamomile (*Anthemis nobilis*) is a creeping low-growing perennial, with identical flower type. Both plants show variable contents in the flower 'cones' (the parts used medicinally), but for our general purposes here their medicinal effectiveness is very similar. The German Chamomile is certainly more bitter, and stronger in its action on the nervous system and on the development of bones and teeth in young children, but both varieties are often found together in commercial preparations, and in the dried flowers used to make a Chamomile tea.

Traditionally, Chamomile is taken by every member of the family from the youngest baby to the most senior of grandparents. Its effect, for both young and old, is to support digestion, to sedate and calm the nervous system, and to supply calcium salts for the maintenance of healthy bones and connective tissues.

Because its calcium phosphate is high, every part of the body's skeletal structure is well supplied with this vital compound which prevents wear and tear on bone ends and at large and small joints. Whenever the skeletal structures, teeth, hair, nails, etc., are being built, calcium phosphate is essential: but in old age, even in middle age, there is the ever-present risk of rapid degeneration of bones, teeth, etc., in diseases like osteoporosis and osteoarthritis. Chamomile would be one of the most prescribed herbs in my dispensary.

Although there is general nervous-system calming and sedating, with an improvement in sleep and reduction in tension throughout the digestive tract, Chamomile shows at its most effective best in reducing cramps in organs. For period pain, for stomach cramps, even for spasms of pain through kidneys and bladder, it is gentle and safe in the form of tea or prescribed professionally in an individual mixture. It is better for digestive tract and organ spasm and resulting pain than it is for ordinary muscular aches and pains after physical activity. Rosemary oil in the bath, or Valerian tea internally are better treatments for these muscular tensions and spasms.

Chamomile has a particular affinity for the tenth cranial nerve (the Vagus nerve) and all its branches into the body. It is worth exploring this nerve's pathways in an anatomical atlas: originating from the brain itself, it has branches affecting facial areas around eyes, nose, mouth and tongue, then down into the chest with a branch to respiratory areas and the heart, before diving across the lower stomach then ending at the pancreas. Disturbances of any of these multiple branches can often lead to many forms of allergy. These can affect eyes, nose, mouth, breathing, heart-rate; and digestive efficiency, especially of sugars. It is characteristic of such a Vagus-nerve origin that the allergies are most obvious when there is anxiety, fear, apprehension, even panic, and it is then that the eyes become puffy, the nostrils itch, the tongue and mouth swell, swallowing becomes difficult, breathing irregular, heart-rate speedy or louder, and various foods taken produce 'allergic'-type reactions.

'Chamomile' person-picture

The Chamomile person lives their stresses twice at least, and sometimes over and over. Chamomile often *dramatises* in re-telling the day's doings to Mum, or spouse, or the household in general. They bound through the frontdoor, flustered, with 'What a day I've had. You'll never guess what happened . . .' Beginning with a missed bus, worrying headlines in the paper, an office crisis at five past nine, and another at morning tea, you'll get a blow-by-blow description of every event, large or small. Hands may be waved about, and the facial expressions and voices of all the cast of players in the day's doings acted out. It may be an *entertaining* experience for the listener if nothing much has happened to them that day and they welcome the diversion, but it is often true of 'Chamomile' that their day has really been quite ordinary. Their listeners may have had a much worse day, and all the dramatics may just annoy by their inconsequential nature.

Luckily, it is seldom necessary to really listen attentively to a 'Chamomile' in full flight! 'Mmmm . . .' you answer, in rising or falling cadences. 'Really?' you interpose when they stop for breath. You continue preparing dinner, dusting the furniture, thinking about something else entirely. 'I'm listening — go on,' you lie as they follow you from room to room. To ease your conscience, it really doesn't matter to a 'Chamomile' if you listen or not: for them, catharsis occurs via the mouth! As soon as the last drama is told (an unfriendly dog between the bus-stop and the frontdoor) poor exhausted 'Chamomile' collapses in the nearest armchair, physically tired out from living the day *twice*. While 'Hops' (pages 186–7) plans for tomorrow and crosses bridges before they appear, 'Chamomile' crosses and re-crosses the same bridge, sometimes three or four times, so every household member can hear the detailed story in all its anxious and fraught moments.

Children are often 'Chamomile'-types. Bursting in the door after school, there may be an explosive need to communicate all the day's events. 'Mummy, guess what happened today . . .' or (even without a 'Hello, Mum, I'm home') 'that awful boy in the class got found out today . . .', etc., etc., etc. Verbal diarrhoea it may be, but it is an essential part of de-stressing, or de-briefing, for this personality-type.

The wound-up 'Chamomile' having run down, a breathless collapse into an armchair, on the floor, or a flat-out sigh on the lounge will signal the end of the story, but also the beginning of the next phase, 'I don't want any dinner', or 'I'm too exhausted to eat anything', or 'I'll just have to shut my eyes for a minute.' Having lived their day *twice*, or more, it's no wonder that processes involving hunger, eating and digestion are too much to contemplate straight away. Worse yet, if they *do* try to eat anything, the tummy can bloat up in no time, with wind, indigestion, cramps and even real pain occurring. 'I've got a pain in my tummy,' says the 'Chamomile' child, 'I don't want anything to eat.' It's *un*-wise parents or other household members who insist on food or a full meal as soon as a 'Chamomile' has finished reliving the day. *Wait* a while! Give sympathetic and parasympathetic nervous systems time to re-balance and calm down. Better yet, hand this drooping 'Chamomile' a nice warm cup of Chamomile tea, preferably just inside the frontdoor!

They are the opposite of 'Valerian' (pages 296–7) who pride themselves on saying nothing at all about their day's doings, keeping their stresses internal and communicated to no one. Perhaps they should marry each other!

Negative-chronic 'Chamomile'

Constant over-communication has not only precluded eating and digestion, but also sleep. Painful cramps and spasms may occur internally from the oesophagus to the anus. There may be a constant 'cold' feeling in the stomach, and any food forced down may feel like an oppressive weight at the pit of the stomach. Not a happy state in which to woo sleep!

The deeper and more emotionally exhausted 'Chamomile'-person can suffer 'allergic' reactions almost from top to toes. Typically, this patient has a long list of foods, contact-substances, 'house-dust and moulds', perfumes, cosmetics, animal products, hair, fur, feathers, even flowers, to which they show allergic responses. It is hard to tell them so, but it is true that if the expensive allergy-testing was done every week for any period of time they would show *different* allergy triggers each time they were tested! These people don't have real allergies to a few substances, they have a trigger-happy allergic response!

They are allergic-reactors, full-stop! Nervous exhaustion will produce a *tired* Vagus nerve: first the eyes will itch with pollens, or air-conditioning; then the nostrils will inhale tobacco smoke or the perfume of tuberoses; the mouth and tongue encounter wheat grains, or prawns, or strawberries, and swallowing may become difficult, throat sore and neck swollen. Some folk may experience breathing difficulties and heart palpitations from chocolate, or salicylates, or the Solanacea family of fruits and vegetables (potatoes, tomatoes, capsicums, etc.). Others may become 'hyperactive' on sugary foods, or on food additives, colorants, etc. All these patients share one common factor in their 'allergies' — emotional exhaustion at the time of encounter with the substance(s) concerned.

The classically-trained herbalist should have been taught that emotional factors can be uppermost in producing body-process changes. Eating the very best of good food with an arrogant client who's giving you hell can produce an allergic response in no time in the true 'Chamomile' person. A child with a new unsympathetic school teacher can spend a year of hayfever, food allergies and asthma, until a new more empathetic teacher the next year sees the whole 'allergic child' syndrome disappearing. A child who gets 'asthma' at grandma's house but not at home has emotional reasons for the breathing difficulties, as well as grandma's air-conditioning or bags of sweets. Asthma which develops after moving house may be from loneliness and insecurity as much as from the new nylon carpet. The 'Chamomile' person has *emotional exhaustion at the time* as the real reason for a long list of foods not to eat and substances not to contact.

It is hard for my clinic practitioners to turn around in these patients' minds their thinking on allergy responses. Almost proudly, they display a long list of foods they may not eat, and a 'restricted' list of contact substances. It is worst of all when the patient is a young child or teenager whose social life is made impossible by foods which can't be eaten in friends' homes and dietary restrictions which reduce their choices for life. I have seen a three-year-old reduced to such a restricted diet that even her mother was at the point of desperation. 'Can you write me out a list of what she *can* eat?' she begged me, almost in tears. 'She seems to be allergic to everything I make for her.' Mum had observed well, without knowing it. The child's parents had separated and there was still much bitterness and wrangling over custody. The lass preferred her father's company, but the courts had awarded custody to the mother. Further discussion was unnecessary: the child was emotionally drained by the wrangling. After the introduction of Chamomile tea daily (for Mum too!) and a clearer understanding all around of the emotional turmoil of the child, her mother was able to report enormous improvement after six weeks, and 'allergy-free' after twelve.

Certainly there is such a problem as an 'allergic response' which may seem to be clear cut on a real trigger, not an emotional one. But it is still fascinating to trace back in time to the *first* encounter with this substance, and what emotional framework that patient was in at that time. Re-exposure to the substance, even years later, may also trigger off again an echo of the exhausted emotions coincident with the first exposure.

Chamomile tea is certainly not a magic potion to remove all allergies! Where the allergies are of the type listed, and the patient has a 'Chamomile' character, then this herb will be amongst those used in an individual mixture. Dandelion, Alfalfa, etc., may be added, too, to support liver function and help the body deal with the physical component of the 'allergy' more efficiently.

Positive 'Chamomile'

All of us have times when we can't wait to get home to tell the family or friends what a full and fraught day we've had. On such a day, a cup of Chamomile tea *first* can be a good idea. While sipping and sitting, the compulsion to act it out all over again will become less. Better yet, there'll be relaxation beginning before dinner, and a quiet sleep, undisturbed by indigestion or spasms, afterwards. In France, Germany and Central Europe Chamomile tea can be a traditional night-cap for young and old alike. For a teething child or a dyspeptic grandma, its carminative effect can be soothing and comforting, while the calcium phosphate it contains begins repair of frayed physical nerves and irritable digestive tract. A 'nervous stomach' needs Chamomile, if such symptoms make eating impossible when emotionally distraught.

Positive 'Chamomile' is aware that eating and digestion should be kept separate from action and excitement. Digestion is a process of relaxation not direct activity: a relaxed nervous system at the time of eating is the best 'allergy' prevention ever!

Dosage

1   A cup of Chamomile tea at any time when emotions may disturb digestion and sleep. For painful period cramps, a cup of Chamomile tea can soothe and warm. After work, and a stressful day, a *weak* Chamomile tea before dinner. (Don't forget its sedative effect: you may not want to fall asleep over the souffle!) Chamomile is not a morning tea: save it for later in the afternoon or evening. On the other hand, if you're a shift-worker returning home at 5 a.m., drink a cup before sleeping, especially if the rest of your household wakes at seven!

2   As a mixture ingredient, Chamomile is included together with other herbs for the liver, the digestive tract, the reproductive system and the cranial nerves. For 'allergy' sufferers of this type, it can, with other herbs, reduce too-sensitive responses.

3   As an external wash for the skin, the used Chamomile tea bag may be put into the bathwater with you for a relaxing soaking. This is excellent for sensitive skins, for wind-burn and sunburn and for those with eczema, dermatitis, psoriasis, etc. Skin irritations of many kinds will be soothed. Insect bites and stings, even blisters, tired feet, and itching skin from too-acid perspiration, can be soothed and calmed down this way.

Out of the many thousands of patients prescribed Chamomile in some form, I have only ever had *one* with an 'adverse' reaction to it. This young lady berated me soundly over the telephone for the headaches, nausea, etc., she had suffered from the Chamomile tincture I had prescribed for her. Astounded, I advised her to discontinue taking it until her next visit in a few weeks time. Then the truth came out: she had added her Chamomile drops to a glass of white wine at her mother's house whilst they continued a long-running argument as to whether she should give up her flat (which she enjoyed) to live again with her mother who had developed kidney stones, angina and migraines since she left home!

Cleavers or Clivers

Galium aparine

A northern hemisphere plant, Cleavers has not spread to Australia to any great degree. I suspect it is not only our lack of hedgerows and perhaps the soil differences, but also the opposite magnetic polarity in the southern hemisphere. Many climbing plants are rigid in their directional needs, twisting their tendrils as if on sky-hooks. Gardeners training climbers over pergolas and walls can be frustrated by the plants' determined deflections one way or the other. Charles Darwin conducted some painstaking experiments of these plant behaviours. In his book *Climbing Plants* he documented hours of patient recording, observing stem rotation, leaf alignment and climbing direction. Phytosteroids (plant hormones) play their part as the signal-carriers for plant direction-finding. Flanders and Swan, the English musical satirists, wrote a sad little song about the Honeysuckle and the Bindweed, madly in love but climbing one towards the right and one towards the left, fated never to meet. Perhaps some English reader can tell me in which direction Cleavers climbs.

This whole plant is rough, hairy and with incurved hooked seeds, all of which tells the observant herbalist that the plant is rich in silica. It thrusts its way upwards to the light, forcing through undergrowth, over fences and shrubs, in its smothering progress. Its country name, Goose-grass, may come from it being fed to poultry, especially geese, but its groups of rough leaves, rosetted around the stem, are also similar to the impression left in damp ground by the feet of geese.

Farmyard animals, rodents, even birds, spread its sharp clinging seeds all too readily. Perhaps it is a very good thing that we *don't* have it rampant in this country as it could quickly strangle bush and scrub with its dense mat of growth.

The whole herb (except the roots) is used medicinally. It is highly astringent, containing citric acid, and two others — rubichloric acid and a variety of tannic acid. These acids make it cleansing and toning too.

Cleavers is prescribed for irritations of the kidneys, bladder and genito-urinary tract, especially in males. It is most specific for chronic or recurrent urethritis, especially if accompanied by gravel, stone or inorganic calcium deposits. Although this is its primary use, as always there is the small print to be read and the most accurate treatment picture possible to be arrived at.

'Cleavers' person-picture

Primarily for male symptoms, Cleavers is occasionally used for its same cleansing and soothing properties in females, but Phytolacca and even Buchu are more used for the female. It certainly has more application to the longer male urethra.

Think of Cleavers, twisting upwards and irritating as it goes: the urethritis experienced is often from a genital infection lower down anatomically. This infection gradually climbs up further and further into the urethra, the bladder, even the kidneys and adrenal glands. Gonorrhoea will cause it, so will various viral infections. Sometimes irritating organisms present in female vaginal secretions will also transfer to the male. It is certainly true that multiple sexual encounters make urethral irritation more likely. So Cleavers has long had a reputation for treatment of venereal infections.

Equally, the infections and irritations which inflame and enlarge the prostate gland may also need Cleavers. (Syphilitic enlargement of this gland may produce sterility in males.) Later surgery may be needed as pressure from it can interrupt urinary flow and cause more back-up irritation.

So the person-picture is of a male, with irritable bladder and urethra, possible intermittent discharge from same and enlarged and painful prostate gland. The causes for these symptoms may be either directly from infection locally, or from a genetic or inherited parental exposure to venereal infections.

It is interesting to note that Cleavers is also prescribed *internally* for resistant or inherited skin diseases like psoriasis, scrofula, etc., which may have ancestral reasons for their sudden and unexplainable onset in descendants. Reading of diagnostic medical texts published anywhere between the 1850s and the 1930s may explain today the 'unexplainable'. A child with infantile eczema, a sudden onset of adult psoriasis on elbows, knees or around the hairline, may have way-back ancestral origins. Much was written and taught then in medical schools about the relativity of skin diseases to earlier genital infections, especially if the latter were poorly managed, incompletely treated, or ignored altogether.

The 'cooling' effect of Cleavers can be noticed from the very first dose as inflamed 'hot' irritated organs are soothed by its soft mucillage. Extract will be prescribed if the symptoms are recent and acute, tincture if there is intermittent recurrence of symptoms over a long period.

Negative-chronic 'Cleavers'

Perhaps one of the greatest moral and medical sins we can commit is to hand on to our descendants a poor genetic track record. Certainly, say the disciples of personal freedom, personal liberties and personal choice, we should have the right to sleep with whomsoever we please. Nature answers with one of her inflexible rules: there may be a price to pay in future generations if a child results from one or two venereally infected parents. Our newer concern, AIDS, has not yet defined its course of genetic damage for descendants of AIDS-positive parents. Although personal choice may lead to self-destructive results, does one have the right to hand down to a child a genetic horror-stretch? I believe that in amongst our bureaucratic regulation and control should be a self-imposed obligation to check for venereal infections and their results, and *have these treated* before contemplating a possible child-productive union. Life is surely hard enough without genetic damage from the cradle!

Positive 'Cleavers'

Human beings are amongst the most wilful and cussed of God's creatures (or Simian development)! In spite of all that we *should* do, we often close our eyes: it's short-term thinking, and very selfish. If a sexual encounter has resulted in irritation, discharge, pain or even a local skin rash, seek professional help immediately. Don't think it will go away; it may and it may not. Generations unborn may be better off for your caution! A herbalist's job is to treat illness *in its early stages*, and before there needs to be, in this example, prostate surgery, cancer of the bladder or children with severe genetic skin disorders. If early symptoms are uncomfortable, Cleavers, Buchu, Cornsilk, and several other plants may be given in a mixture to wash through, soothe, and de-inflame the urogenital tract. If you want to bounce healthy whole grandchildren on your knee, have *early* treatment when urogenital symptoms first present.

Dosage

1   Although Cleavers tea is often mentioned in North American and European herbals, it is rarely used in Australia.

2   As the symptoms which need its help can be destructive in the long term, it is better to have it prescribed for you than to self-medicate. Although not a dangerous herb in any way, its high silica needs watching in dose assessment. Silica being the powerful eliminative mineral that it is, there's no need to take more than you require.

3   Occasionally, Cleavers is listed amongst the ingredients of herbal underarm deodorants. To me, this indicates strong hormonal activity in the plant, but I have not as yet found any reliable research or analysis to corroborate this.

Coltsfoot

Tussilago farfara

*I*t is astounding to me to know that, as I write this, Coltsfoot is being considered by various medical and pharmaceutical academics as fit only to be placed on the poisons schedules in this country and others because, in theory, it contains pyrrolizadine alkaloids! The authorities concerned are adamant. They refuse altogether to recognise the Arndt-Schulz law.

The 'Arndt-Schulz Law' was formerly taught in orthodox chemistry, especially since Hahnemann's use of it circa 1800–1830. I can't find the exact dates, but later Rudolf Arndt, a biologist, and Hugo Schulz, a pharmaceutical chemist, formalised it as follows: 'To any given stimulus, thermal, electric, chemical (e.g. drug administration), protoplasm reacts differently according to the dosage of the stimulus. Small doses encourage life-activity; large doses impede life-activity; very large doses destroy life-activity.'

After the Comfrey débâcle world-wide, Coltsfoot also is possibly to be classed as 'deadly', and for the same wrong reasons. Although there have been *no* recorded dangerous effects or distressing symptoms from herbal treatment with Coltsfoot anywhere in the world today, this helpful and beneficial plant may be made inaccessible to professional herbalists and placed in the hands of pharmacists (who have never had one whit of training in its use!) via the poisons schedules classification. Moreover, we have all been told 'anecdotal evidence from herbalists, well patients, and hundreds of praise-laden writings on its benefits for centuries' will not be considered at all! Rest assured that also as I write this there is massive professional and public protest, and measures are very much under way to counter such actions.

It seems that seldom will pharmacy and chemistry budge from a man-made theoretical base no matter how much *practical* evidence from centuries of use is produced. Perhaps it would be more beneficial to mankind if academic research was undertaken as to *why* and *how* so many chest and respiratory complaints *improve* when Coltsfoot is prescribed, *without* hepatoxicity resulting in any of these patients. Coltsfoot actually *improves* liver function in the doses used by herbalists.

Coltsfoot flowers are amongst the first to raise their bright chrome-yellow flowers on brownish stems which look like asparagus spears at the first suggestion of early spring. The leaves and long underground runners appear after the flowers have died down, a back-to-front plant. It grows in damp beech woods and deciduous forests, amongst the fallen leaves of the previous autumn. It has also spread as a common weed in the UK, in Europe and in America. It does not grow naturally in Australia: all plants I've attempted to grow in Sydney soils have been eaten by snails, birds and beetles, and what leaves that remain have withered in our fierce sun and ultra-violet exposure. It does not thrive in the southern hemisphere.

There are specific ingredients present which apply to all irritated, infected, scarred or inflamed tissues in lungs and bronchial tree, and which also support liver function so that the two protective Vitamins A and D can be better metabolised. There is much mucillage; there are some tannins for toning mucous linings and loosening accumulated phlegm; there is a bitter glycoside; resinous substances: and grape sugar for fast energy replacement in lungs and respiratory tree. There is phosphoric, citric and malic acid, and several other sugars. There is also inulin, a muscle-sugar found in grasses and in several other medicinal herbs. This muscle-stimulant improves the 'pumping' action of the lungs, stimulating expectoration of hard or old mucus, and loosening a cough.

'Coltsfoot' person-picture

I call Coltsfoot the 'overcoat remedy'. The person-picture is one of winter chill winds, cold temperatures, and a person leaning into the gale with overcoat collar up, with scarf around ears and sore chest, with a handkerchief to the mouth or nose, and a dry, hard and painful cough. In this country, it is hard to find overcoats in the wardrobe! We tend to believe that our winter sunshine always means *warmth*, but a blustery south-westerly wind in July can send temperatures to zero and a chesty cold or respiratory virus can take advantage of our 'chill' and attack us. Keeping warm in cold weather sounds self-evident commonsense, but it's amazing how we shiver and freeze in T-shirt and jeans, convinced we live in Paradise.

Negative-chronic 'Coltsfoot'

Repeated bronchitis year after year can erode and scar the respiratory organs and pipelines. Actual tissue-scars may be present from an old TB contact, from pneumonia, even from whooping-cough. There may have been chronic asthma for years, or worse, infected asthma with wet greenish mucus clogging respiratory passageways. The long-term 'Coltsfoot' person may need slow and gradual exposure to the plant in any medication given, as its expectorant stimulus is strong. It is *not* a good idea to overdose or even give a high dosage initially, as the powerful expulsion of mucus may be too sudden and may clog bronchial pathways somewhat before it can be coughed clear. Especially for a chronic wet asthmatic, Coltsfoot must be *gradually* added at an initial low dose, increasing at the second visit when much old mucus has been safely removed.

Positive 'Coltsfoot'

Wrapped up warmly in cold weather, positive 'Coltsfoot' wears gloves, a windproof coat, and often a scarf. There is little likelihood of chill. Even when they put out the rubbish-bin on a wintry night, they put on an extra layer and wrap it across the chest.

These people do not get chest colds and viruses, being well aware that chill winds and sudden lowering of body temperature invite the arousal of viruses and bacteria dormant in the nose, throat and bronchial tree. However, Coltsfoot is only to be used *after* damage; it has no use preventively at all. Better use Garlic, or Cod Liver oil, for avoiding initial infection: after the damage has been done, even *long* after, use Coltsfoot.

Dosage

1 Traditionally, the dried leaves were used domestically on cooking fires to avoid contagion. In the days when TB was common, and

pneumonia an ever-present terminal illness, its use could be life-saving for children and adults. The pain of pleurisy and the dry cough of children with rickettsial deformity of the chest cavity could alike be improved.

2   Coltsfoot tea is unusual. It is more commonly used as an extract or tincture added with other chest herbs like Elecampagne, Horehound, etc., in an individual recovery mixture after chesty symptoms.

3   It is a prime ingredient in herbal smoking mixtures. (See *The Book of Herbs*, Pan Books, 1976, page 160.)

> If you by any chance *can* grow Coltsfoot in a cool area of Australia, throw some of its leaves on the barbecue in cool weather. Don't be surprised if there is a bit of productive coughing from some of your guests as the smoke is inhaled! They may never have otherwise removed those old deep-seated mucus-residues which have insidiously made breathing inefficient and demanding of more effort.

Cornsilk

Zea mays

The grain of ancient South American cultures, yellow corn kernels are now used world-wide. Tinned, frozen, dried, ground into polenta, flours and meals, they keep well without nutritional loss. The hard outer covering of each kernel can make corn indigestible for some folk, but it is a different part of the corn plant (also called maize) that we are concerned with here: the soft tassel of pale golden 'silk' at the end of the ripened cob.

Cornsilk to the herbalist means mucillage first. Its soothing demulcent properties are obvious from the initial dose. Its particular sphere of operations is the urinary tract and also the kidneys which feed into this.

Silica has been found in the soft golden 'hairs' of the corn-tassel. So have salts of sodium and potassium, as well as calcium and magnesium phosphates. All these ingredients together add up to a powerfully soothing and mildly diuretic stimulus to kidneys and bladder. It is most prescribed today for cystitis, both recurrent and acute.

'Cornsilk' person-picture

More a symptomatic pattern than a holistic one, there are still some person-characteristics for Cornsilk. There may be a very irritated and over-acid system generally: the professional iridologist expects to see in the iris the overstimulated nervous system and whiter than white nerve fibres which represent excess acid waste products and irritation produced with their excretion via the urinary system. Indeed, the 'Cornsilk' person may have an irritation around the bladder orifice too, and the feeling that urine is too 'hot', even burning. This may be acute, from an infection or an irritation, but it can also be from a mechanical cause, the cheerily-named 'honeymoon cystitis'. Affecting mainly women, frequent or too energetic intercourse may cause a mechanical irritation of the bladder and the urethra, especially if there is poor natural vaginal lubrication as well. Quite painful swelling and inflammation can result in the mucous linings. Many a new and promising relationship has been called off in its earliest days because of vaginal and urinary soreness and discomfort. Even the male may experience burning and soreness around the urethral opening at the tip of the penis.

Negative-chronic 'Cornsilk'

These poor souls can suffer burning irritation and real distress on every sexual occasion. Life can become a nightmare of pleasure–pain balancing. It may not be a 'headache' that prevents intercourse but the genuine distress of inevitable burning discomfort for days afterwards. Many folk who eventually consult marriage-guidance counsellors because their sexual-encounters are painful physically, so that gradual reluctance has caused emotional and psychological problems between them, may *both* need Cornsilk gently to soothe irritable and inflamed organs. This is prescribed in an *internal* mixture to be taken three or four times daily, but Cornsilk extract can also be used as a douche for a gentle regular 'washing' of the vagina too. (See Dosage.)

Positive 'Cornsilk'

After treatment with Cornsilk, and possibly other ingredients like Buchu, Celery and Juniper, Alfalfa, etc., there should be comfort in the urogenital tract as never before. Many women become accustomed to a general acidity, discomfort and the mucus discharge this produces, and seem quite surprised to discover that this need not be a 'natural' phenomenon at all!

Males who have been chronically plagued by non-specific urethritis find Cornsilk comforting and soothing too. It is *not* antiseptic, and does not inhibit any infection sources or kill off bacteria, etc. It is purely and simply soothing, washing through tiny irritating pieces of calcium gravel or dead tissue, and lining the sore and inflamed areas so healing can begin.

Dosage

1   Cornsilk tea is not the usual way to take this herb. I would not buy corncobs, rip off the tassels and make a quick cuppa. This is simply because the cornsilk may have been sprayed or exposed to adulterants on the way to market. By the time your greengrocer receives the cobs, the tassels may be a sticky and disintegrating brown! Of course, if you grow your own corn, knowing that it is unsprayed, you can cut the silk tassel when it is pale golden coloured. This can be dried, or used fresh. One corn-cob 'tassel' will make two or three teapots-full. Take a cup of this, warm or cool, three times daily for three days, in acute attacks.

2   The professional herbalist prescribes Cornsilk extract (together with other ingredients) to be taken maybe every two hours in an acute cystitis attack, until comfort returns; then three or four times daily thereafter for a further week or two.

3   Ten drops of Cornsilk may be added to the juice of a lemon and a cup of warm water, as a gentle vaginal douche.

> **Seek further help from your professional herbalist if soreness persists! There may be much more damage than simple irritation and inflammation. In fact, it is *always* better to consult first, then do it yourself after a trained person has assessed your causes of urogenital discomfort.**

Echinacea

Echinacea purpurea,
E. angustifolia

This comparatively recent intro-
duction into common use by herbalists world-wide originated in
the prairie lands of the North American continent. While *Echinacea
angustifolia* was the original plant evaluated and used there, a second plant and a close relative of the first, *Echinacea purpurea*, has
become even more favoured and widely prescribed. This latter
plant became the darling of European homoeopaths and herbalists
towards the end of the last century, and has become deservedly
more and more popular with every passing decade. Today, with our
immune systems depleted by marihuana use and with growing resistance exhibited to antibiotics by more and more viruses, up to
and including the AIDS horrors ahead of us, Echinacea will be more
and more needed with every passing week.

Where to start with this complex and multi-use plant? One of
the best and most complete textbooks for the professional herbalist
has recently been re-published in the USA — *King's American
Dispensatory*, Felter and Lloyd (Eclectic Medical Publications,
Portland, Oregon, USA, 1983). The authors devote seven close-
printed pages to Echinacea, its contents and uses. I agree whole-
heartedly with every line!

The thickish root-parts of Echinacea are the therapeutically
useful pieces. The medicinal properties of *E. angustifolia* are
variable indeed from plant to plant, whereas *E. purpurea* shows
more consistent properties and is probably preferred for this
reason.

Echinacea is listed simply as 'alterative' and 'antiseptic', but
this does not do justice to its particular and unique properties. First,
it raises the leucocyte count in blood — the process a body does
naturally when an infection source is recognised and a fight is ahead

for the immune system. Second, its line-up of fatty acids is even more impressive than those of the much-acclaimed Evening Primrose oil. It contains oleic, linoleic and palmitic acids, vital nutrients for the immune system, the liver, the lymphatic circulation and the blood. Third, its inulin, a muscle-sugar, stimulates muscle tone and provides better energy, together with a more even distribution of blood-sugar. And fourth, its high iron content is partnered by the necessary copper and cobalt traces, so that the iron is quickly and completely absorbable. To its other already discovered properties I would add further its undoubted ability to raise and protect Vitamin B_{12} metabolism. This appears to be via its cobalt traces, as this mineral is an integral part of the DNA–RNA mechanisms which are responsible for the transference of genetic characteristics. It is *not* the answer to all the ills of mankind: no single plant is ever that. Nor is it such a fabulous herb that all others should be discarded. *Don't* make the mistake of planting out forty hectares of it to corner the market and save the world! First, it grows poorly in the southern hemisphere: second, its specific uses, although spectacular in treatment, are narrow and limited.

'Echinacea' person-picture

Echinacea is indicated whenever pus is present anywhere in the body. The presence of pus shows that the immune system is fighting hard: the pus itself is composed, amongst other things, of dead white blood components, like leucocytes. These build up around a source of infection, especially if the fight against the invading organisms is a tough one! Types of staphylococcal bacteria, some viruses, bacilli and spirochetes can all result in pus around the septic focus of the infection itself. The most dangerous infection of all, perhaps, and a fast and deadly killer of otherwise apparently 'healthy' people is septicaemia. Even an insect bite or a small cut or wound can introduce violently active pathogens into the blood, and a resulting septicaemia can kill quickly. It is the bacterial and viral waste products, the toxins produced (not the infective agents themselves), that are so lethal. Infected wounds, 'hospital staph', a mosquito carrying malaria, or an abscess anywhere in the body can cause a septicaemia; 'blood poisoning' is an apt name for the condition. This is when a herbalist will prescribe Echinacea preventively so that such a potentially deadly condition may be reduced rapidly by improving the body's defence systems.

It goes without saying that Echinacea is *never* prescribed by a trained herbalist for a leukaemic patient's support-mixtures. This patient already has the condition of *over*-production of white blood components as part of their disease: an immune system which won't stop and is producing a distortion of natural defence mechanisms.

Negative-chronic 'Echinacea'

So far the person-picture shows infection, blood change and toxic wastes carried around by the blood, and pus-formation. Follow-up symptoms may include secondary infection following a first attack, because the immune system has been so depleted in the first onslaught that it cannot handle the second. Death from secondary infection can be the final result.

This grim picture *can* be brightened. A professional herbalist may prescribe and include Echinacea preventively whenever possible infection threatens. I include it in my personal overseas travelling-mixture with other ingredients to minimise infections from Cairo to Djakarta. Against mosquito bites in Syria, or tropical parasites and their toxic wastes in Bali, Echinacea goes in preventively each day in a tiny prophylactic dose.

If a dental diagnosis is 'tooth abscess' or if you share the miseries of Job with an outbreak of boils, or even if cross-infected acne results in pus-filled pimples around face and neck, Echinacea is indicated. Its ability to protect against secondary infection hitting you while you are down has been proved time and time again in practice.

Many extremely useful medicinal plants today entered our Materia Medicas by way of the North American Indian's application of them. Echinacea was used by them as a corrective and preventive of venereal infections like gonorrhoea and syphilis. Its alterative and antiseptic properties were peculiarly effective in treating the septic sites of entry of these diseases, the syphilitic 'chancre' and the gonorrhoeal discharge. A wash externally from dried Echinacea-root extracts was added to its internal consumption.

Positive 'Echinacea'

A quick *and complete* removal of the toxic waste products of infections indicates a healthy and well-balanced immune system. Too many case histories at my clinic tell the story of health deterioration after some resistant infection. Antibiotics failed to halt the assault and toxic waste products accumulated. These may have been 'sealed off' and encapsulated by the body, building rubbish-dumps in which random cells may later find fertile surroundings. The *completion* of any disease process, any infection or invasion, leaves the body as if that disease had never occurred. If a strong (but not over-active) immune defence is naturally mounted by the body, even the most dangerous of infective contacts can be dealt with by the lymphatics, the blood and the organs of excretion, and completely eliminated. Half a defence may leave the pockets of pus, dead bacteria, etc., that may fester away for years. Such sites can even cause a type of 'arthritis' half a lifetime later. The unique action of Echinacea is not duplicated by any other plant. With our immune systems under more and more threat as mentioned in newspapers daily, last century's discovery and early use of this herb may be opportune indeed!

Dosage

1   Do *not*, repeat *not!* self-prescribe Echinacea. It is not available (nor desirable) as a tea, ever. Its natural acrid and bitter taste precludes this anyway. What's more, some of its most useful ingredients are only extractable by alcohol preparation, so a tea from it would not be effective.

2   The professional herbalist spends time, money and brain-dizzying study-hours learning the trade. The 'cautions' and the 'contra-indications' are part of this training. Consult an experienced professional if you feel that a septic focus of infection may be at the root of your resistant and debilitating symptoms of ill-health.

Elecampagne

Inula helenium

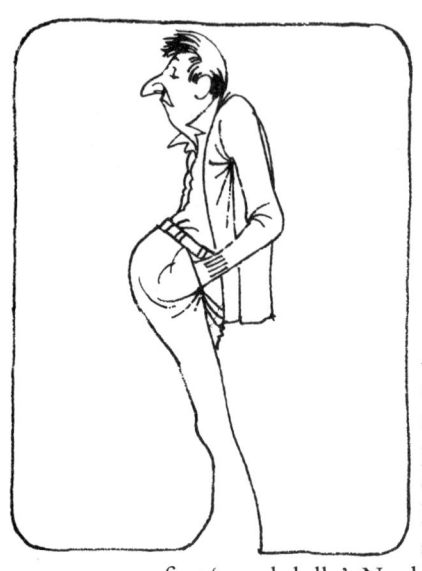

A wonderfully long history of simple usage of the roots and rootstock of this tall herbaceous plant dates back to the fourteenth century, and earlier, in Northern Europe, where as a lozenge or a sugary-based confection it became our first 'cough-lolly'. No doubt the travelling monks brought its growing roots gleefully back to their monasteries in France, Italy and the British Isles. But even earlier mention is made of it by Dioscorides, and by Pliny, and there are records too in early Indian Pharmacopoeas. Centuries of continued use of any plant mean that the plant is a truly effective remedy: humans are not stupid enough to continue using therapeutics which don't work!

Wherever tuberculosis was a killer disease, Elecampagne was one of the simple and effective tonics and antiseptics prescribed. Its powerful action on lungs, stimulating blood flow and increasing the strength and energy of each breath taken, made the plant almost specific for the pulmonary distress, the oxygen deprivation leading to physical exhaustion, and the eventual haemorrhages and anaemias of advanced tuberculosis of the lungs. Prescribing it in the earliest stages of the infection, even for the families and close contacts of tuberculosis patients, often meant that the dreaded disease passed them by, their lungs being capable of active removal of the bacilli they inhaled. When TB was a killer all over the world, and its method of contagion was understood, improved hygiene and awareness began to relegate it to a low-profile disease. But as the world's less-developed populations explode, and conditions of cramped housing and poor sanitation return, expect the current new strains of the TB bacillus to become a terrible threat. As a radiographer from Sydney's expanding western suburbs told me, telltale X-rays of boat-people and immigrants to this country from Vietnam, Korea, etc., are beginning to record this disease again.

'Inula', another commonly used name for Elecampagne, has given its name not only botanically to the plant, but also to its major starch-like ingredient, inulin. This is a powerfully active principal ingredient, stimulating expectoration of wet mucus, infective residues and dead tissue from the bases of the lungs, and producing larger lung capacity and therefore more oxygen available. With more efficient oxygenation, the blood has better oxygen-transport and more likelihood of burning out the infection quickly. (The siting of TB sanatoriums in mountainous districts was to *force* the lungs to expand more fully in the thinner air. Perhaps Elecampagne used as well would have reduced treatment time dramatically?)

Other ingredients in Elecampagne read like a tailor-made prescription for breathing efficiency. The volatile oil from the plant volatilises at blood temperature and becomes directly available in the lungs, loosening phlegm and debris. This oil is also antiseptic. Vegetable sodium chloride adds its expectorant and antiseptic properties too. It contains Alantoin (also high in Comfrey), so that damaged tissues can heal rapidly and safely. Alantoin is a cell-proliferant and is demulcent as well, increasing the rate of healing in the damaged lung-linings.

Together with Garlic, and perhaps Echinacea, Elecampagne is prescribed for all respiratory infections of the lower breathing mechanisms. For tracheatis, for bronchitis, for threatened pneumonia even, it is a powerful agent. It should only be prescribed with very great care for bronchial asthmatics: too sudden or powerful a respiratory stimulus may be counter-productive, loosening too much wet and waste matter and actually provoking an asthma attack. Let your herbalist decide how much Elecampagne you need.

'Elecampagne' person-picture

'Elecampagne' breathes shallowly: the lungs are often lifted up by the shoulder girdle from above, not lifted by the diaphragm from below. Many of these people when asked to take a deep breath raise their shoulders with the effort, instead of pushing from below with an intake of air beginning from the diaphragm. Yoga breathing exercises can be a positive necessity, to retrain this patient.

Skin colour may be pale, without a pinkish tinge. 'Elecampagnes' may *sigh* a lot: they may also hunch down posturally over their solar plexus area, restricting the diaphragm and the pulmonary channels. They may even feel stabs of pain or an uncomfortable oppression in the chest and sternum areas, causing more tension and apprehension about a possible heart problem. 'Sit up straight and take some deep diaphragmatic breaths' is good advice to this person-type. Young Australians often slouch their upper torsos forward and down, inhibiting valuable oxygen-supply organs. The Australian slouch may even produce an asthma-like respiratory problem, or 'exertion-asthma' symptoms.

Negative-chronic 'Elecampagne'

Most of us feel some degree of negative-'Elecampagne' after a long period of sitting still in a classroom, in an armchair reading, in an aeroplane seat, or in front of the television; all for far too long and in a bad postural position for the respiratory organs. If you fall asleep in front of television, your health may be better served by a brisk walk with the dog or with your children or flatmate. Chronically shallow breathing can make you permanently 'tired'.

Pale skin can also deteriorate further: extremities may feel cold, even in hot weather. Hair may be limp and lifeless because oxygen transport is poor and the gravitational top of the system, the scalp, misses out. Chronic tiredness can lead to memory lapses and concentration difficulties. And although you may expect to be less energetic, balding and forgetting things past ninety, you should not expect these symptoms (or put up with them!) at thirty!

If added to your symptoms are multiple days off from school or work while you gasp for air and reach for your 'puffer' to keep breathing, as well as maybe recurrent bronchitis attacks and lack of energy, then Elecampagne may be a necessary ingredient when your herbalist prescribes for you.

Positive 'Elecampagne'

This person remains active, energetic and enthusiastic well into extreme old age. They have straight backs and twinkly eyes, and often a shock of fast-growing hair. They *walk*! In fact they often prefer a walk to a sit down! Their stride lengthens and they take long deep breaths rhythmically and without conscious effort.

When they return home, or to the office after a lunchtime stretch of the legs, their faces are pink and their eyes bright and clear. Oxygen has refreshed them from top to toe, and in the process, all sorts of day-to-day wastes have been moved towards organs of excretion for elimination. Lymph has been pumped, sweat-glands stimulated, and a powerful excretion of carbonic acid has cleared the lungs. These people, breathing deeply and well, often seem like youngsters in their attitudes to life, even well into old age.

Dosage

Elecampagne tea is not a good idea, nor does it exist in tablet form. Alcohol extraction is usually needed from the dense and heavy root areas of plants, so alcoholic extract or tincture is the usual form of dose. As a 'chest' herb, for respiratory improvement, it relieves symptoms as well as treating cause factors. Invaluable!

One of the taller-growing medicinal herbs, Elecampagne is a big and generous plant. Stems of 1–1½ metres are crowned with deep yellow-orange open flowers, like a cross between a dandelion and a sunflower. Nature often colour-codes to help us choose appropriate foods and medicines. Many of the bright yellow-flowered herbs are effective in protecting mucous-lined organs and body-structures, and the evidence of carotene, a building-block for Vitamin A, is often indicated by a clear yellow flower-colour. Just as the orange and yellow-coloured tropical fruits and root vegetables, even spices, are indicative of carotene's presence, so some of the herbaceous plants, too, give us the clues if only we will open our inner eyes and observe.

Eucalyptus

Eucalyptus globulus

It would be remiss of me, in an
Australian herbal, not to mention one of the very few native Australian plants which is now used medicinally world-wide. It is
surprising to me to find that it is more highly regarded and more
used in other countries than it is in our own! In Germany and
France Eucalyptus oil is included in many proprietary medications,
in inhalants and lotions, even in ointments. In many other
countries, when I introduce myself as an *Australian* herbalist, the
response is 'Oh yes; where our Eucalyptus oil comes from.'

There are many Eucalyptus species from which the resinous
aromatic oil can be extracted, but *Eucalyptus globulus* is the best
source. The traditional method of extraction is primitive, but very
effective. The young tips are harvested (sometimes after coppicing
the tree first to stimulate better growth and oil content), tipped into
a ground pit, and heated by an ordinary woodfire. The rising steam,
containing the oil, is collected then re-distilled, and the final oil is of
strong odour and a pale golden colour. This may or may not be
refined again, or may be added to other oils or broken down in
strength. The pure oil, like most other aromatic essential oils can be
caustic to skin, eyes, etc., if not used advisedly.

Eucalyptus's fame spread also to the Middle East, and it is
common to find roads lined with 'gum trees' in Syria, Egypt and
Jordan. As the tree grows, it cycles through itself a tremendous
quantity of water each day. A paradox reveals itself: in other
countries eucalypts are planted to *drain* swampy areas and reduce
the breeding of malarial mosquito populations. (The oil is also used
for other blood-parasites like hookworm, etc.) It may be that
Australia dried out in the outback from too many eucalypts taking

up the groundwater. It's worth a thought for gardeners who want an Australian bush-garden: don't be surprised if your soil dries out, depriving other plants of formerly available moisture!

The main ingredient of the leaves, eucalyptol (almost identical to cineol in some aromatic spices), changes chemically, and quite rapidly, on oxidation. It is a powerful antiseptic because of this. Users often remark on its change in odour after a day or two of application to skin, to infected cuts or wounds, or to fungal or viral skin lesions. This odour is of ozone, produced as a breakdown product. Clothing or wardrobes can also smell somewhat musty and like a beach at low tide if Eucalyptus is left in contact with materials which have been sweated into and have then been hung up again, unwashed! Used Eucalyptus oil has a very different chemistry.

As a household antiseptic, Eucalyptus is without peer. Its ability to free up oxygen can be seen as it bubbles slightly when in contact with bacteria, funguses, etc. Festering pus-filled sores or wounds can be gently wiped over with it, and many an Aussie soldier has used it protectively in Middle-Eastern and tropical theatres of war. One drop, in a gallon or two of suspect drinking-water (left to stand overnight), can kill off all sorts of potentially dangerous uglies.

There is no real person-picture, either negative or positive, for Eucalyptus oil, though perhaps an Aussie countryman, boiling the billy with a eucalypt-leaf or twig suspended in the rising steam, would be an appropriate image. There are so many roadside fire-places and rest-areas now on our national highways: why not resurrect our billy-boiling past more often? A leafy twig of eucalypt above the boiling water can do more than just evoke an atmosphere. It can improve the breathing, clear the throat and chest, and generally refresh. Its pungent oil is now used throughout the world in respiratory infections, in asthma, in croup, in emphysema, pneumonia and bronchiectasis. Even cystic fibrosis sufferers have found improvement in their breathing using it as a household inhalant.

Dosage

1 One or two drops *only* in a basin to which 500 ml of boiling water are added makes an excellent antiseptic inhalation. Put a towel over your head and the basin, and breathe in the steam until

the water cools off. Great to clear and decongest in upper or lower respiratory infections! Children can do this too, especially before bedtime when breathing can become most obstructed. If there are respiratory infections in the household, other members can use this procedure preventively.

2   Add a *few* drops to warm water when bathing a cut or wound, or when washing any pus-filled sores, fungal infections like tinea, ringworm or paronycia (fungus under the nail cuticle).

3   Use as a powerful household antiseptic. Wipe over bathrooms, toilets, kitchen sinks, etc. Again only a *few* drops of the oil, well mixed with a litre of water is plenty.

4   Although many herbalists prescribe the *internal* use of Eucalyptus oil, I would hesitate to advise this in a household sense. 'A few drops on a lump of sugar' is a commonly found treatment in do-it-yourself herb-books. I have too much respect for the powerful essential-oils from plants to suggest this. Contact by the undiluted oil with throat, stomach-linings, etc., could be uncomfortable, to say the least, and may even cause a 'burning' or later ulceration. Your professional herbalist will advise you and prescribe for you if there is any need for *internal* use of Eucalyptus oil.

Fenugreek

Trigonella foenum-graecum

As its name implies, this annual herbaceous plant was beloved of the Greeks and in the Ptolemaic period of Greek influx into upper Egypt it became almost a staple food there. It is still grown today in the Nile Delta, and all around the eastern Mediterranean where it is believed to have originated as an indigenous plant. Often wrongly called a 'grain', it is botanically a legume, and as such it shares with other legumes a high vegetable-protein content. Rich Vitamin B and phosphorus compounds (like lecithin) make it not only a digestive-system herb but also an excellent food-plant for nervous system health. As it also manufactures in its growth Vitamin A and a vegetable-form of Vitamin D, it is supportive of liver function too, and protective of all mucous-lined body organs. There is much sulphur present; and also choline, a support for cholesterol metabolism. Several glycosides make it an energy-supportive plant and, although the seeds contain not even a trace of starch, they have abundant mucillage. It is therefore a multiple remedy and a powerful one. Its properties may best be summed up as supportive of liver function, protective to mucous-linings all through the body, and giving renewed nervous energy. There is a fourth benefit, however, and one which is becoming more and more necessary today: Fenugreek clears and promotes the drainage of the body by the lymphatic system. As lymphatic vessels and lymph-fluid movement are essential parts of our immune system, Fenugreek may become a valuable plant for the future.

Although there are local area exceptions, Fenugreek would grow very well indeed in many parts of Australia as a commercial crop. Consult with your local Department of Agriculture officials for advice on growing conditions.

Fenugreek seeds, hard little yellowish-brown rhomboids, can be stored for long periods of time in screw-topped glass containers, without losing any of their aroma-packed punch. It is certainly better to buy them whole rather than to buy the powder crushed maybe months or years earlier which will *not* hold its freshness nor its chemical integrity. Ask your health store staff for the freshest of Fenugreek seeds, and sprout these. So many easy sprouting contraptions are also available now that this process can become a regular part of your kitchen activities — especially interesting for the children who will begin to acquire good nutritional habits early in life. (See *The Natural Health Book*, pages 132–3.)

One good reason for sprouting Fenugreek seeds is that their pungent curry-like odour and taste is removed by the chemical changes in the sprouting processes. Even those finicky family members who turn up their noses at Fenugreek tea will cheerfully eat Fenugreek sprouts in the salad bowl or on a sandwich with no criticism. This pungent savoury smell and taste of Fenugreek seeds makes it an essential ingredient in curry mixtures and as one of the spices in the rich ancient dishes of the Persians, the Turks, the Greeks and Arabic tribes. As 'helba' the crushed seeds were cooked and pounded into a pastry cake in Egypt. In all desert and dry countries where dehydration can be a daily danger, Fenugreek has become part of the culinary tradition. In Australia, we should learn its benefits quickly.

When vegetarians feel unable to take Cod Liver oil to tone up mucous-linings and protect against colds, 'flu, viral attacks and bacterial infections, Fenugreek is a vegetable look-alike, almost identical in the balance of its ingredients and in the body-areas in which it is effective. Keep up the Fenugreek sprouts, or the daily cup of pungent Fenugreek tea, all through the autumn and winter months.

Fenugreek is diaphoretic and slightly diuretic too. If a spicy curry makes you break out in a sweat on the face, the forehead or neck, or even the hands or whole body, then your lymphatic fluids needed a kick along anyway. Slow-draining lymphatics are really stimulated by this herb. The skin 'breathes' better too, and excess fluid retained in tissues is hurried along towards kidneys and bladder. 'A good clean-out' one patient described it as, although Fenugreek has no laxative properties whatsoever. Its direct effect is through liver and lymph.

If you take Fenugreek tea as a household remedy, be aware that the powerful diaphoretic effect may cause you to smell less than rose-like for a few days! Shower frequently and exercise in moderation too to speed up this initial clearing out of formerly 'blocked drains'. (Your plumber experiences the 'Fenugreek-effect' frequently when a sluggish clogged fluid-waste system is flushed through!) The good news is that a human flushing-out will lose its disagreeable odour through the skin after the first few days of Fenugreek use. Plan a Fenugreek-and-solitude weekend, then open your door on Monday morning with a well-flushed sweet-smelling you to greet the world again.

'Fenugreek' person-picture

'Fenugreek' doesn't exercise much. Perhaps called 'lazy' or even a 'slob', 'Fenugreek' lives a sedentary existence where 'exercise' becomes a dirty word, and 'work' is equally repulsive. 'Fenugreek' drives kilometres, but won't walk a hundred metres from the parking place to the shops. In short, there is an obvious reason why this person is a bit poddy, a bit overweight, a bit slack in muscle-tone and even more obviously a little *yellow* in overall skin-colour. Typically, they don't sweat much at all, and may seldom think of using their bladders. Fluid circulations, especially lymphatic circulation, are *slow*. Strangely enough, they often eat the very worst foods for their type — fatty, fast-foods, deep-fried potatoes, rich buttery sauces and then wash it all down with dry wines, or other alcohol-based fluids. Alcohol is dehydrating anyway! No wonder their livers slow down, excess fats are stored in tissues, and it becomes harder and harder to find the energy to even think of regular exercise let alone a walk to the corner-store or around the park with the dog.

Negative-chronic 'Fenugreek'

After all this fat-plus-alcohol-minus-exercise for years, you can picture our Fenugreek-needing person. Overweight, flabby, with an upward-creeping blood-pressure through arteries narrowing from fatty-plaque deposition in their walls, it's not a picture of the sun-bronzed sporting Aussie that we see! The sedentary Australian is too common, driving everywhere but walking hardly at all, being a spectator at the sporting events or a television watcher of other people's sweat and strain. After constant sitting around, the effort needed to begin any activity becomes greater and greater, and the pressure changes in blood flow more and more dangerous if any exercise *must* be done. A flight of stairs can become difficult, even a downright hazard for heart and major circulation.

Handfuls of vitamin tablets may be resorted to, or a naturopath may be consulted in a burst of guilt or with family prodding, but when *exercise* is advised as part of a treatment programme, chronic 'Fenugreek' loses interest. Or, even worse, in a fit of self-disgust out they race in brand-new jogging-shoes at 5 a.m. — and drop dead three weeks later from the too-sudden major changes in circulatory pressures and fluid flows. Typically, their skin colour goes yellowish-grey after any too-sudden exercise.

Positive 'Fenugreek'

This person perhaps leads a life where compulsory sitting and limited movements during working hours are balanced by *regular* exercise.

Positive 'Fenugreek' goes for a brisk walk in the park in the lunch-hour, or a swim before or after work. After sitting for hours in a business conference, you'll find them running upstairs two floors, not waiting for the lift. Graphic artists, fashion designers, authors and office workers, telephonists, machinists, even dentists, need to *change* their limited postural stances of the day and exercise physically to keep fluid circulations moving. Curry for dinner may also be a favourite!

Dosage

1   Fenugreek sprouts are becoming more regularly available from the greengrocer. Cultivate the sprout-habit in every salad you make.

2   Fenugreek seeds are available from health stores. A flat teaspoon of them should first be pre-soaked in cold water for five to ten minutes to soften their hard coating, then pour a cup of boiling water on top and leave to brew as for any tea. Strain and drink, with a pinch of vegetable salt or a twist of lemon added. You should perspire more freely afterwards!

3   When prescribed in extract or tincture form as an ingredient of a personal patient's mixture, Fenugreek helps to treat sinusitis,

hayfevers, upper respiratory tract infections, 'glue ear' and middle-ear clogging, catarrh in nose and throat, etc. It also stimulates liver and pancreatic enzymes, and aids fat metabolism. When iridological examination shows pearly-white or yellow lymphatic-rosary signs, Fenugreek is indicated to promote lymph flow and fluid excretion through skin and kidneys.

4　　There are few cautions on the use of this plant, but I would not recommend more than one or two cups of the tea a day unless personally prescribed for you by your professional herbalist. Always remember, *too* much of a plant medication may produce not a better or a quicker 'cure', but an *opposite* effect in the same body parts and processes.

Children do not find the flavour of Fenugreek tea as strange as do some adults. Make it half-strength for a child under five, and full-strength for older children. A cup at body temperature, or hotter, can be a safe and quick home remedy to reduce a fever in any infectious disease of childhood. There will be natural sweating, reduction in temperature, and it can also reduce the itchiness and discomfort of the skin rashes and pustules which accompany many of these diseases, as a welcome secondary effect.

It has *no* use externally applied.

Gentian

Gentiana lutea

Most people think of Gentian Violet, the antiseptic paint, when this herb's name is mentioned, but the internally-prescribed Gentian used by herbalists comes from a different Gentian. This is a tall-growing yellow-flowered plant, a stately perennial, which is found above the snowline in southern European mountain chains, especially in the Pyrenees and the Alps. You may have tasted 'Genzian', a beautiful tonic liqueur which is bottled in white glass with the red, blue and yellow Gentian flowers depicted. If you like a 'cordial' after dinner, read on and see if your best tipple would be 'Genzian'.

Many of the cold-district mountain plants used by herbalists seem to have an energy quality which is superior to plants grown at sea-level or in the tropics. Such plants seem to act more quickly and more obviously. The patient really notices the process of getting well again with a positive feeling of improvement after each dose.

Gentian is one of the most bitter of all our medicinal plants. The root is the part used, its fleshy paleness oxidising to a darker and darker brown as it is dried. It is almost never used fresh, and rightly so, as its lively chemistry needs to be attenuated by careful drying.

It is a rich source of potassium, iron and sodium, and is directly effective in the stomach, the liver and the portal vein. One of the best digestive tonics, it stimulates enzymes, tones up stomach linings and helps decongest the liver and liver circulation. As an appetite stimulant, it has been used safely and effectively by medical doctors and herbalists continuously for centuries. It was almost as popular as Chamomile, as a bitter, carminative, digestive aid. It is especially indicated where illness, shock, emotional upset or severe debilitation make the patient feel too tired to digest, and where appetite is non-existent.

'Gentian' person-picture

'Gentian' reacts to traumas by losing all desire for food. Even a mouthful cannot be swallowed, let alone digested. There is great *ennui* and depression, and the effect on the liver can be very evident. There may be biliousness even at the smell of cooking, and pronounced nausea and difficulty swallowing. This person shows dismay on their face when an over-full plate is plonked down in front of them at the end of a stressful day, or indeed after *any* day which was other than perfect! Eating with someone they dislike can bring on violent dyspepsia. A family quarrel around the dinner table can see them pushing back the plate with the meal hardly touched.

They often describe their stomach–liver–emotions reactions to you by a gesture where one hand grabs at the stomach–liver midriff and *twists* a handful of gut. At the same time their face, especially the mouth, will mirror their uncomfortable emotions. The mouth may turn down, or tighten, or close firmly shut so the words don't come out — but the food won't go in, either. 'I've got a nervy stomach', they say, or 'I can't swallow all that emotion', or 'I'm a worry-guts'. Whatever they say, they cannot digest food and emotional experience at the same time. For these people, more than for any other person-type, *peace* around the dinner table and congenial relaxed surroundings are essential. *Never* suggest a business lunch to a 'Gentian'! They will go through agonies of dyspepsia, real pain, bloating and general digestive impossibility for hours, if not days, afterwards. Present them with small, pleasant-looking meals, in congenial company and their digestion will be perfect. But introduce even the slightest note of discord, like too-loud music, a noisy drunk's party at the next restaurant-table, or even a difficult child or complaining teenager or grandma at their own table, and their digestions will rebel. If food *is* eaten, everyone around may suffer the irritability, the self-pity and the induced guilt of their indigestion for half the night.

These people are not putting on an act; they are genuinely suffering. Sensitive is not the word; there's just a very close correlation between the digestion of food and the digestion of the day's experiences. Days later, when the original emotional traumas have been forgotten by all those involved, 'Gentian' may tell you what upset them.

Negative-chronic 'Gentian'

These people's digestive apparatus tyrannises their whole life. Almost any small occurrence puts them off their food. A frown from their nearest and dearest, an imagined insult, a genuine *faux-pas*: all can cause 'Gentian' real intestinal discomfort. They become picky eaters, with likes and dislikes that terrorise the household cook. Be aware that such a person *may* go on to use their digestive difficulty as a weapon, and may spread around them some of their own pent-up and unvoiced emotions, upsetting all and sundry. 'Handle meal-times with care' should be hung around their necks so prospective friends, lovers, acquaintances and business associates will know what to expect.

These negative 'Gentians' may insult waiters, ruin a restaurant's reputation and lash out, *later*, with the tongue at all those present. This reflects only their own inability to digest emotion and food at the same time. But it can lose them many friends! Portal-vein congestion may be a constant problem. The heart may also suffer from this chronic congestion, and 'heart-burn' is a common name for their midnight forays in search of dyspepsia remedies, sleeping pills and emotional reassurance.

Positive 'Gentian'

Giving *Gentiana lutea* tincture or extract as a mixture ingredient for this person can produce the rapid opposite of the above rather dismal dinner-guest. Although it needs to be taken regularly, and in combination with other herbs like Chamomile, Alfalfa, Hops, Dandelion, etc., there should be digestive improvement noticed from the very first dose.

Positive 'Gentian' gets invited back time and time again, and is a joy to cook for. What's more, any real *faux-pas* from the cook, the other guests, the family or the customers, are overlooked and even made into a funny story or fascinating anecdote so everyone around the meal table digests better after a good laugh and a good story.

Positive 'Gentian' *feels hungry*! It's surprising how many patients admit to seldom feeling such a signal! Positive 'Gentian' makes everyone's eating experience not only comfortable but easily digested. A good host or hostess is known for the positive 'Gentian' they dispense. Fun as well as food; interest as well as a perfect soufflé, and a funny story while the coffee-pot boils dry upsets no one at all. On goes the tea-kettle, and everyone enjoys tea instead.

Four hours later the guests leave, giggling and relaxed, and positive 'Gentian' says, 'Gee, I'm hungry; I'll just have a cheese sandwich before I turn in.' No dyspepsia, no walking the floor: the digestion of food has been kept separate from negative emotional digestion, and life's irritations have been put aside while food is easily digested. For those patients who have genuinely suffered from severe emotional traumas, shock, depression, etc., Gentian can provide a positive way back to a healthy appetite.

Dosage

1   Gentian root is *never* prescribed as a tea. Its bitterness alone would preclude this.

2   It will be prescribed by a professional herbalist for lack of appetite after emotional, physical or environmental traumas have temporarily made food uninviting.

3   For a true 'Gentian' person, whose stomach rules their life and ruins their social relaxation, the herbalist may add various nervines, Bach Flower remedies, etc., to condition this patient to keep emotions and food separate. Digesting both together is a next to impossible task without Gentian for this person-type.

> Some patients do complain about the strong bitterness of Gentian. Bear in mind that a fairly 'bitter' person may be behind that complaint! Persevere with the Gentian, plus other digestive herbs; if necessary add a little honey to the dosage-glass, or cloak its bitterness with a sweet fruit juice. 'Gentian' is a sensitive soul, but don't let their own touchy feelings upset the entire kitchen and dining room!

Ginseng

Panax quinquefolium

We must turn towards the 'East' and away from our general European ancestry to learn about the fabled Ginseng. (Of course, from Australia, the direction is north-west!) From India, Tibet, Mongolia, China and Korea come the stories and the claims, the magical lore and the medicinal miracles of Ginseng growth and use. When any plant re-locates from the countries where it grows naturally, and is incorporated into other cultures, into different racial-origin groups and traditions, we must expect *changes* not only in the plant's usefulness and applications, but in its suitability to the new conditions.

Wild Ginseng, growing high in the mountains, amongst huge ancient forests and in misty waterlogged air, is obviously different from cultivated plantings of the herb, row beside row, under shade-cloth and with irrigation. The *quality* of the plant is different, and although it may be unfashionable to talk today of aristocrats and peasants, wild mountain Ginseng is rightly a treasure beyond price, and the cultivated plants can be ordinary indeed.

In its wild state, mountain Ginseng can glow at night with an eerie phosphorescence. This was how it was originally discovered, and it was sought at night, marked with an arrow and dug in daylight — with as few helpers as possible! The prices paid for such plants would transform the peasant into a wealthy lord for three generations to come, at least!

As the outside world began to hear of this revered plant, rich Chinese merchants and travellers brought with them a single precious root to strange lands, or bid huge amounts to obtain such a Ginseng root from northern China, Korea, etc. There is on record a price of US$200,000 paid for a single high-quality root by a wealthy West Coast expatriate Chinese. Don't waste your time sitting in the dark staring at your Ginseng tea bag waiting for it to glow with magical lustre: the difference between a processed tea bag, made from commercially grown Ginseng, and the wild mountain plant is the difference between twenty cents and $200,000: what you pay for is what you get!

In a Chinese pharmacy in Hong Kong I spent a fascinating hour at the Ginseng counter. All shapes and sizes of the greyish-brown roots were displayed, cut in slivers or whole; boxed or plain; wrapped in gold and red or sealed in ornate packages. The price range amazed me. Some Ginseng-classer knew much more than I ever would!

In 'Eastern' tradition, the Ginseng root is used, life-long, in a particularly simple way. Kept in a trouser-pocket, or on the person, the dried root is not used at all when that person is *well*. But when energy slumps, when there is trauma or shock, when an infectious disease strikes, or when advancing years see enthusiasm for life fading, then the Ginseng root is nibbled at, sucked, or a few precious scrapings from it are used to make a series of teas over a few days. In the old Dutch trading city of Batavia (now part of Jakarta, in Indonesia), I enjoyed a cup of Ginseng tea made from a few scrapings from a huge Ginseng root preserved in alcohol in an enormous glass cylinder which was *locked* through a tightly closing lid. Such a Ginseng root would provide restorative 'teas' for many many years. I certainly felt my energy zoom up within an hour, my physical strength return, and my mental interest too, after a bout of dysentery which had previously ruined a week of my holiday there. There was no need for further cups of the precious tea either and this taught me the truth of what I had previously read in Oriental herbal lore; Ginseng is a *short*-term booster of body functions. It does not need repeated doses day after day for a mild illness, nor should it ever be taken this way. A Ginseng-'hit', accurately prescribed when indicated, acts like an engine booster: once the revs are up, they stay up.

The eerie phosphorescence of mountain Ginseng was formerly thought to be from naturally radioactive soil in which it grew. More recent analyses have shown that the plant itself produces this phenomenon. Its contents are complex indeed, but compounds containing iodine and phosphorus are involved in this 'magical' ability of the leaves to glow. Loosely-bonded but highly active chemical changes characterise this plant. A few tiny particles from the root, where those iodine-compounds are stored, are a massive thyroid and pituitary stimulus. I personally believe that *all* the multitudinous body effects attributed to the use of Ginseng are directly attributable to its effect on the two principal hormone-regulators of the body — the thyroid and the pituitary systems. If you read the testimonials, Ginseng has 'cured' everything from an underactive stomach to terminal tertiary syphilis! How could one plant do so much good in so many different ways, and be prescribed for such widely-different diseases as bronchitis and kidney failure? Is it just a giant Oriental placebo con-game, or does its reputation rest on real results? Before you decide, read up on just how many body-systems and functions are dependent on healthy strongly active pituitary and thyroid glands. The list of their control mechanisms is a long one. It is certainly claimable that improvement in these glandular functions can cause improvement too in hundreds of major and minor symptoms of disease, especially in *degenerative* processes of advancing old age. Ginseng's traditional use by older males, to improve and rejuvenate their sexual organs and to continue to father children into their eighties and nineties, may have validity. It is certain that a balanced and active pituitary gland produces long life and an old age without loss of faculties. Maybe 'honourable Oriental gentleman' is smiling inscrutably for very real reasons!

There is not a paintable person-picture for Ginseng. It is such a multi-purpose plant that its uses are too many to identify quickly visually for you. I would consult a qualified Chinese herbalist if you feel this plant may suit your symptoms. We are newcomers to its prescribing. The experts have centuries of experience with it.

Like most other medicinal plants, there are cautions about Ginseng's use. With an *over*-active pituitary gland or thyroid, it is not only *not* needed, but may be contra-indicated. Don't believe for a minute that everyone can and should benefit from Ginseng use! For a Western-trained herbalist, iridology can be an excellent diagnostic determiner if Ginseng is a possible therapeutic choice. Those with hyper-white pituitary or thyroid zones should not take it indiscriminately. Because it 'made a new man' of your best mate does not necessarily mean it is applicable to *you*!

There are many and varied forms in which Ginseng is commercially available in this country. See your professional herbalist first before you look for eternal youth in a capsule or in a bottle! I know of one tired 'cello player whose girlfriend gave him a Ginseng 'tonic' for his birthday. He sure stayed awake — sometimes around the clock! — but he consulted me later for shaking hands, depression, insomnia and outbursts of emotion not formerly typical of him. His iris showed me the brilliant white markings of a borderline hyperactive person. He needed calming down with Mugwort, Valerian, Chamomile and Passiflora, not a massive further 'hype' with Ginseng. The bane of a professional herbalist's life are those who 'want to help' but have no formal training in all the cautions, the care, and the appropriate prescribing for each individual. A desire to help needs study and experience to guarantee that the helpee truly benefits!

Dosage

1   Added to the above cautions and contra-indications must be care to be taken with the dosage levels. What is effective for one person may need either one-tenth of that dose, or ten times that dose, for another. Years ago a yoga teacher in my herbal class ignored my warnings and took a half-teaspoon of ground Ginseng root three times daily for a week or two. He missed three weeks of classes, and when he finally returned, he yawned his way through the two-hour session. His Ginseng dose had given *opposite* results to what he sought. He had slept the clock round, his wife had shaken and shoved him to wake him each morning, and he had actually fallen asleep during one of his own meditation classes, much to his chagrin. If you have read well the Arndt-Schulz law (page 141), you will recognise the pattern: he had taken a grossly too large amount *for him,* and his individual reaction was *opposite* to that intended. Nature's laws can be tested by all of us: they hold good in every case.

2   A Ginseng tea bag should be regarded as you would any other mild stimulating warm drink. It is a fact of the Ginseng commercial economy that the lowest grade of available Ginseng root is processed for the tea, the higher grades being reserved for therapeutic preparations. Don't expect an instant erection after a cup of this uniquely pungent brew!

3   *Always* consult a professional Chinese-trained or Australian college-trained herbalist before you outlay what may be a considerable sum on over-the-counter Ginseng. Friends and neighbours, well-meaning though they may be, do not have the necessary skills to prescribe this herb.

Golden seal

Hydrastis canadensis

King's Dispensatory, one of the finest and most completely presented Materia Medica of all time, concentrates heavily on the North American continent's indigenous plants. Only to be expected from its American authors trained in the Eclectic medical schools of the time (1898), it has been updated and reprinted in the last two years (*King's American Dispensatory*, Felter and Lloyd [Eclectic Medical Publications, Portland, Oregon, USA, 1983]). It devotes no less than nine of its substantiated fact-filled pages of analyses and uses to one of those herbs which entered European herbal medicine via North American Indian traditional lore. A source of some of the finest and most effective plant medicines in the world, the various Indian tribes gave freely of their accurate and experiential knowledge of these plants to the new white flood of humanity which inundated their cultures and their continent. I am disappointed that our own Aboriginal people have withheld since our arrival here the greater part of their centuries of knowledge of plants used as medicine. What filters down to us today is tantalisingly general and incomplete. It makes our country the only one left in the world where we must painstakingly begin from scratch to identify, list and begin to use *local* Australian native-plants for herbal medicine. In my travels, I am constantly asked for information on the medicinal plants of Australia. Aside from a dozen or so recent books, still very general as to preparation of the plant, parts used, dosages, symptoms, cautions, etc., I cannot refer to much hard data, pharmacognosy, experience or research which could place our own indigenous-medicine Pharmacopoea on a par with the rest of the world.

Golden seal, often just called 'Hydrastis', is a rhizomatous plant which grows in upland forests and mountainous territory (contrary to its botanical name, it is *not* found in marshes or in wet boggy ground). The American Indians used the dried powdered root-parts as a face-paint, giving a strong chrome-yellow stain to the skin. They also used it around eyes and ears. Interestingly, its medicinal uses may have been originally observed from this practice, as locally applied to eyes or liquid preparations of the root dropped into ears have strong but gentle antiseptic action, stimulating mucous-linings to throw out invading organisms, dead cells, pus, etc. As an ear, nose, eye and skin remedy, locally applied as an ointment or an aqueous lotion, it is unsurpassed.

There are three alkaloids found in the rhizome: hydrastine, canadine, and berberine (the last also found in Barberry, *Berberis vulgaris*). Caution must be advised therefore on its internal uses. It should only be added to individual mixtures in quite small proportion, as due to its resinous sticky character (lignin being another constituent), it will adhere to wet mucous-lined surfaces as well as to skin, for many days if not weeks. Internally, if too heavy a dose is taken initially, upsetting liver and gall bladder, stomach and intestines, the effect of this too-large dose may also last for days or weeks. Better get it right beforehand: Golden seal in *small* quantities always.

It is one of the most expensive of all herbs on our dispensary shelves and I have never discovered why it should be. It yields its properties readily to water and alcohol, and does not need specific or difficult processing. Perhaps it has something to do with its scarcity, for it will only grow undisturbed in wild areas, and cultivation, or any attempts to begin commercially-valuable plantations of it, are not possible. Disturbing the soil with ploughing, other crops, etc., will see Hydrastis disappearing from the locality altogether. It is a prohibited export from the USA, and does not germinate from seed at all well. So I guess we must pay the high price so that its mountain gatherers will keep looking and gently lifting each individual rhizome.

If ever a herb had a 'detergent'-like effect, this one does. Its resinous adhering powers internally and externally lift debris, infection residues and excess mucus away from skin and mucous-lined organs. Such wastes and pathogenic materials can be then washed away externally or can pass out through the alimentary tract.

Hydrastis also contains much carotene, the yellow building-block for Vitamin A production. This explains its suitability for a mucous-linings and skin tonic and its protective long-term effect for these body zones. It also explains another reason for the *small* doses internally, as too much Vitamin A can have an upsetting and over-stimulant effect on the liver. Altogether, another plant to leave to the professionals when used internally, but externally, as an ointment or in an eye-wash, it can be a valuable and safe addition to the family medicine cabinet.

One of its best applications is in teenage acne, and in various eczematous and itching skin rashes it is not only soothing but healing as well. In erysipelas, impetigo, infected sores, boils and carbuncles, unsightly infected 'blind' lumps, styes on the eye or crusted sore nostrils, it gently reduces throbbing and pain as it cleans and renews. It is wonderful for what used to be called 'bride's spot', any one large disfiguring pimple that erupts just when you want to look your very best. Don't squeeze and prod; just apply Golden seal ointment and leave it be. The irritation will lessen in minutes; infective material can be wiped away within the hour, and a second application can reduce deeper swelling and redness too.

Golden seal is prescribed internally for long-standing slow-healing under-active symptoms, and has a pronounced tonic effect not only on the liver but also on the muscular tone of arterial walls. It is added to internal mixtures when there is chronic atony, but should *not* be used when there are acute active inflammatory conditions involved. Needing very special care in its choice as a therapeutic substance, there is a fine dividing line between its ability to soothe and heal as well as stimulate and wash out, and its ability to irritate an acute inflammatory process even more. I do not prescribe this herb very often for internal use. Although it has undoubted value, its unpredictability makes it a difficult choice. It is *not* the job of a well-trained professional herbalist to make patients unduly uncomfortable during a treatment period. There may be unavoidable discomforts as alteratives remove wastes and debris, but Golden seal is always a critical choice. Some patients seem able to tolerate it well and improve rapidly. Others feel nauseous and flatulent. When there are other safe and comfortable liver and bile herbs like Dandelion, Fenugreek, Fennel, Alfalfa, etc. to choose from, Golden seal to be taken internally may not be necessary.

As an external ingredient in eye-wash, ointment or lotion, it has yet another external application as a douche mixture ingredient. Like Calendula, its antiseptic properties and its high Vitamin A potential, together with its stimulant and tonic effect on vaginal walls, make it a better and easier choice used this way than systemically. (See Dosage.)

Golden seal
person-picture
Not perhaps as clearly defined as are other person-pictures in this book most of 'Golden seal's' inner catarrh and mucus is hidden from easy identification. So is a pelvic area which may be atonic, and any haemorrhagic tendencies internally, like endometriosis. But the person may show their picture clearly by constant or recurrent skin and middle-ear infections, by sore red eyes, a runny nose and over-heavy menstrual bleeding.

Predominantly a female herb, 'Golden seal' may show only the external symptoms to the world, feeling constantly 'drained', tired without just cause, with sore and tender spots over stomach and abdomen, and over pelvic organs. There may be some typical comments made like 'I feel I need a good clean-out inside', or 'I feel kind of yellow-yukky', or even 'I feel everyone is looking at my dreadful skin.' There may be a very poor self-image, a door-mat personality, even a resentment that life seems such a succession of disfigurements and sore intestines and pelvis. One of the most complicated of personalities, these person-types can trek from therapy to therapy, from practitioner to practitioner, bemoaning their inability to be diagnosed by anyone. Their emotional life is often disappointing, sex may be uninteresting or even irritatingly painful, and they cry 'There must be more to life than this!' Disappointment seems to be a constant companion, but they may appear unable to break its cycles.

Negative-chronic
'Golden seal'
Severe liver and gall-bladder symptoms may follow the earlier terrible skin, sensitive red eyes and menstrual exhaustion. Difficult digestion may be traced to the pancreas, or to an under-active stomach. Sugar-metabolism may also be disrupted. Life seems to put these people behind the eight-ball. Emotionally they may go from wrong partner to wrong partner, and each time a spotty skin or an eye or ear infection may follow. Their emotions may be difficult to balance, but their out-

ward signs are easy to read. When they fall in love, their eyes are clear and their skin improves; when disappointment and disenchantment result, their skin breaks out, the stomach becomes 'sore' and tender, periods change character and eyes lack lustre.

Positive 'Golden seal' A healthy liver, both physically

and emotionally, leads to far better life quality. Nor have I ever yet met a really *un*healthy person with a healthy skin! Positive 'Golden seal's' skin is clear and glowing, not a murky yellow-grey. Mucouslinings are comfortable and strong so that infections in ear, nose and eye occur rarely. If they do, a quick topical application of Golden seal heals them rapidly.

Digestion is comfortable and flexible, without any prohibitions on fatty foods, etc., especially if the emotions have just taken a tumble in life's traumas. This person feels that life, love and the experience really have been rewarding and satisfying, no matter if a little rain has fallen on the emotions now and then. 'Overall', they'll say, 'I've had a good life, and I've enjoyed the whole experience.' You may be surprised to find that they've had just as many troubles and upsets as the next person, but these are written off as 'experience' and not dwelt upon, blamed and resented. 'Wouldn't have missed life for quids' one twinkled at me, bright clear eyes alert in his sun-browned face. No matter that his share of emotional loads had been high, he had 'put it all down to experience'.

Dosage

1   Leave all internal usage of this plant to your professional herbalist (who will have a hard enough time deciding!).

2   Externally, use the ointment as necessary to skin, eyelids, vaginal entrances, etc. (Remember there may be a little staining on clothing or bed-linen from its yellow-resins. Use old underwear and linen if large skin areas are to be covered, or cover with a clean dressing.)

3   Add ten drops of Golden seal extract to a cup of warm water as a vaginal douche. No need to use this more than say weekly or fortnightly as a prophylactic treatment, or ask your herbalist for instructions if there are actual vaginal or uterine symptoms.

4   You will not buy this herb over the counter, nor as a tea — and rightly so!

Do not confuse Golden *seal* ointment with a proprietary pharmaceutical eye-ointment, Golden *eye* ointment. This second preparation is based on mercuric chloride, and shares no chemistry at all with Golden seal. One cannot and should not be spoken of in any connection with the other.

Guaiacum

Guaiacum officinale

This forest-tree is not a suitable denizen of your backyard herb-patch! A native of the West Indies, it is slow-growing and not a pretty garden specimen either, so it has remained comparatively little known botanically. But to ship builders it has been commercially valuable: its tough dense hard wood has been used as a friction-lining between propeller-shaft and stern-tube since the old steam-boat days. I was involved with its pungent characteristic odour and its long lasting resins many years ago as I cleaned up a factory where a rush order for stern-tube reliners had been filled. I have never forgotten the smell! It can best be described as a lemony liquorice-molasses experience!

Guaiacum is almost impervious to salt-water, holds high heat and friction without sudden breakdown, and withstands high pressures. A tough one! It is used medicinally for people who are just as tough!

There are resins in abundance in this timber given the common title of 'guaiacic resins'. As a medicine, the wood shavings are heated and the gummy resin skimmed off as it rises. It mixes readily with various alcohols for the making of tinctures and extracts; the resinous exudate is now preferred to the whole wood.

This herbal remedy takes us back to the swashbuckling Caribbean pirates, to the Spanish Main, and to general thievery, debauchery, captured foreign maidens and ensuing high jinks. Errol Flynn may have been well cast as he leapt from shrouds to deck, sword swinging, while the nubile heroine below panted with longing!

Guaiacum was a Caribbean remedy for syphilis and for the acute inflammatory processes in joints and in the blood that this disease may leave as a potential inheritance for future descendants.

'Syphilitic rheumatism?' you cry aghast. West Indians knew its causes in the sixteenth century, and used the wood and resins from a native tree to clear the blood and reduce the inflammatory legacy in ligaments and joints, especially when a gouty form of the rheumatoid pattern was later found. Even late last century, medical textbooks described vividly the legacy of a 'rheumatoid pattern from venereal-disease origin'. Gonorrhoeal infection could produce related symptoms too but bacterial foci were the causes here, not the syphilis spirochete. Out of Edinburgh and Glasgow, from some of the greatest medical schools since Alexandria and Verona, came the classic symptomatology of syphilitic rheumatism, either immediate or in store for later descendants. Guaiacol was incorporated into nostrums, pastiles, and medicinal liquids. The British Pharmacopoea listed it for decades.

Herbalists preferred, as always, to use the *whole* plant part, not its individual extractives. We still use it today, and for similar, if not identical, symptom patterns.

'Guaiacum' person-picture

'Guaiacum' always feels 'hot'. That is, of course, when they're not feeling an odd 'coldness'. It's like the experience of peppermint; a sensation of heat, but an underlying cold. Typically, their body is hot to the touch; they spend cold winters in shirtsleeves, and throw off the bed-clothes, poking their feet out to 'cool' them. A radiator can be torture to them; an over-warm room a problem. But in summer they may add on a jumper or coat when everyone else is in shorts and T-shirt. This heat–cold distortion is common with 'Guaiacum' people.

Typical also is their difficulty in mobilising joints first thing in the morning. 'I'm all right as soon as I've had a warm shower and I loosen up,' they'll say. They'll also enjoy outdoor activities, and are *better from movement*. Consequently, they seldom 'relax' or remain in the one position for long. 'I need to move about a bit' they'll say as they shift in the chair, and then take the dog for a run or dig the potato-patch. The aches and pains *worsen* when in the one position for too long, and their joints tend to seize up when immobilised. *Lubrication* is their major skeletal requirement. Anti-friction herbs like Guaiacum are ideal for them, preventing tightening ligaments from locking and 'freezing' dry hot joints. *Mobility* is essential. This extends to fluids, too, where uric acid crystals may deposit out otherwise in toes and feet, fingers and hands, as gouty rheumatism.

Emotionally, they are tough rather than feeling. Like the dense Guaiacum timber, they may avoid emotional 'waters' if possible. 'None of that nonsense', they'll decide if an emotional storm breaks in their environment, and off they'll go to water the garden, chop some wood or clean out the kitchen cupboards. They are doers rather than feelers.

Negative-chronic 'Guaiacum'

*A*ll this heat and activity leads to fluid difficulties. Drying joints may burn out their synovial fluids and lock into position. Heberden's nodes may form on fingers and toes, making movement difficult and stiff, with increasing 'itchy' discomfort or pain. Worse, and typical of long-term 'Guaiacum', the large bowel shares in this drying out of fluids, and chronic constipation can result with haemorrhoids, and even intestinal bleeding as hard, dry faecal matter tries to move out without natural fluid lubrication. Imagine your motorcar engine running for a long period without sufficient water and oil. Eventually, a cylinder jams with the unlubricated heat and pressure. So does your skeleton, when its articulated parts try to move without sufficient lubrication!

Chronic 'Guaiacum' suffers pain and immobility which inevitably worsen. Confinement to bed in geriatric homes is the cruellest of torments to them, as they inevitably have clear and active minds into very old age. Intellectually, 'Guaiacum' is often above average, even brilliant. The old syphilitic gene which may be buried amongst the ancestors produces geniuses as well as capable and reliable people who relish key jobs and responsibility. However, the syphilitic gene can also produce sterility, some schizoid symptoms, nervous system degeneration and the dropped weakened previously hyper-mobile ligaments in feet and wrists which are typical of the actual disease as well as in its hereditary legacy.

Some medical as well as naturopathic researchers believe diseases like Multiple Sclerosis, even genital and other Herpes, are more likely to be found down the syphilitic inheritance pathway. Guaiacum can be used in individual mixtures when the symptomatic and ancestral history points to ancient causes of today's symptoms. I have even prescribed it for young people who show mental rather than rheumatoid symptoms, but whose irises show the dark muddy-brown overlays which need alteratives to clear them, and in whose case histories the ancient patterns appear. Some severely retarded patients have also shown mental as well as physical improvements and changes once their ancestral cause factors have been treated with this, and other, alterative herbs. It is also interesting to note that some forms of epilepsy have in bygone days been treated with Guaiacum, especially if chronic constipation is a presenting symptom as well.

Positive 'Guaiacum'

Bowels move as regularly and predictably as does the rest of the skeleton. Faecal matter is soft and moist. There are no 'aches and pains' to be expected as a result of advancing years, nor immobility and 'hot' inflammatory symptoms. Positive 'Guaiacum' is well-lubricated — and not only over the tonsils! (Speaking of which, Guaiacum was also formerly used for a dry, inflamed and swollen throat!) Emotionally too, positive 'Guaiacums' 'oil the wheels' of those around them at work and at home. They 'keep their cool', knowing when quick action is required but also able to relax mentally and physically when it's not. Strong, tough and dependable people, they are quick and responsive both intellectually and physically into old age. They just love to be relied on and asked to help!

Dosage

1   Thank God there is no such thing now as Guaiacum tea! I could certainly never be prevailed on to drink it, let alone prescribe it for others. However, a soaked decoction from the chips of the wood and with the resins present was its original sixteenth-century method of prescribing.

2   Included in personal mixtures in an alcohol–water extraction, its strange taste can be masked by other ingredients. As a 10 to 20 per cent inclusion, the patient's dose of the Guaiacum would be only a bare one to two drops in each ten-drop dose of mixture, added to a little water. At this dilution, the taste and smell is negligible, but its effectiveness is adequate. One of the best alteratives when rheumatoid symptoms are present.

Early-life acute rheumatoid disease can be more easily understood when the distant or recent hereditary component is recognised. Rheumatoid arthritis tends to 'run in families' and, like any other genetic component, can sometimes throw out as an exaggerated concentration of ancestral experience. Some young child today may suffer life-long for 'sins of the fathers unto the third and fourth generation'. A syphilitic sailor, centuries ago, may have programmed in today's 'sudden unexplained onset' of rheumatoid diseases in child, teenager, pregnant woman or healthy athlete. Shocks, hormonal changes, as well as physical traumas, can 'call out the old Adam' as ancestors claim a part of your body relating to them generations earlier. We can change and improve many of our own body's processes, our experience and life quality. We can never change our ancestors, and their voices in our cells. How important, therefore, for us to leave for our children and their children as clean an ancestral slate as possible! Every health improvement we make today, every positive and honest emotion, every environmental change for the better, is a more *positive* ancestral start for tomorrow's world and far beyond.

Hops

Humulus lupulus

*I*f you're a beer drinker, at least be aware of the herbal-medicine origins of what is perhaps the next oldest drink after water; the fermented fluids from plants. In ancient Egypt barley-beer was the tipple; in Japan, China and India rice-ferments were used. Almost every plant which has calming or relaxing properties has been used as a beer-base. While the beers of antiquity were mostly sweet in taste, later European preferences were for a bitter quality, believed to be more thirst-quenching from its very bitterness and astringency. The bitter flavour also produced appetite stimulation and increased gastric-acid production. So beers of various kinds were drunk before, or with, meals.

Hops entered the herbalist's repertory, as did so many plants, as a pot-herb. The young emerging shoots of the first-year's growth were boiled or steamed and eaten like asparagus. This is often how medicinal properties of plants were first understood and developed into a therapeutic system — from their effects on people when eaten as a vegetable. It is only a short step from the kitchen-garden to the still-room, and not a long road either from a vegetable on the table to a water and alcohol extract on the herbalist's dispensary shelf.

As Hops dries for longer and longer, the female flowers (or strobiles), the parts used for beer and medicinally, develop more and more Valerianic acid (see Valerian, pages 294–5). Much of the skill of yesterday's herbalists rested on their abilities not only to know which plant to use, but how the particular plant parts should be treated to produce the best therapeutic effect. If Hops is to be used for sedation and calming-down of the central nervous system, the Valerianic acid is the constituent most required, so longer drying is necessary: if Hops is to be prescribed as an appetite stimulant or a stomachic-bitter to improve digestion, its effect is actually better if dried less. 'Old wives', often criticised for their tales, used to know such small-print qualifications well. It can annoy today's herbalists mightily when some blanket-regulation on a plant's use completely ignores the great differences in a plant's chemistry and medicinal effects as it follows a cycle of seed, growth, flowering, fruiting, drying and processing by alcohol or water extraction. At each stage, vastly different chemistry presents itself as that characteristic of the plant.

I re-learned this lesson well on a recent return visit to my favourite English pub which still brews individual beers and stores them in oak casks. It's also the preferred watering-hole of bandsmen from the Household Brigades, many of whom are old friends now. They gave me a good lesson in herbal medicine. One was going home to bed after an exhausting three days on duty, so he specified one particular beer; a second was on call and organising several complex band performances in the next few days — he ordered quite a different brew. A third had to evaluate applicants for a vacant position in the percussion section in an hour's time; he ordered a light beer. From long experience, these men knew the effects on them of different stages of Hops fermentation. From the same plant, it was possible to gain either restful sleep after long duty, renewed alertness and managerial co-ordination, or critical evaluative sensitivity in judging the quality of musical competence of a prospective bandsman. I often wish the small breweries of England would bring their ancient recipes and skills, as well as their knowledge of plant processing, to this country. A can of Fosters really doesn't give you the complete Hops experience!

The Scandinavian countries produced the alternative name *öl* or 'ale', the Vikings' drink, and by Saxon and Scandinavian invasions the name entered the English and Scottish vocabulary. The British were several centuries behind in adding Hops to their brewed drinks; the Vikings used Hops in many ways as the plant grew naturally in their northern climate. In Australia, Tasmania and parts of Victoria have ideal latitudes for Hop-growing too. They don't thrive or give of their best medicinally if planted in warmer or tropical zones.

Would you believe, even Hops has felt the stigma of 'evil' and 'danger' suffered by so many useful plants when their properties are imperfectly understood. Both Henry VI and Henry VIII forbade its addition to ales and beers for a time, not for its danger to health but for its change to the *taste* of British beers. These had formerly, like earlier cultures, been sweet: hops added its *bitter* principles and was promptly assigned to the Devil and his attempt to pervert good British palates! Too many of us dread change and the unfamiliar, and attribute to it devilish energies which may be threatening to our present comforts and established ways.

Male and female flowers occur on different plants. As it is the female flowers only that yield the powdery resinous Lupulone, the bitter principle, only a few male plants are necessary in a whole field. It's a wise manufacturer, too, and with long experience in the trade, who can assess the quality of a bag of dried Hops flowers which should not contain any of the male plants.

Hop-beer was (or should have been!) an end-of-day drink, as its two active principles, Humulone and Lupulone, combine both tonic and relaxant effects. After the day's work, a Hop-beer could produce that lovely expression, 'unwinding'. Adrenaline which had been pumping out all day would begin to subside, and muscular relaxation could then also begin. The effect of a Hop-beer or two could see the day's cares receding, and energy for play, pleasure or relaxation and hobbies returning. Hops as a nervine produces an easier change from active, competing, striving and exerting, to a *calmer* state. As tense muscles relax, and your coiled spring loses its tension, there's energy of a different kind available for hobbies, for chat, for creative skills and interests, even for *pleasurable* competing in training or sporting activities. In line with nature's fixed rules of balance, one or two naturally brewed Hop-beers, made in the old ways from real Hops, yeast and sugars, and varied with other malted grains added as well, can, and do, produce this effect; five or ten beers can produce the *opposite* effect in the same body-parts! Instead of relaxation and energy renewal, there could result aggression and irritability followed by exhaustion! Does this sound like anyone you know who drinks *too much* beer? Especially if it's of the differently-made commercial kinds?

Home-brewed Hop-beer is a different entity altogether. Make up a batch from time to time, have one or two glasses after a tense day, and notice the difference. Recipes are available in many books on home-brewing, with multiple variations and additions to the basic recipes and methods.

'Hops' person-picture

Are you the manager and co-ordinator? Do you lie awake at bedtime tense and with the job still on your mind? Do you review today with irritability at all you *didn't* get done? Do you spend the first few hours in your bed planning perfectly, and with complete organisation all that lies ahead of you tomorrow? Sleep is hard to find as imaginary conversations keep you still adrenally-active. 'I'll tell Bill to meet Jim, then both will go in the one car to meet Fred. After Fred decides how he wants the project to proceed, Bill will leave and meet Doug back at the office and Fred will then have time for three customer-calls before he leaves for the airport. I'll call Bill for a report at 10.30 p.m. at his interstate hotel' . . . and all the *details* of tomorrow, beautifully meshed and smoothly efficient, are planned and re-planned. The only problem is that you've *pre*-lived tomorrow, and it's now already here: it's 2.45 a.m. and you're still not asleep! And, as you secretly fear (and the adrenaline keeps pounding to cope with the anxiety of it), what if Bill wakes up late, misses Jim altogether, and Fred's taken a sickie? Off goes Plan Two in your head!

Hops is the nervine for the pre-worriers and the pre-planners and the co-ordinators of projects; the 'managers'' herb. Medical herbalists prescribe it in extract or tincture form for those who *pre-live* their stresses, and whose sleep only comes when every detail is in place in their mind's eye. Unfortunately their *real* eyes may be still wide-awake watching the moonlight on the wall, and planning, planning. Comes the morning and a haggard face stares back from the bathroom mirror. That telephone call from Bill in ten minutes time will trigger irritability and tension, possibly letting loose a full adrenal-temper on the poor man: an *un*planned-for event — Fred's skipped the country with your secretary! All your sleepless hours have been for naught.

Negative-chronic 'Hops'

Constant irritability and criticism of the poor-planning of everyone else becomes part of the personality. Muscular tension increases and aches and pains begin here one day and there the next. There is increasing fatigue in the muscles, even to the point where you are *more* tired when you finally wake in the morning than when you went to bed. Fluid retention can cause 'weight' problems next as the adrenal overloads become constant. Depression follows an apparent over-confidence. You drink perhaps more and more alcohol (beer?) and even smoke more and more as adrenal glands demand crutches to keep adrenal output high. The so-called 'nervous breakdown' can follow: one morning, the adrenals refuse altogether, and you huddle in bed, shaking, even with tears, as life has spoiled so many of your perfectly laid plans.

Positive 'Hops'

The British general, Wellington, who outsmarted Napoleon, never needed Hop-beer, or even Hops extract prescribed by a profesional. 'I make my plans of string,' he answered one of his officers enquiring about the order of the day for the next morning's battle. Wise general! He didn't quote 'Murphy's law', but he knew it well: if anything at all can go wrong and foul things up, it probably will! Accordingly, he remained *flexible*, knowing from experience that if string broke it could quickly be re-tied in another place. And it is recorded that he slept well on the eve of Waterloo! Perhaps he used a Hops pillow? I can hear my grandmother now: 'And what's your alternative plan for fog or mist?' she'd twinkle, when as a child I planned and re-planned a holiday outing. I slept more easily when I learned her lesson: don't worry; it may *never* happen!

Dosage — household uses

1   From dried hops flowers, make a small flattish pillow. Place this under your normal pillow at night, and as you turn and move your head the aroma will ensure continued muscle relaxation and restful sleep if you are the 'Hops'-type.

2   Homebrewing can be fun for all the household. Remember though, too much of a good thing will produce the opposite effect. Save your Hops beer for nights when tomorrow's plans, excitements, challenges or adventures could keep you unusually wakeful and adrenally-charged. And follow the old recipes now available in bookshops and health stores.

— professional uses

Hops can be added as an ingredient in a general nervine mixture. The herbalist may blend it with Vervain, Scullcap, Valerian, etc., depending on how badly the adrenal glands have become suddenly or chronically overloaded and exhausted. One patient kept her 'arthritis' at bay by drinking *one glass* of homebrew every few days! On the other hand, it's also possible — and likely — that excess Hop-beer consumption will *cause* aches and pains, especially in hips, knees, ankles and feet. It's the herbalist's professional task to establish the dose of either tincture or extract suited to each 'Hops'-personality patient. The right dose-level, and 'Hops' sleeps soundly, wakes refreshed, and with flexible and fast adaptation to the new day's events.

Horse chestnut

Aesculus hippocastanum

This chestnut is not the edible variety. Its bitterness precludes any food uses of the nut, although in its history the crushed pulp has been used all over Europe as stock fodder, after initial treatment with lime or other alkalis.

A comparative newcomer in herbals, this beautiful decorative tree, with its triangles of pinkish flowers held like a candelabra, and growing steadily to a height of 15–20 metres over many years, came into prominence through the German and central European schools of herbal medicine, but it is a native of India and parts of Asia. Perhaps some observant Bavarian farmer watched his cattle growing fatter and even more fertile on the pulped chestnut fodder and, understanding nature's laws of opposites, reasoned that small doses of the same should be effective for those humans with *too* much muscular bulk (especially around lower torso, hips and thighs), with congestion on softer organs and difficult fluid-flow because of it. In large amounts, it seemed to *increase* prostate size — and usefulness — in the male animals. This far into a herbal, you should now be deducing its *small*-dosage use in the human male and, different in degree only, for the human female.

Aesculin and Aesculetin are two glycosides found in the fruits and the bark of the Horse Chestnut — the parts used medicinally, so there is certainly muscular-energy available from its use. Fraxin, found in all the Ash family of trees, is an astringent tonic. Allantoin, found in several other herbs like Comfrey and Elecampagne, is a

189

cell-proliferant and healing agent, ensuring that as routine cell-death occurs every day, the new cells will be accurate carbon-copies of the original *healthy* cells they replace. Allantoin appears to have an inhibitory effect on the continued existence of random or badly formed new cells, and a stimulatory effect on the normal DNA-RNA code, encouraging accurate new cell growth. For cattle-breeders in Europe, what could be more useful than a blood-line protector from the male side?

There is also a digestive enzyme, lipase, in the nut-flesh; resin and a fixed oil, ensuring even spread and continuity of its effectiveness; albumin for kidneys, and several sugars; Vitamin C and iron. An impressively useful combination for the person described below.

'Horse Chestnut' person-picture

The body, either male or female, is thickest around the lower torso, hips and thighs and usually strongest, too, in those areas, in early life. I've heard Horse Chestnut called the 'Hungarian Herb', and it also applies to the Czechoslovakians, Albanians, Yugoslavs and even into the southern Russian states.

Physically active people in health, there is good muscular co-ordination in the lower part of the body, which is always the heaviest and strongest. These people love walking, climbing, mountaineering, and tend to be adrenally cheerful first thing in the morning — sometimes too much so for the rest of the household! Early mornings tend to be their best time of day for strenuous activity, but the strongest of them are still leaping up on the tables at midnight, singing loudly and waving their arms about. 'Horse chestnut' is a frightfully jolly person!

Negative-chronic 'Horse Chestnut'

All this energetic leaping about in early life can lead to adrenal *over*-charging and a constant strain on other endocrine glands because of it. In the male, especially, there often seems to be great development in the physical and athletic use of the adrenal glands, sometimes at the expense of the sensual and sexual uses for the prostate gland. Such males can be gladiators in the sporting world, but find great difficulty with the softer and gentler hormones used in emotions, in sexual activity, and in physical comfort. They can, and do, become martyrs to physical competency, training hard and vigorously to achieve 'perfect' condition. They run up sandhills and three flights of stairs at the office, thoroughly enjoying their 'excellent' health. They can even regard sexual activity in a 'performance' sense, notching up the quantity, and not necessarily aware of the quality — especially for their partner! If ever a herb reflected macho-maleness, it's Horse Chestnut!

The female 'Horse chestnut' can be fearsome! Large arms pummel you on the massage-table, and you can bet she'll run round the block at the end of the day, just to use up all that excess hip and thigh energy. When it comes to childbearing, though, the lady can have a serious pelvic tension history, with painful periods and spasmodically slow or uncontrollable flooding. Pregnancy can be traumatic for such women, with varicose veins appearing early and remaining and worsening after the birth.

Pelvic congestion, in both male and female, can cause varicosity not only in legs, but in the rectum and the anus. Haemorrhoids are the classical affliction of 'Horse chestnut'. Constipation can be a consequence, and it's only a short step from there to severe prostate congestion, inflammation and even gross actual enlargement in the male. Not a happy prospect for that perfection-seeking Hercules in later life! This pelvic and rectal congestion can sometimes occur simply because the prostate is not emptied enough. More (and more *relaxed*) sexual activity is sometimes a circumstantial relief for the 'Horse chestnut', even well into their usually healthy and strong old age, but it's sad that their personality-type often rejects such activity. Sometimes it's willpower, sometimes it's a cold shower, sometimes it's a twenty-kilometre bushwalk: emotional or sexual tensions tend to be released in rather a self-punishing hair shirt way.

The long-term negative 'Horse-chestnut' may face either ovarian or prostate cancers, chronic and severe constipation or even lower-bowel tumours, and varicose veins like twisted tree-roots; and, of course, intermittent or chronic haemorrhoids — 'the grapes of wrath'!

Positive 'Horse chestnut'

*T*reatment with 'Horse chestnut' as one of the ingredients in a general herbal mixture for such complaints can be a kindness to this person-type. This herb is certainly not enough on its own to reverse long-term developed or chronic symptoms, and will be just one of the ingredients used; other herbs will be needed with it for general endocrine balancing and fluid flow through the pelvic zone.

Positive 'Horse chestnut' is physically (and sexually) active until at least eighty if not ninety years of age. A strong sense of humour and the ability to laugh off the inevitable failures and weaknesses that we all suffer at times, no matter how 'perfect' we'd like to be physically, ensures relaxation as well as 'performance'. It's a happy and healthy octogenarian yodelling his way up the mountainside who can also relax by the fire at night with his beloved. The lesson to learn is that perfection does not exist in this world; weaknesses flaw even the strongest of us; but it takes *real* strength to admit it and laugh. Then on your horse for a gallop across the plains and a Cossack dance all day and all night!

Dosage

1   It is not usual to take Horse chestnut in any nutritional or household form, nor as a herbal tea.

2   Prescribed medicinally as extract or tincture, relief from symptoms should become obvious fairly quickly, even within days, when prescribed for prostate symptoms of inflammation or infection. Varicosity and pelvic congestion may take much longer to relieve; weeks, even months.

3   In Germany and Switzerland injections of Aesculin have been given medically directly into varicose veins to shrink and straighten them. Such treatment is not at the moment available in Australia from herbalists.

Horseradish

Cochlearia armoracia

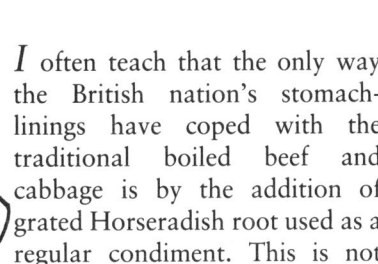

I often teach that the only way the British nation's stomach-linings have coped with the traditional boiled beef and cabbage is by the addition of grated Horseradish root used as a regular condiment. This is not only the traditional way to take Horseradish, but also the most efficacious in many ways. Eaten with stodgy food, or with dry overcooked meats or, in this country, 'burnt offerings' from the weekend barbecue, the herb the French call 'German mustard' stimulates gastric juices, stomach linings, liver, pancreas, even gall-bladder. Whatever was indigestible before becomes more readily and easily turned into chyme and chyle with this plant's pungent stimulant action added.

One of the most active and obvious of all medicinal herbs, the Horseradish root may be *too* active for some folk. It is powerfully diuretic, diaphoretic, and even a strong laxative, as well as being a digestive tonic. I will never forget the astonished look on the face of one of my guests when a too-eager consumption of my home-made Horseradish relish with her meal hit her formerly-slow digestive tract. Almost with her legs crossed, she excused herself suddenly from the table and then streaked towards the toilet! 'I just about made it!' she confided to me over the washing-up. It cured her of too-enthusiastic adventures into the herbal-medicine world: start *slowly*, and gradually introduce small amounts of improvement and change. Even if it is for the better, bodies need time for acclimatisation to these new experiences.

193

The hot, biting, breath-catching taste of Horseradish stems from its allyl and sinigrin contents. These two substances are also found in the vegetable radish, mustard, cress, nasturtiums, etc., all of which plants join Horseradish in the Cruciferae order. Cabbage, sprouts, etc., are from the same family. All do a similar stimulant job with stomach linings, enzymes, and even with other mucous-lined areas like throat, nose and respiratory passageways. As a protective strengthening stimulant for mucous-lined organs, Horseradish is most suitably prescribed when any of these zones is *under*-active. Iridology can quickly indicate the state of individual mucous-lined zones, with the greying tones of hypo-activity most needing this plant-root. *Over*-active stomachs may find Horseradish just too stimulating, causing hyper-peristalsis — as happened to my surprised dinner guest!

In another of nature's provisions for therapeutic plant use, an enzyme called myrosin is present in this root in separate cells from those in which the sinigrin is found. The root's cells need to be broken for the intermixture to produce the allyl. When dug from the garden the whole root can be stored for some time, but when grated for use as a condiment or in the preparation of extracts, tinctures and tablets, the broken pieces rapidly oxidise and begin their breakdown cycle of enzyme-action. (Many of the livelier herbs are given the prefix 'horse' in their common names, indicating their grosser activity and lively results. This also distinguishes them from commonly used vegetables with similar names.)

Its mineral content is also high; in iron, silica and sulphur, it almost rivals Garlic. Diabetics have found that gradual everyday use of Horseradish as a condiment can stimulate pancreatic enzymes and improve digestion.

The plant's origins are obscure, but it grows well in eastern European countries, in the south of France and in Germany. It can tolerate marshy acid soils, but needs this soil to be deep and stone-free to avoid the developing root splitting sideways into smaller rootlets, lessening its commercial value. It is used in traditional Hebrew ceremonies, being one of the five bitter Passover herbs. You can always buy the grated root, preserved in vinegar, from kosher delicatessens.

'Horseradish' person-picture

As 'Horse Chestnut' typifies the Germanic nature, 'Horseradish' may be said to typify the British.

This person-picture is one of leathery and inactive stomach linings, maybe from too much alcohol taken as gin, Scotch or brandy, or even slivovitz or Vodka! Think of the bygone Victorian era, the Kaiser, the Czar, and you have a picture of 'Horseradish': phlegmatic, dogmatic and pragmatic were the codes of behaviour, with rigid public moral principles and Lord-knows-what private repressions and inhibitions. Emotions were *out*! To cry (even to laugh at the wrong moment!) were social disasters indicative of 'poor breeding'. Stiff upper lips were part of the required facial expression when photographed with the regiment or the family. Grimness of visage matched rigidity of principles and stereotyped behaviour. 'The British love their dogs and train their children,' was a Shavian comment. 'How much better for their descendants if these habits were reversed!' But the British didn't have it all on their own: the rest of the European world, the Americans, and even our Australian founders and pioneers kept their faces, their morals and their stocking seams straight — in public anyway!

Negative-chronic 'Horseradish'

This narrow rigid code of behaviour and emotional deprivation produced the inescapable effect of all life's experiences in the body as well as in the mind. Its controlled attitudes led not only to suppression of the emotions, but to suppression of those organs and systems related to emotional 'feeding', as well as to cold beef and boiled cabbage intake. Iridologists find the relationship of organ and system to emotions and attitudes of mind clearly displayed in iris recordings. The naturopathic principles hold firm: experiences of mind and environment will in their train produce changed body processes too. The liver, which reflects the complexity of emotional nutrients passing through just as it reflects basic metabolism of food, may become slow and inefficient. A life deprived of an emotional range of experience, as well as coping with stodgy over-boiled food and too much spirits in a glass, will eventually cause hypo-function of body assimilation systems. Paucity of emotional feeding, plus unimaginative, overcooked, physical feeding produce between them the greyish-eyed person, whose grim philosophy 'Life wasn't meant to be easy!' is reflected in hypo-activity of the gastro-intestinal tract. How some of them love curries, hot spicy casseroles, highly salted meals, pepper, chillies and Tabasco sauce! Worcestershire sauce, an English answer to a slow liver and an under-functioning digestion, is beloved by 'Horseradish' types. Anything that will give a sharp kick to the digestive system they pour over, sprinkle on, or add in cooking. Some of them were medically routinely prescribed diluted doses of hydrochloric acid with each meal, because hypo-active stomach linings could no longer produce enough. Wind, bloating, pain and discomfort could too easily follow a cold cooked meat and hot boiled vegetable meal. Cabbage, sprouts, etc., gradually became unacceptable to them. Why? Without Horseradish, mustard, cress, etc., such a meal would just upset a hypo-tonic stomach, not re-stimulate it to better activity.

If you don't use it, you lose it! The diets of these people, like their lives, became plainer and plainer. 'I can only eat very plain simple food, dear', one of my prim elderly single British expatriate patients told me. I thought in terms of fresh raw vegetables, salads and fruit, and began to advise her. She bridled in horror, her gloved hands clasped. 'None of that *raw* stuff', she looked shocked. 'I like everything I eat really well-boiled.' No 'raw' emotions had been allowed to pass through her life either. She had been a 'good little girl' for her seventy-four years, nursing aged parents, foregoing proffered marriage, living alone, with rigid stoicism. Her steely-grey irises challenged me. 'In all my life, I've never allowed myself to cry', she told me proudly. 'Don't fancy all that emotional stuff. It's silly.' She had consulted me for wind, digestive troubles, sleeplessness and increasing throat catarrh every morning. For her, the introduction of Horseradish medicinally needed to be very slow and gradual indeed. A lifetime of poor emotional feeding was also reflected in an iris registration of under-active liver and pancreas, poor enzyme activity, hypo-tonic stomach, and mucus-laden throat and respiratory tract. Her 'spirit' had not been an alcoholic one, but gained from numerous cups of tea each day and with every meal. Her rigid self-denial of any 'pleasures' in life was pathetic. At least I could improve her digestion of food; a little Horseradish relish as a condiment she could understand *if* I described it as 'medicinal'. Otherwise she refused to 'dress up her food' as she put it 'just as a self-indulgence'.

Positive 'Horseradish'

This person knows that emotional stimulation and digestive stimulation run hand in hand. A satisfying emotional range of experience can promote a healthy digestive tract, a good appetite, and positive enjoyment of each meal, as well as more complete digestion and easy elimination. Those who are comfortable to laugh, cry and feel, need no 'sauce' to digest their raw foods, or their fresh fruit. Life's more 'raw' experiences are well digested too, with active and positive elimination of these from the character as well as from the bowels.

Dosage

1 As a regular table condiment whenever there is underactivity of mucous-lined organs, digestive system, etc. *A little* can be taken with any savoury meal.

Caution! Horseradish is contra-indicated for persons with *ulceration* present in any parts of the digestive tract, mouth, throat, etc. Its strong, stimulant action could cause pain, even inflammation in such sensitive areas, especially when there is an increase in acid secretions. Check with your practitioner!

2 Available as tablets for travellers and for midday doses away from the home dinner table. Stay well within the labelled-dose range! Again, check with your herbalist and begin *gradually*.

3 In extract or tincture, this root is processed fresh rather than dried, so that the sulphur will not be unlocked too early. It is added to digestive tonic mixtures as individual diagnosis may indicate. It is best taken in small doses over a long period of time; at least twelve weeks may be required to re-establish permanent improvements unaided.

> Horseradish is also prescribed for the type of hayfever sufferer where the cause of the problem can be traced to over-sensitive mucous-lined organs and passageways. This person is also somewhat over-sensitive or over-reactive to emotional experiences as well. It doesn't take much to affect their mood or their feelings: nor does it take more than a grain or two of air-borne pollens or dust, or chemical pollutants, to cause mucous-linings of eyes, nose, throat, and perhaps digestive tract too to over-produce mucus. A course of Horseradish, professionally prescribed, may need to be taken periodically, before spring pollens bring the sneezes and sniffles and the runny nose and swollen eyes. Don't wait until it happens! Protective and preventive treatments are easier, faster, and more permanent.

Horsetail

Equisetum arvense

This strange ancient plant dates back to the Carboniferous era of earth's vegetation. Gigantic primitive Horsetails, related to the ferns in their botanical characteristics, propagated both from unwinding their spirally packed springy spores and also from their creeping underground stolons. Survivors extraordinary, their much smaller relatives today inhabit marshy wet forests, twisting their spirals tightly against the flowering stem-head when conditions are dry, but uncurling rapidly when humidity rises or when rain falls. Perhaps this ability to withstand the changes from a wet, misty, rain-saturated early earth to a continuous and progressively drier spread of deserts and denuded land masses has assured the plant's continued growth. More like dry plastic or an imitation made in silk or paper, its dry rough stems are like sandpaper to the touch. It has been called Pewter-grass, or Scouring-rush, containing so much silica that it can polish metal. A strong plant! Animals generally avoid it and won't eat its coarse erect stems, which also contributes to its survival. However, the occasional horse will chew off a few gritty green parts and appear to relish them. Cows' teeth deteriorate if they are deprived of other pasture and may in desperation eat a little: our Arndt-Schulz law (page 141) should explain to you once again its opposite *protective* effect on human teeth when prescribed internally in the very small doses used by herbalists.

It is our most concentrated source of silica compounds. Luckily, these are balanced by magnesium and calcium also present. Because of its strong concentrations of silica, it should *always* be professionally prescribed for each individual's needs. Silica is not a quiet mineral! Powerful elimination through skin, kidneys and bowels can be expected. Added to its eliminative properties are its calcium-protective 'hardening' of bones and teeth, and its tonic effects on the hair, and on finger and toe nails.

Many different Horsetails remain on earth from pre-history: *Equisetum arvense* is the commonly used medicinal one.

'Horsetail' person-picture

A bit droopy, with lack-lustre hair which is thin and grows slowly, too-flexible fingernails which also bend, tear and break unnecessarily, is the physical outward appearance. A history of thin dentine-enamel, of early dental caries, and of slow healing after a broken bone, may also be present. In early life and into adulthood 'Horsetail' bites (and swallows!) fingernails, chews at strands of hair and 'picks' at acne spots. A broken bone may not only heal slowly, but may heal imperfectly, causing an overgrowth of calcified spurs or lumps. For ever afterwards, the person may be afraid of putting weight on the former fracture area, feeling it to be 'weak' in some way and needing permanent 'favouring'.

Silica is an essential mineral for nervous-system resilience too. It is stored in the nerve sheaths, the protective 'insulation' which produces quick nervous-energy recovery after mental and physical effort. Enough silica, and 'Horsetail' can talk all day, teach half the night, fall asleep quickly and bounce to life again in the morning, refreshed. But deprive this person of silica, and hair (and patience!) becomes thinner, a fingernail tears, the back droops, constipation can become a problem and kidneys slow down to a crawl. Urine may become scanty, dark and strongly odorous. In personality, these people are communicators; either in their jobs or by choice, they talk a lot, and rapidly. They think rapidly too, their mouths keeping pace with an active brain. Mental exhaustion may follow, and they may need solitude, peace and quiet, and *no* need to talk, to recover their energies. You can often see them physically bending forward and lower as they talk, and talk. Their *backs* get tired from over-use of the mouth — and of the brain behind all this communication. Worse, as they tire, bending forward, they lose co-ordination and become accident-prone. Some of the broken bones they suffer have resulted from mental tiredness causing physical falls, slides, mishaps and stumbles. Typically, they want to become active again, both mentally and physically, before the fracture is completely healed. Such impatience produces only disturbed healing and postural misalignments as the body compensates for the weakened structural member.

Negative-chronic 'Horsetail'

As posture slumps, nervous system tires and energy flags, 'Horsetail' can become chronically bent and stooped. As the back rounds, spinal changes begin to put pressure on kidneys via the lumbar spine. The body appears to be leaning forward, and even the gait may change. Accidents and falls may become more frequent.

At the same time, hair thins and loses bounce. It takes longer to grow, and you need fewer visits to the barber or hairdresser for a trim or cut. Fingernails also take longer to grow. There may be a regression to biting fingernails again. Nervous *tension* increases; it takes longer to recover from mental effort. Too tired to talk, the formerly mentally agile and physically quick 'Horsetail' begins to solidify: there may be calcium metabolism distortion, kidney stones, lower-back aches, osteoporosis, falling hair and underactive skin. 'Old before his time', friends say. 'Worn out and burnt out mentally.' The last step may be physical and mental 'breakdown' from a nervous system which can't bounce back any longer.

Positive 'Horsetail'

If your nails are so tough and thick and hard that your emery-board hardly makes any impression on them, if your hair grows so fast and thickly that your barber drives a Bentley, if your skin is young and elastic and positively glows, and your dentist by comparison with your barber is lucky to see you at all, then you are unlikely also to have broken bones which heal leaving a weakness, nor any osteoarthritis or osteoporosis. You are likely to bound around, interested in life, and quickly recovering from mental effort. You are also likely to be *patient*, especially with those who are mentally slower. Still loving to stretch your mind and flex intellectual muscles, you can also turn right off and think of nothing, staring at the sunset or the receding tide, giving your brain a rest. Your posture will be symmetrical and your back straight into old age. If there *is* an overload, and you fall and break a bone, it will heal quickly, accurately, and with no loss of load-bearing strength.

Dosage

1   Some years back, an article on the 'dangers' of herbal teas mentioned 'Horsetail' as causing 'back-ache and pain over the lumbar spine and kidneys'. By this far into herbal medicine, you should understand perfectly that the person suffering such 'symptoms' has taken an inappropriate dose. Surely, kidneys will *suddenly* work harder, and maybe an arthritic lower spine with porous bones will begin to tingle and send stronger signals out when Horsetail tea is strongly introduced. In smaller, weaker and more gradually-introduced doses, the *opposite* effect would have been obtained. However, Horsetail is still one of the richest sources of silica for a herbalist; explanation of its possible 'stirring' effects will overcome patients' fears that such stirrings are symptoms of disease rather than signs of returning healthy activity.

Drinkers of Horsetail *tea* must expect elimination as part of its action.

2   As a tablet, Horsetail has been sold to stimulate growth and strength of hair and fingernails. Adhere closely to the labelled dosage! You may even want to start at a half-dosage, and increase gradually.

3   As an ingredient in individual medicinal mixtures, Horsetail extract or tincture is added to other herbs rich in calcium, magnesium and phosphorus to relieve both the pain and the continuing degeneration of osteoarthritis, osteoporosis, scoliosis, post-fracture weaknesses, and general physical-nerve debility brought on by mental overstrain. Sluggish elimination from kidneys, bowels and skin may also call for it; the 'person-picture' must fit closely.

> It constantly surprises me how many 'Horse'-named herbs suit Sagittarians! Horsetail, Horse Chestnut, even Horseradish, quite often provide the person-picture identification for this Zodiacal sign.
>
> Part of the classical training of herbalists is in pattern-recognition as much as in recall of facts and knowledge of contents. The *old* brain must be used in the business of observation, recognition and diagnosis, as well as the newer faculties of intellect and factual recall. The patterns overlap and reinforce each other. Even the prime activity area for Horsetail, the lumbar-spine, is the anatomical position of the *Cauda equini*, the 'Horse's Tail'! At this zone, the spinal nerves leave

the spinal cord and splay out unshielded. Our vestigial 'tail' area is where you will feel it first as Horsetail begins to stir, eliminate, strengthen and protect.

Do you ever get the uneasy feeling that we have thrown away much useful practical knowledge in our mad hurry for increasingly complex intellectual brilliance? Perhaps our scientists should drink weak Horse-tail tea occasionally; the ensuing discoveries may not then be cleverer and cleverer ways to destroy our planet, pollute our air and water, and build up wastes and residues which can remove our ability to reproduce our species and also destroy our food sources. Intellect may need to listen to the *old* brain occasionally; intellectual brilliance is often gained at the expense of common sense. Dare I say, of *horse*-sense?

Hydrangea

Hydrangea arborescens

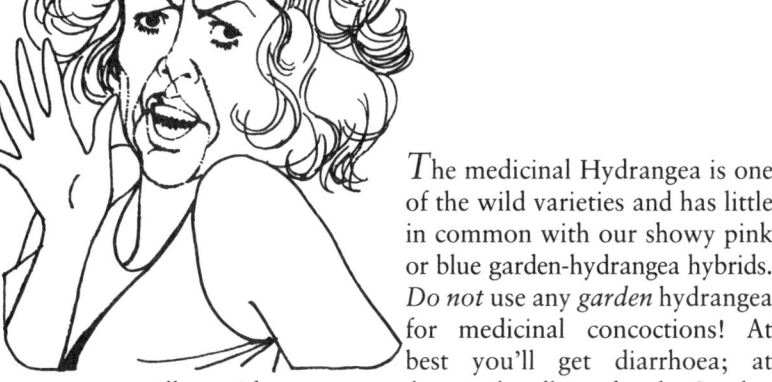

*T*he medicinal Hydrangea is one of the wild varieties and has little in common with our showy pink or blue garden-hydrangea hybrids. *Do not* use any *garden* hydrangea for medicinal concoctions! At best you'll get diarrhoea; at worst, you'll provide some more banner headlines for the Sunday papers!

The medicinal Hydrangea, although only attributed to North American origin, is also native to China and Japan. From it as 'stock', the huge-headed garden varieties were later developed and crossed, re-crossed, and developed further. All through herbal medicine runs the same story; hybridised garden varieties carry little or none of any original medicinal qualities. Bloom size, and genetic engineering for hardiness, longer blooming period, disease resistance, etc., become more important. The plant's quality changes altogether, and its chemistry does too.

The name 'Hydrangea' means 'water-vessel'. Although this refers to its natural liking for wet sheltered sites in the wild, it has an interesting correlation to its medicinal activity. Many herbals mention its effectiveness in kidney diseases of various kinds.

Its contents are best evaluated from the mineral point of view. Extracted from the root and root-bark are compounds of calcium, sulphur, magnesium and phosphorus. These compounds cause breakdown and re-combination of calcium oxalate and calcium carbonate stones in gall bladder and in kidneys. Chemical changes lead to physical ones too: 'softer' compounds of sulphides and sulphates are formed slowly and gradually. The stones can reduce in size and hardness, but the time taken to complete this may be longer than the patient would wish. The 'water vessels' of the kidneys must work harder to excrete the remains, and the bowels too are stimulated by the sulphur to work harder. Hydrangin is a powerful glycoside, which helps both.

'Hydrangea' person-picture

Often holding on to grudges, resentments and old hurts, 'Hydrangea' can become set in a pattern of bitterness and cynicism. I often think of it as the 'messy divorce' herb! Every fault in the partner is exaggerated and dwelt upon; every hurtful word uttered is repeated to friends, neighbours and family. Bitter arguments develop over joint property, joint bank accounts and the children. Selfish streaks and stubborn stands show increasingly. Criticism is implied in every facial expression and in every taut muscle. Just waiting to say 'Yes, but . . . ', former partners disagree on principle. It seems to be obligatory to get in first, telling all and sundry of the partner's deepest character flaws before he or she can get in first and do the same. Bitterness and life-long rock-hard prejudices are fostered. It is a *hard* time for all concerned, especially if children are involved.

A life episode of this type may be temporary in a person who is not otherwise bitter, selfish or stubborn. But when emotional defeat is the experience, many people show their hurt by vicious counter-attack.

Negative-chronic 'Hydrangea'

If the facial expression becomes fixed, and the diatribes go on for years after the divorce arrangements have been settled, this is a more serious matter. Instead of putting the past behind them, negative 'Hydrangeas' hold it constantly close, nursing every aggravation to feed it. Everything adverse in their lives is placed on the account; every compulsory child-access day is a cause for further concern. What if your children are turned against you? Should you get in first and turn the tables? The bitterness grows and sets hard into rock-like points of view, inflexible standpoints and stubborn determination.

Of course, not only divorce causes such resentments and such fiercely possessive attitudes. Many of life's disappointments over the actions of others are taken out each night and reviewed again while sleep slowly tries to creep in and block out this negative and unproductive use of the brain, mind, nervous systems and emotions. After all, none of us can undo what's past: living back in it can stop any progress forward into what could be a much better future.

The wholistic view is that it's impossible to have a hard attitude of mind without the body creating rock-like changes too. Bitterness and resentments about the past (or the present) may bring gall stones, kidney stones, bladder gravel, etc., as their physical manifestations. 'I'm looking after No. 1 from now on', may prevent a person from ever making another twosome. Certainly, bruised feelings and lack of confidence may make solitude and 'looking after myself' for a while a natural action. But wounds should heal and the future should replace the past. Where a growing cynicism, selfishness and stubborn will to 'get my own back' carry on for too long, the physical chemistry may also change. Inorganic salts of calcium begin to precipitate out: the 'water vessels' fill up with stones. Stasis and obstruction results: pain can be extreme if such stones move. One of the most excruciating is that of a kidney stone passing through delicate ureters or, worse still, stuck part-way.

Positive 'Hydrangea'

Leaving the past behind them, positive 'Hydrangeas' come to an end of hurt, bitterness and resentments, and *drop* the experience. 'What's done is done, and can't be un-done', they declare. 'Best to look forward now. The future could be a different story. Who knows what good things may be around the corner?'

Positive 'Hydrangeas' learn that the whole world doesn't share their grief, their let-down, their resentful seething and compulsive reviewing of who was 'right' and who was 'wrong'. 'Why *me*?' moan the negative 'Hydrangeas' as fatty foods and red wine cause gall-bladder problems, or kidneys slow as impacted stones cause obstruction and lumbar pain, even 'arthritis'. It needs to be realised that others have problems and disappointments, emotional traumas and hurts too. Positive 'Hydrangea' doesn't feel singled out by fate for the heavy end of the load: philosophically, these people move away from the past, dropping negative backtracking. They do not set hard into rock-like ways of thinking or of action. Remaining flexible, they pick up the pieces and begin anew when fate deals a heavy blow. They know they have not been singled out for special attention by Lucifer.

Nor do they moan, 'It's my Karma this time', and accept a negative 'way' of past suffering repeated over and over again. 'Karma' after all means 'work'; working through an experience, learning from it and going forward. If you don't want to carry a load of heavy stones in your emotional water vessel, Hydrangea may be a necessary ingredient in your individual mixture.

Dosage

1 While the bitter resinous taste of this plant's rootstock does not suit a tea, past generations often took it this way for gravel and stone. As well as the taste, its purgative and eliminative actions make this form of taking it a little unwise unless professionally supervised.

2 As a mixture ingredient, it joins other herbs like Horsetail, Pellitory-of-the-wall, Uva Ursi, etc., in mixtures to soften, chemically change or loosen gravel and stone. As such concretions often may be large, sharp-edged and unsafe to move suddenly, I personally have often requested x-rays or scans first to evaluate the options. Long months, even years, of treatment are better than emergency surgery for a ruptured ureter or blocked bile duct!

> The one and only time I have ever received a money donation from a grateful patient was for painless and gradual removal altogether of kidney stones. She had been threatened with inescapable surgery. She chose to do it slower and less traumatically. After several months of treatment, her x-rays (which had previously showed considerably larger stone-formation) showed clear. Joyfully, she showed her doctor the results. 'The first x-ray must have been wrong,' was his terse reply. Her cheque for $500 arrived in the mail. My practitioner and myself really didn't know what to do with it! Herbalists don't receive named bequests, foundations, research grants or legacy windfalls. We just bought some clinic plants, put the rest into clinic funds, and wrote her an embarrassed 'thank-you' note!

Juniper

There are some herb partners which seldom appear alone. Juniper goes with Celery like cheese with olives, or dates with walnuts. One partner balances and complements the other, so that giving both *together* acts differently and even more effectively than giving each one separately. While Celery supplies a boost to the body's necessary sodium requirements (sodium is essential for blood balance, for kidney function and for the liver's metabolic jobs, as well as in preventing dehydration and excess fluid loss), Juniper provides the potassium compounds to counter-balance. Sodium and potassium together maintain the 'pump' into cells of vital cell nutrients and the 'pump' out again of cell wastes. Both minerals play their balanced roles in the nervous system, too, as they control the sinapse — the 'gaps' every nerve signal must jump as it races along a nerve pathway. Kidneys also need sodium-potassium so that fluid excretion is not excessive, nor too scanty.

The smoky-black round berries of the common Juniper are the medicinal parts. Together with Sloe berries, Juniper berries were formerly the plant-base for Gin manufacture. The oil of Juniper, resinous and sticky, gave to Gin its oily-sweet pungent flavour. As a rich source of potassium salts, Gin became an excellent muscle toner and relaxant at the end of a physically demanding day. Of course, *too much* Gin produced the *opposite* effect, in accordance with nature's inescapable laws. The muscles — and the will power! — weakened greatly: the habitual heavy Gin drinker gained only waterlogged kidneys, nervous-system lapses, incontinence and eventual oedema and heart symptoms. It should not now surprise you to find that Juniper berries are prescribed medicinally by herbalists for kidney slowness, puffy ankles, 'tree-leg', bladder weaknesses and eventual heart insufficiency. The law of opposites is just as valid today as ever it was when pharmacy espoused it as the Arndt-Schulz law (page 141).

No, I'm not advising you to become a bedroom Gin-drinker! Juniper berries extract or tincture will do very nicely as a herbalist's tool for treating these complaints.

Lignin is present in the berries, ensuring that the effect produced is a lasting one. As Juniper berries are particularly effective at the kidneys, this lignin also adheres to the same tissues well. There are records of removal of chalk, gravel, etc., as this resinous material smooths the way through ureters. The berries have long been used in infusions and decoctions for gonorrhoea and its associated deterioration of ureters and kidneys, even of the bladder. Now that the newspaper brings us warnings of 'resistant strains of gonorrhoea' throughout the Australian population, perhaps it's time for a few Juniper berries to be added to stewed meats or spicy hotpots; there are many recipes for their use. Bearing 'aunty's ruin' in mind, *don't* be over-liberal with these pungent additions to casseroles, etc. Remember that inverse law, not only of opposites but of small doses and large doses, and their contrapuntal effects.

'Juniper' person-picture

'Juniper' has legs like Minnie Mouse. Swollen with fluid, the feet and ankles almost overflow from the shoes, and because of the friction of waterlogged thighs against each other when walking, 'Juniper' may develop a waddling gait, legs apart and rear end waggling like a duck. Extreme examples of oedema are now more rare than in generations past, but the disease called 'dropsy' medically still exists. I can feel nothing but pity for these extreme examples of 'Juniper' as every step can be an effort.

Even in less obvious 'Juniper' pictures, there may be little definition between ankles and feet. Fluid retention may be obvious too in upper arms, around the waistline, in the face, under the chin, etc. 'Juniper's' kidneys are not doing their job!

Negative-chronic 'Juniper'

*F*luid retention leads on to massive disturbances in adrenal glands too. In fact, adrenal-hormone insufficiency may also *cause* the dropsical condition. Either form of diabetes (*D. mellitus*, *D. insipidus*) may be involved as a cause factor, or may result from the adrenal aspects. Diabetics who 'float on fluid', with gross bodies and the characteristic fluid-engorged legs, typify the extreme negative of long-term 'Juniper'.

Don't rush out to self-medicate if you have such a serious disease pattern. Don't believe either that Juniper berries will remove diabetes! They won't: what they will do is provide abundant potassium to promote naturally the excretion of more fluid, to stimulate kidneys and to flush out the bladder.

Kidney failure is a serious disease with acute danger involved. A consulting herbalist will seldom see such potentially terminal patients. However, past history of kidney and bladder infections, gonorrhoea, adrenal insufficiency, etc., may have left slow fluid-waste removal as a legacy. This residual pattern herbalists can treat. Juniper, plus Celery, will be used in the patient's individual mixture. Buchu may be added, or Dandelion, amongst others.

Positive 'Juniper'

'*W*hen you have to go, you have to go!' they chortle, with a brisk exit towards the toilets. No fluid retention here! They are leaner and more sparely-covered, but perhaps still with the rounded 'Juniper' bottom protruding, and the tendency to build up a spare-tyre around the hips in later life if too much alcohol — especially Gin! — is indulged in.

But their bladder empties positively, with clear signals given beforehand. When they drink more, they urinate more. Whatever fluids go in, others come out in proportion. And there is no strong sweetish or ammoniacal smell to their urine either. It is clear, straw-coloured, and without pain, irritation, burning or interruption.

Dosage

1   An occasional recipe including a few Juniper berries as flavour-enhancers can be added to your kitchen repertoire if you are a

chronic fluid-retainer. Don't overdo it, throwing the balance in the opposite direction!

2   As a mixture ingredient it is prescribed in extract or tincture form. Its action can be powerfully stimulant, so leave it to your herbalist to judge the proportion for your mixture, and the level of dose.

CAUTION

If kidney stones are known or suspected, Juniper may produce such a kidney stimulus as to cause some small movement of these hard concretions, even expelling small or tiny particles. Naturally, this may cause not only discomfort but real pain, and some risk of bleeding, etc. I do not advise the inclusion of Juniper unless stones can be absolutely ruled out. If Juniper causes discomfort around the lower back, even around hips and in bladder areas, then this may be the result of applying a stimulus to what previously may have been a 'lazy' kidney. Many people have one kidney which functions strongly and does the greater part of the fluid-waste separation, while the other floats along as a 'passenger' almost. There may be tissue protest as a lazy kidney is stimulated. Contact your practitioner as soon as possible if prescribed Juniper causes discomfort.

Juniper, Jupiter, jovial, joyful: herbalists who attribute Zodiacal characteristics to plants as well as to people class Juniper as a Jupiterian herb. Certainly there are many resemblances.

'Fat and jolly' may be the personality-summation; a hearty, jovial, fun-loving person who is not only expansive by nature but also by waistline! Falstaff, Shakespeare's wine-bibbing, red-faced, rotund declaimer of stories and fun, was a classic 'Juniper'. In later life, dropsy would follow.

Lady's mantle

Alchemilla vulgaris

The most ancient and enduring schools of medicine teach that *causes* should, and indeed must, be treated, not symptoms alone. Only this way may lasting benefit be gained. The doctrine has always been that symptoms show only the various processes and functions which have been the body's methods of *reacting* to a disease, not the disease itself. In this form of herbal medicine, as I have taught and practised it for most of my life, symptoms disappear, almost like 'magic', when basic causes are uncovered and primarily treated. By removing the base, the whole pyramid of developed symptoms collapses away. Knocking the disease down stone by stone from the top can be a much longer exercise.

It will surprise you then to read that Lady's mantle is a herb for *symptoms* only but these symptoms can be so weakening and so distressing that it may be necessary and beneficial for the patient to remove them quickly. Lady's mantle is prescribed internally for excessive menstrual bleeding, for too much bleeding after curettage, for flooding menopausally, even for prolonged blood loss when uterine fibroids cause any extra bleeding or sudden floodings. The loss of iron and Vitamin B12 in such haemorrhages may allow other infections elsewhere to begin and to gain hold. The blood loss may also cause dangerous lowering of blood pressure. The excessive tiredness of chronic blood loss can be extreme.

Obviously, to stop or reduce this bleeding is a prime objective. Other herbs may also be given at the same time for whatever *causes* need to be treated.

This plant is a common English and European wild herb, but it does not grow naturally or well in Australia, needing deciduous trees around it and chalky soils for preference. The leaves are shaped like the inverted folds of a cape, hence its common name. In the centre of these leaves the dew remains longer than on most plants. Growing only to ankle height, with its beautiful pale-yellow flower clusters, this herb would perhaps be prized as an exotic garden groundcover if it were not originally such a common weed. It is classed as Rosacea family, many plants from which have affinity for blood in all its aspects.

Its botanical name (and it's often just called 'Alchemilla') is a carry-over from the Middle Ages. Its speedy anti-haemorrhagic properties made it seem indeed an 'alchemic' miracle. We now know that its tannins are the reason for its styptic and astringent effect, especially active on the uterine wall — the endometrium.

I am often amazed at the stoic story of a patient who for years has endured fourteen-day periods, or massive floodings for the first few days of menstruation, and has accepted this as 'normal' because it keeps on happening! It is certainly *not* necessary to suffer major haemorrhages every few weeks of life! If you bled this much from a wound, you'd be rushed to Casualty for transfusion! Blood loss for any reason at all is still a major trauma, and a herb to stop this, while causes are searched for more slowly and carefully, is an excellent therapeutic.

Lady's mantle does not treat the *causes* in any way at all. Other herbs like Phytolacca, Sarsaparilla, Pulsatilla, etc., will be needed if the problem is a hormonal one, or a weakness of the uterine linings. A curette, with the shock of scraping away at the uterine walls may call for other herbs for tissue repair as well.

Dosage

Do not attempt to self-medicate with Lady's mantle. Excess bleeding may certainly stop, but without your herbalist's assessment and diagnosis of the reasons behind the bleeding, you may be lulled into feeling it's all 'better', and take no further action. There may be many and serious causes behind these symptoms. Responsible herbalists may refer you on for further examinations. In the meantime, the debilitating blood loss can be gradually and firmly minimised.

Linseed

Linum usitatissimum
Flax

One of my late husband's most treasured volumes of Egyptian agriculture was a map of Thebes, painstakingly drawn on linen, in the careful and accurate style of 1830 by J. Gardner Wilkinson. One of the greats, this archaeologist drew meticulously field after field planted with Indigo to provide the deepest of blue pigments, and Linseed — Flax — from which the finest of linens were woven. Centuries earlier, in the City of the Dead, artists, anatomists, priests, embalmers, builders and architects first planted these fields of Flax from which mummy-bandages, as well as gossamer-fine linens for nobles and their households, were crafted.

Not only were the stem fibres of the plant used for clothing, but the seeds were treasured too. In such an excessively dry climate, oils were a daily cosmetic as well as being used in cooking and in the food itself. Linseed oil rubbed on the skin saved many a desert-dweller from dehydration, just as its addition to paints and pigments long ago has helped preserve for us the tomb and temple decorations. After the hard outer covering of the seeds had been crushed by stone rollers and the oil had been expressed, the creamy mush that remained was pounded and formed into 'cakes' of protein-rich solids and valuable carbohydrates. No local plant could better provide for its human ecological partners!

Today we see Linseed oil still in artists' suppliers and in hardware stores to be used in paints and varnishes. But its medicinal uses are not so well known. You may see Linseed meal on the cereals shelves at your health store, and wonder what it does in your breakfast muesli. Internally, Linseed meal makes a nutty slightly bitter food laxative. Enough of its oil remains to lubricate the lower intestinal tract gently, and to keep faecal matter moving. If a *dry* bowel is the reason for constipation, a little Linseed meal can also be added to flour and used in general cooking. As well as its oil, the inner part of the seeds contains about 25 per cent of vegetable protein, so it is ideal for vegetarians. Its fats are rich in lecithin and other phosphorus compounds. Ascetic acid is present, to balance blood-viscosity and stimulate enzymes. Waxy and resinous substances lubricate the whole digestive tract, but especially the lower bowel.

As a household herb, it can be added to other cooking oils when bought in its *refined* and clear cold-pressed form. Don't add hardware-store *raw* Linseed oil to any foodstuffs, or you'll have an internally-'varnished' bowel! *Raw* Linseed oil has another external use which I find one of its most beneficial aspects: whenever ligaments are strained, torn, cut, too relaxed or too tight, *raw* Linseed oil massaged into the affected area has a tonic effect. A few drops need to be well rubbed in until absorbed; otherwise excess will form a sticky surface film which remains for hours, impregnates clothing and is impossible to wash out. *A little* is all that's needed.

It is gentle and effective in renewing elasticity after burns have caused ligament or tendon shrinkage and contraction. Gently applied and rubbed in until it disappears, it can actually soften and restore flexibility to tendons and ligamentous tissues. It needs to be regularly applied and rubbed in well day after day, especially after trauma like sprains or athletic activities. I will not charge insurance companies for the information, but repetitive strain injury would be minimised, even removed, with regular massage into wrists and hands of raw Linseed oil!

More necessary when tendons or ligaments are cut by surgery, or in car accidents, sports injuries, etc., regular applications each day can gradually treat tennis elbow, footballer's knee, and turned and twisted ankle joints. It should be in every gymnasium for weight lifters, for high jumpers, and for any sportsman or sportswoman who punishes and pushes the body past anatomical limits. Marathon runners, please take note!

Linseed oil has *no* heating or anti-inflammatory properties like Wintergreen oil or Rosemary oil. It *lubricates*, pure and simple. It is not indicated where tense muscles are the problem, nor where painful sciatica or other nerve pain is the problem. But where body 'elastic' is involved, the ropy tough connective tissues which bind muscles to bones and which often determine the positions to which bones will be returned after muscular contraction, then externally applied raw Linseed oil acts gradually to put snap and bounce back in your elastic.

Be patient and regular in its use: it will not be effective overnight at all. Gradually, day after day, the improvements will be noticed.

Although there is not a specific person-picture for Linseed, my husband was an excellent example of its almost daily use over many years as a restoration artist with the British Museum and then in interior decorating and mural painting. At the end of every working day he would clean off paint spots, varnishes and solvents with raw linseed oil rubbed into hands and arms, face, neck and chest. Not a wrinkle was to be seen, even in his late fifties. He had not a twinge of arthritis nor any aches and pains after long days of precarious balancing on ladders and scaffolding. I have seen him astonish passers-by as he did a 'cartwheel' off a ladder just because he felt good!

Occasionally at home he would do a back-flip to reach a book on the other side of the lounge room. 'Nothing worse than sloppy elastic', he'd joke. Long hours over the drawing board with calligraphy or illuminated script produced no RSI in hands or elbows.

Perhaps those ancient Egyptian artists overcame the desert-dryness and the hours of cramped posture in tombs and temples with Linseed oil from the Flax-fields of Thebes, while the Valley of the Kings behind them scorched and desiccated even the scorpions!

Dosage

1 Linseed meal as an ingredient in cooked porridge or in muesli. Add grains like oats, wheat, millet, etc. Linseed on its own is bitter and a little unpalatable.

2 Linseed *seed* tea for constipation if a dry bowel is the cause. Follow the labelled instructions on the packet, and bruise or crush the dark-brown, hard outer covering of the seeds before brewing as tea. *Do not eat the seeds whole.*

3 *Raw* Linseed oil applied externally each day as prescribed above.

> Although it grows in dry climates, Flax must also have groundwater. The plant is a dainty annual, with open pale-blue flowers. It seems almost too fragile to produce the armour-sheathed seeds and long-lasting oil.
>
> Remember, the *raw* Linseed oil externally; the refined and clear oil if being added to other cooking oil for internal use.

Liquorice

Glycyrrhiza glabra

*E*very child knows the flavour of this plant from its extensive use in sweets since mediaeval times. As a home remedy the juice from its roots and rootstock was used all over Europe and around the Mediterranean, spreading across to Persia and India — even to China — from which last country most of our present commercial supplies are now obtained.

The plant is of the legume family, and capable, like all legumes, of fixing nitrogen from the air. Like peas and beans, and even peanuts, such plants have always been used as a rich source not only of food, but of specific calcium and potassium compounds as a medicine. The black, sticky, molasses-like juice, boiled out from the fresh plant-roots and root-runners and allowed to cool and set, can be processed into either hard glass-like pieces or flexible rolled strips. Be wary, however, of any 'Liquorice' sweets bought today: much commercial sweet manufacture duplicates the colour and flavour by using aniseed oils, or synthetic flavourings, black colouring and gelatine. *Real* Liquorice will stain the tongue (even the lips if you suck it!) to a yellowish-black colour which remains for hours, even for days. Real Liquorice is also laxative, and stools may be yellowish-black too after a Liquorice-binge when you eat a whole bagful.

Glycyrrhizin is the 'active principle' beloved of pharmacy, and gives the juice its sweetish taste and its energy-boost action. Iron is obviously present, and some sulphur, but the potassium-calcium combination is also medicinally powerful. Liquorice is laxative, demulcent, tonic, stimulatory and alterative. One of the safest and most commonly used herbs world wide, it is astounding to find that some evaluation committees are trying to portray it as 'dangerous', restricting it to various poisons schedules, and therefore medicinally available only from retail pharmacies! All herbalists would be laughing in disbelief if the game was not so deadly serious. To be consistent, your corner-store should put an 'S1' or 'S4' label on the sweet-jar. This will not, of course, happen: herbalists may find Liquorice restricted *to them*, while the public must perforce go to the corner pharmacy — or the sweet shop! — for this 'deadly' plant!

There is not a clear 'person-picture' for this plant, but there is a very clear symptomatic frame of reference for its use. With its demulcent, and some expectorant, properties it is included in the extract form in cough syrups, in mixtures for bronchitis and chest colds and viruses, and for smoker's cough, emphysema, bronchiectasis, etc. It was formerly used extensively to loosen accumulated hard mucus and 'wet' material from the lungs in tuberculosis. As a preventive against TB, it undoubtedly saved many family-members and close contacts from contagion. Sucked or chewed in London smogs last century, who knows how many children avoided bronchial disorders of major kinds?

A secondary indication for its use is when constipation results from either a *dry* bowel or when adhesions form after an appendectomy, after abdominal surgery, even after childbirth or a Caesarian birth. Many bodies build up strong ligamentous bands of connective tissue after such surgery or trauma, and the bowels may increasingly be held in constricted and restricted tension by these adhesions, making bowel movement difficult and causing pain, bloating, wind, constipation and a drying out of faecal matter. When faeces are retained too long, there may also be weight gain, blood occasionally with faeces, and haemorrhoids; and in the male there may be painful and dangerous pressure against the prostate gland.

If any person relevance there be, the 'Liquorice' person is dried out, bound up (in more ways than one), and distended abdominally.

There is a third major use of Liquorice, becoming more and more researched upon and written about in eminent and respectable scientific journals as well as in naturopathic literature; its effect on adrenal glands which is protective, restorative, tonic and stimulatory. Long used medically as a diabetic-safe extract, especially for diabetics with exhausted adrenal glands and massive fluid retention because of it, Liquorice is coming into its own again today. For patients whose exhausted adrenals must depend only on a cortizone drug to function at all, Liquorice is being re-evaluated as support therapy. It has been shown to reactivate several hormones which are effective through liver and adrenal glands, and there is also a possibility of pituitary stimulus as well. Maybe that instinctive childhood craving for the real Liquorice was a strong protective signal! A lot can be learned about the body needs of children, even teenagers, when they show sudden strong desire for a new or different food, plant, fruit or vegetable. Even basic knowledge of what these foods contain can teach you what nutrients that young and growing body urgently needs at the time.

Liquorice is often prescribed by herbalists for rheumatoid arthritic patients whose 'hot-dry' body demands lubrication and fluid movement. Many of these people have chronic haemorrhoids and intermittent or persistent constipation.

Dosage

1   Some health stores still sell real Liquorice; in lozenges, in hard little lumps, or in strips or rolls. Don't forget, if 'Liquorice' does not leave your tongue blackened, there may be very little real Liquorice extract in the product.

2   Prescribed in an individual mixture, Liquorice should join other herbs like Guaiacum, Burdock, etc., as a lubricant and a demulcent for the 'hot-dry' patient, especially when this pattern involves chest, adrenal glands and bowels.

3   You *may* find the rootstock twigs from the Liquorice plant in a herbal pharmacy, but this will be a find indeed, and a rare occurrence. Liquorice tea from these twigs is not really strong medicinally, and I do not recommend that it be taken this way.

Most plants which will grow in Spain, in Greece, in parts of Italy, even in Egypt or in Jordan, will grow happily and well in the temperate zones of Australia which match the Mediterranean climate, or in hotter and drier country districts. Even *cool* dry districts may succeed in being host to Mediterranean plants, especially Spanish ones.

Liquorice may be suitable for commercial growing in Australia. Ask your local Department of Agriculture for advice on this. Because underground stolons from Liquorice rapidly spread and acclimatise it into quite an extensive patch over an initial three-year growing period, there may be some aspects of 'weed' involved, which are always frowned on in this country. But controlled and contained commercial growth should be considered. World supplies of wild Liquorice are dwindling as civilisation creeps inexorably over the former growing areas. Many medicinal plants would *not* retain their properties with the same effectiveness if grown in this country. Liquorice not only *would*, but Australian quality could actually become higher if grown in the appropriate areas. It is an undemanding plant; poor soil suits it fine, and even sandy soils if given humus and organic materials.

The news about vanishing plants is not always bad! There are some opportunities not only for improvements but to encourage rural producers to improvise and diversify in difficult times. Australian-grown plants, half a world away from Chernobyl and nuclear accidents, will become sought-after on world markets; this trend has already begun.

Any takers for a Liquorice plantation? Any Department of Agriculture executives with vision?

Marshmallow

Althea officinalis and
Common mallow *Malva sylvestris*

Do you remember when Marsh-
mallows could be toasted over an open fire? I tried again a few
years back, but the pink and white confections melted right off the
fork and dripped away! Logic told me that things had changed, and
that a good imitation is not the same as the real thing.

I vividly remember foraging trips around the foreshores of Hen
& Chickens Bay on Sydney Harbour, one of my grandfather's
favourite haunts, and on the flora of which he wrote several long
and learned papers for the Royal Society (of which he later was
made a Fellow) and for the Linnaean Society, copies of which are
amongst the most treasured in my library. As a teenager, I went
back again to find Marshmallow and Common mallow plants, to
bring home for kitchen brewing up into a skin ointment for acne.

The root and the leaves of the Marshmallow may be used
separately; the root is taken internally as an extract for ulcerated or
over-acid stomachs, for duodenal ulceration and for mucous colitis,
etc. Any sore or irritated linings in the digestive tract are eased and
begin to heal with its useful combination of calcium phosphate,
pectin and mucillage. The leaves have a more stimulant effect on
enzyme production, and may even be prescribed together with the
root in a joint extract where over-acidity is partnered with low
digestive enzyme population. There was a very real reason, in some
households, for following a meal with a 'marshmallow' made from
the real thing! Not only a sweet, but a digestive aid, the white milky
juice crushed from the root, boiled up with raw or brown sugar,
was poured into a shallow sweet tray where its pectin helped it set
quickly. I used to enjoy the job of cutting it into squares, rolling
them in white coconut and storing them in containers, ready for a

'toasting night'. These real Marshmallows didn't drip away, but the coconut browned and the white rubbery insides melted only in the mouth as we juggled them off the fork. 'Sweets' are not always sinful! It depends entirely on their real ingredients. Comfortable tummies and complete digestion produced sound sleep and better energy for the next day.

Professional herbalists prescribed Marshmallow root or leaves extracts together with perhaps Papaya, Alfalfa, etc., where difficult digestion is made worse by ulcerated areas in the digestive tract. A follow-up treatment may be a course of Slippery Elm powder or tablets to complete the healing process.

Dosage

1 Medicinally only, as a mixture ingredient, not because of any dangers or cautions on its use but because it is not as effective as a water-extracted tea.

2 Many digestive tablets and proprietary herbal compounds contain Marshmallow root, and sometimes the leaves too. Over-the-counter sales of these self-prescribed remedies may still not be as accurate and appropriate as a professional consultation first to establish each person's different needs.

Common mallow

Malva, as it is often called (*Malva sylvestris*), is the Common mallow that grows as a shrubby weed in waste places made by man. Wherever rubbish accumulates around disused old factories, derelict houses, railway sidings and industrial estates, Malva will soon follow. Like Castor oil, it thrives and grows large on land which is not only inhospitable but down-right poisoned. Even after Council weed-spraying, or land-clearing, up will spring the rounded geranium-like leaves of the Common mallow. As if to emphasise its decadent habitat, insects often tear at and eat holes in the leaves, giving it a most bedraggled appearance. In cold climates its flowers are larger, darker plum-coloured and even up to a finger-joint across. In Sydney, and further north, it may hardly flower at all, or produce only pale tiny pinkish flowers, scarcely visible.

A member of the Hibiscus group of plants, Malva's deeper purple flowers are sought after in Europe as Hibiscus tea. These same flowers are often added to Rosehips tea to enrich its colour and to add even more Vitamin C, copper traces and iron.

Malva leaves make an excellent poultice for boils, for old infections where pus is present, and for pimples, eruptions and infected acne, even for cystic acne.

Only recently, research has shown this whole plant to be an excellent source of Vitamin C, and a very concentrated source at that.

Dosage

1   Do *not* eat fresh leaves of the Common mallow! Not only are they coarse and somewhat tasteless, but you may also get a mouthful of those insect predators! Worse, you may pick the leaves of the wrong plant! Take a branch, with flower and green small fruit if possible, to your local nursery or Department of Agriculture first for accurate identification. Only then should you select the best of the leaves, simmer them for a few minutes to soften the texture, then apply to the infected areas of skin and cover with an absorbent cotton dressing, fastening well. This is best done when you are able to sit down for an hour or more with the poultice in place. For facial application, mix the simmered green leaves in a kitchen blender with a small jar of a simple cold-cream, vaseline, even lanolin, and apply gently to the face while you're at home. A little bit of 'glugginess' is worth the softening, soothing and cleansing effect produced. The leaves have great cooling and anti-inflammatory properties as well.

2   Drink the German 'Hibiscus tea' or 'Malva tea' for an occasional cuppa. Similar in most ways to Rosehips tea, a blend of the two is an excellent pick-me-up.

Maté

Ilex paraguayensis

I often wonder why this South American tea has not caught on in the rest of the world. Tea and Coffee ('herbal' beverages both) are certainly economically stronger, with vast plantations and world-wide marketing. However, this shrubby Paraguayan native could easily be grown in the same locality and climate, and could begin to provide a third option in the questions 'Tea or Coffee?'.

Almost the only liquid traditionally drunk in Paraguay, it is consumed in vast quantities, even today. The leaves are dried and broken up, and it is brewed like an ordinary tea, strained, and drunk *without* adding milk, sugar or lemon. The flavour is perhaps best described as 'hay-like' and a little bitter, but ordinary tea has an unusual bitter-musty flavour too if it is abstained from for years and then drunk again. Only common usage makes its flavour 'acceptable'.

Like ordinary tea and coffee, Maté contains tannins, theobromine and caffeine. I'm just waiting for scientific accusations against Maté use because of its 'dangerous' alkaloids: our commonly accepted and freely drunk tea and coffee contain the same 'dangerous' ingredients. A vast commercial empire ensures that neither of these is restricted to poisons schedules and therefore available only through pharmacies: I do hope the same 'fair' treatment will be extended to Maté tea if its safety is ever in question!

My long-lived grandmother brewed up a ritual cup of Maté tea each day as she passed the sixties, then the seventies and eighties.

Stubborn to the last, she cloaked its unusual flavour with 'just a drop of milk, dear'. When I brew up a cup for myself every so often now that middle-age is behind me, I think of her twinkly clear-blue eyes and her boundless energy and enthusiasm right up to the day that she died. Maté is a stimulant tonic for circulation in general and heart in particular. In the high mountains of Paraguay, where the air is thin and oxygen-deprivation a daily danger, Maté was a protective and preventive means of taking the load off the heart. It is certainly *not* necessary for us to drink such large amounts of it at sea-level and without any oxygen difficulties. But when an aged heart is labouring unevenly, or when a flight of stairs causes puffing; if a long brisk walk on a cold winter's morning leaves you panting and your heart audible in its exaggerated beating, then a cup of Maté tea *before* such exertion might have been a good idea. For athletes and footballers, for Granny as well as for marathon runners, for weightlifters and mountaineers, and also for occupants of geriatric homes, retirement villages, etc., an occasional cup of Maté tea can keep the heart's rhythm strong and even, and can insulate against excessive heart-loads, or possible strains of heavy or prolonged physical activity, or physical heart weakness.

The people of Paraguay are renowned for their physical endurance and their long lives under extreme climatic conditions of pressure changes and oxygen deprivation. A strong heart is a major health benefit to every other part of your physical body.

Dosage

A cup of Maté tea may be taken occasionally. Just as you would vary your other fluid intake, do not take cup after cup of this tea in the belief that you'll live for ever! Too much of a good thing will have an opposite effect: *excessive* consumption of Maté tea may produce dysrhythmias and actually overstimulate the heart to potentially dangerous levels where eventual heart weakness may then result. *An occasional cup* is plenty: only your professional herbalist will have the diagnostic skills and training to advise you otherwise, and possibly change this dose.

> **Maté is pronounced 'Mar-tay'.** One dinkum Aussie weightlifter muscled into the local health store asking for some '*Mate* tea, mate, thanks mate.' The puzzled assistant sold him an odd packet of Billy Tea from the back shelf! Australian pride is a good thing, but remember the name is pronounced 'Mar-tay' and you'll get what you went in for!

Mugwort

Artemisia vulgaris

If you have ever visited a traditionally trained acupuncturist, you may already have experienced Mugwort's affinity for the entire human nervous system. The 'Moxa'-cones which may be placed on a slice of ginger, or of potato, before being ignited to smoulder slowly over a weakened nerve-signal area, are made from the downy white undersides of Mugwort leaves. The leaves are used medicinally, and the root when dug in the cooler months of the year. Extracts or tinctures of Mugwort are excellent nervines. The fresh or dried plant was formerly the basis for beer brewing in Europe and Great Britain long before Hops became the preferred plant-nervine in beers. Its common name may have stemmed from this time, when 'Mug-weed' grew everywhere, and homebrew from it was popular.

It would be hard indeed to convince me that Mugwort is a 'dangerous' herb! Generations of us in Australia today would never have been born if Mugwort beer, drunk then as commonly as the Hops beer that follows it today, had killed off all our progenitors early! The choice of a relaxant but tonic nervine to turn into an alcoholic drink has never been a restricted one. Nervines abound, and blends were common. But Mugwort has unique and particular application, as set out below.

Its mineral content is high, mostly as phosphates of magnesium, calcium and potassium. All three minerals are necessary for nervous-system health and strength, and when Vitamin B6 is also found in this plant, it becomes anti-spasmodic as well as a nerve-tonic, and it regulates some hormones, particularly pituitary and adrenal hormones, as well.

225

'Mugwort' person-picture

'Mugwort' is often highly intelligent and with great acuity of the senses. Hearing may be above average, even to distressing levels so that a car-door shutting late at night half a block away may wake them quickly. A snoring bed-partner can see them desperately creeping with blanket and pillow into another room, and shutting the connecting doors. Taste may also be discriminatory, and a 'Mugwort' knows when the milk is on the turn, or the fish is past its prime, long before anyone else notices. Sight may be very sensitive: 'Mugwort' often puts sunglasses on at the front door in the morning, and can be very distressed in glare and under bright lights. Worst of all, a *flickering* fluorescent tube, a camera-flash, strobe-lights in a disco, even a low winter sun shining in moving stripes through roadside trees, can not only distress them physically but produce a mental change into anger, even violent attempts to stop the offending lights. Flickering lights may even trigger off a type of epileptic 'gap', or a *petit-mal* vagueness, or 'absence', for a second or two.

Sound and sight sensitive, taste and touch sensitive too, their 'smell-a-vision' really acute, these people can suffer sensory stimuli at too high a level to let them sleep restfully. They often have vivid technicolour dreams, and consciousness is never too far away even when they are apparently deeply asleep. They may answer you, or carry on a conversation whilst apparently asleep. You feel they are seldom turned right off at the powerpoint!

Many of them sleepwalk as children, even as adults. Some are astoundingly bad drivers! Their attention to the road has 'gaps' while they are solving a problem or a million miles away on an imaginative return journey from Venus! Often creative and intuitive, they carry on internal head-conversations between right-brain and left-brain, or head-visit a museum in Cairo while washing the car. Wherever you think they are, they're somewhere else.

Being married to a 'Mugwort' for eight years, I learned about them at first hand. 'Just put the cup there and I'll have it later,' said my 'sleeping' husband often in the mornings, or even stretched out on the lounge breathing deeply and obviously 'asleep'. It startled me for the first few years, but eventually I got used to a basic 'Mugwort' trait: they *never* completely switch off, can be awake on their feet and *running* in seconds, after snoring peacefully seconds earlier.

Their positive 'Mugwort' exposes them to sensory and brain

activity which is valuable in ideas, in creative capacity, in artistic skills and in forward-thinking, but eventually this hyper-acuity of the senses, and hyperactivity of certain brain areas can bring nature's inexorable balance laws into action.

Negative-chronic 'Mugwort'

'*I* haven't slept for five nights now,' my husband would say, and he was telling me *his* truth. He had lain beside me, snoring away peacefully, mouth open and eyes closed, with breathing deep and slow; but he had heard every word of the neighbour's violent argument at 2 a.m., and the rubbish-truck at 3 a.m., and the kookaburras at 4 a.m., and could describe it all in accurate detail. About one night in five, exhausted beyond measure by the previous 'sleepless' four, he would tell me nothing of each hour's events night-long. His energy restored, he'd bound around after one night's '*real*' sleep, as he called it, but his desperate exhaustion and over-running brain for the previous four was a constant problem.

Many people will tell you they 'didn't sleep a wink' because of intermittent wakeful periods. Negative 'Mugwort' is different: their body 'sleeps' but their brain doesn't, not completely. The obvious result is 'brain-fag'. Co-ordination begins to slip, and words come out too fast and maybe garbled, or with syllables reversed. The good Dr Spooner, whose name provided a new English word — 'Spoonerisms' — was a tired and negative 'Mugwort'. 'Kinkering congs their titles take . . .' he announced the hymn: the 'conquering kings' were no less for his syllable reversal! To some extent, dyslexic spelling and difficult word recognition is also a negative 'Mugwort' problem. Psychologists and speech therapists will confirm that the person behind the apparent foolishness is often a genius. Remedial teachers know that Isaac Newton would have been in their special class because he couldn't spell, and Thomas Edison would have been considered 'backward' because he spoke not a word until past the age of four!

As a child, the negative 'Mugwort' can suffer ridicule at school, be written off as 'unable to concentrate', and be cruelly tormented by classmates. Not perhaps until university studies does this leaping agile mind, stumbling quickly through slow word-syllable impatience, begin to show through as a brain with four or five forward gears instead of three. The 'absent-minded professor' can become very physically ill indeed because his hyper-active, hyper-sensitive mental apparatus will not let his physical body ever completely rest. He will miss out whole syllables from spoken and written words, and become intolerably angry, even arrogant, when the rest of the world can't follow his leaping thoughts and acrobatic mind.

Negative-chronic 'Mugwort' may settle for silence. Withdrawing into the rainbow mind, a negative 'Mugwort' may choose solitude and silence, their only entertainment the travelling circus inside their own head.

It is not coincidental that the use and abuse of marihuana needs Mugwort as part of a long-term corrective treatment. The *artificially*-produced heightening of the senses, the vivid dreams, the creative flights of fancy, and the feelings of enlargement of being are cruelly negative 'Mugwort'. Any 'happy' is fake-happy; and visions of heavenly colours, flashing forms, and larger-than-life-size achievements, happen as the nervous-system sinapse widens, and brain-cells explode and die. The 'gap' every nerve signal has to jump in transmission around the body, — the sinapse — lengthens, and more energy is needed every time to bridge this widening chasm. 'Spaced-out' is an apt description: marihuana use *fakes* the attributes of genius and the sensory awareness of the universe. The *reality* is a lost job, a failed study course, a hopelessly over-blown ego and no real achievements to back it up. Cloud-cuckoo land is ever present; the real world fades further and further from view.

Positive 'Mugwort'

When I finally convinced my Taurus-stubborn husband of the suitability of Mugwort for his form of insomnia, how our lives changed! A new relaxed and happy Bull took his mixture every night, in which Mugwort was a prime ingredient. The heightened sensory awareness was still present, but *real* sleep replaced a semi-conscious state of debilitating continual awareness.

As a 'Mugwort' takes this plant and gradually subconscious, conscious and super-conscious minds sort out their relative jobs, *real* rest produces *real* energy-restoration.

It is intriguing to note that many 'Mugworts' have experienced massive birth trauma, long labour, late arrival, even apparently ceasing to breathe at or before — or after — birth processes. My own belief is that when foetal hormones send to the mother a signal that birth is now to begin, and if for any reason that signal is stopped, artificially slowed, or even over-ridden by hospital routine or a delayed obstetrician, a 'Mugwort' child can result. Medicine gives Vitamin B6 injections after birth; herbal medicine may give both mother and child Mugwort extract or tincture after such a birth.

Don't write off a 'Mugwort' child as a 'slow-learner who can't concentrate'. Under that little scalp a thought may be forming that will change the world. '$E = Mc^2$' came from the Mugwort brain of Einstein; Leonardo and Mozart were both positive Mugworts underneath, but they suffered the inner torments of its negative side when ill, over-tired and hard-pushed. A highly developed brain and mind is of positive use to send mankind a few faltering steps further: the opposite balance is an early demise, burned out by the white-hot brain activity. 'Doing a Mozart' I call it.

Dosage

Although Mugwort-based beer is no longer available, this herb is better extracted by alcohol and water together, and is now only available in fluid form for dispensing by a trained herbalist.

Do not self-medicate: Personal requirements will vary greatly, and, like any other plant, too much may be worse than none at all.

Nettles

Urtica dioica, U. urens

Every farmer the world over knows that Nettles, like Dandelions, follow human habitation. All around the chicken run, the dairy, even by the farm-implement shed, there are the darkish-green, mint-like leaves of shrubby Nettles, waiting to sting the unwary visitor. English and Scottish farmers have told me that their Wellington boots are more for nettle-protection than for wet ground! Nettles grow easily on any nitrogen-rich soils where animal excreta accumulates.

As a common weed, Nettles are readily available as a pot-herb, and have been used as a spinach-like green vegetable all around the world. The leafy tops are picked (with gloves and secateurs!) and steamed or boiled quickly for just five minutes or so. This is enough time to break down the chemistry of their stinging spines and leave them highly palatable.

Theoretically, *Urtica dioica* is the taller-growing kind, with male and female flowers on different plants; *Urtica urens* is shorter (Wellington boot height!) with male and female flowers together on the same plant. In practice, this identifying line is often blurred, and it can be difficult to separate the two.

Both Nettles are excellent sources of dietary iron. The stinging hairs, hollow little spines containing ammonium bicarbonate (an alkaline compound), lose all their punch when the formic acid found in the juice of the plant is liberated by short cooking. The strong base and the strong acid cancel each other out chemically,

230

leaving iron and phosphorus compounds as the plant's main constituents.

Nettles are stimulatory and alterative in action: they are tonic to arteries, and may cause arterial blood pressure to rise if *over*-used. (See Dosage.) They are prescribed for *low* blood pressure, with poor oxygen transport because of it. Herbalists often choose to pair it with Rue (*Ruta graveolens*); Rue is to veins what Nettles are to arteries. By using both together any too-sudden changes in blood pressure may be avoided. If both arteries and veins improve together, there should be no consequent localised pressure change which may otherwise cause any weak spots in blood-vessel walls to distend.

I have vivid and painful memories of the giant varieties of Nettle which grow to head height in the dense and almost impenetrable jungle of the Townsend Spur in the Snowy Mountains of southern New South Wales. A well-planned two-day walk became a six-day life-threatening ordeal to me as the overgrown walking-track, dropping hundreds of metres down the narrow spur to the Geehi Valley, disappeared altogether. Within half an hour we were hopelessly lost, compass, maps and experience notwithstanding! 'It's tiger country in there,' the Rangers told us after our helicopter rescue six days later! Giant stinging Nettles, tangled amongst long thorny canes of wild roses, tore us to shreds each night as we battled through them to reach needed creek water. In the morning we faced the green wall of them again as we climbed up again to seek another downward-pointing spur to follow. I always carry with me on such walks a small jar of Nettle ointment to rub quickly on ant-stings and insect bites. The law of balance and counter-balance still applies, even to dangerously lost bushwalkers! Nettle ointment (a homoeopathic one) soothed the viciously burning reddened skin areas on face, hands, arms and ankles where we had been lashed as we beat our way through. Without it, the experience would have been a much more painful one!

In Europe and England, even in North America, it is common to find Nettles and Dock growing near each other. Traditionally, the leaves of Dock, placed quickly on Nettle stings, antidote the sting immediately. In Australia (and perhaps in the southern hemisphere in general), Dock not only doesn't grow comfortably near Nettles, but even if there is by chance a dock-leaf available a pad-dock or two away, its effectiveness as an antidote is much reduced in this part of the world.

'Nettle' person-picture

'Nettle' has *low* blood pressure more often than a normal BP range, and is pale of face. Body skin colour may also be greyish-pale, and the spleen may be under-active and somewhat enlarged. Although a blood pressure in the lower end of 'normal' range may please your doctor, there are definite problems attached to *too*-low arterial pressure. Your heart may beat slowly and deeply — again, a supposed benefit — but the risk is always that, if pumping action and arterial blood flow slows, it may take more *effort* to get moving and keep moving, and blood-oxygen levels may be lower than requirements, too. 'Nettle' often looks half-sleep, eyelids drooping and body movement slow. They may *sigh* a lot, especially if in the one position for too long. Sitting in an armchair at night, they nod off in seconds. To assess superficially, they always seem *tired*: although once they *do* get moving, they have good endurance-energy and can keep going at a task for long periods of time, often far longer than someone with a 'normal' blood pressure. Too often they are told to rest more — because they look so tired! The answer is not more rest, but renewed activity to get the blood moving again at a better speed.

Negative-chronic 'Nettle'

*I*f the 'Nettle' person is wrongly told to *rest* because everything seems such an effort to them, they can degenerate quickly with loss of memory, poor concentration and too-early ageing. Speech may slow, hearing become difficult, hair begin to thin and fall out, and their grey face may add twenty years to their real age. And all this may occur at seventeen, even at thirty, if arterial pressure is *too* low! My own second son has had very low blood pressure all his healthy life. He will no doubt live till ninety, with a strong and unstressed heart, but at times he walks around asleep! Even in his teens, one glass of beer, with its relaxant effect, could find him fainted right away under the table as his already low blood pressure dropped even lower. Oxygen deprivation produced the sudden fainting.

Cerebral blood pressure can experience first the deprivation of oxygen that not only causes a faint, but also memory lapses, balding, etc. The brain is at the top end of the arterial pumping system: the lower body gets its blood by gravity-feed, but cerebral insufficiency can result from the neck up if the pumping pressure drops. If cerebral arteries are also narrowed by arteriosclerosis or atherosclerosis, and fatty plaques and calcium salts build up, it becomes even harder to get cerebral blood through. Strokes can happen at forty, or the increasing lack of concentration and mental acuity can mean job-loss and premature ageing. These people may be sick from being too healthy! The idealised low blood pressure may bring physical apathy and mental dullness as a result. If blood pressure is artificially lowered with pharmaceutical drugs, the same symptoms may be observed, though hopefully to a lesser degree.

As a side-effect of too low blood pressure, males may find it hard to produce — and to maintain! — an erection. Herbalists are often consulted by healthy but worried males, sometimes with failing relationships because of it, for a 'magic potion' to increase their virility. In too many cases, they have previously been prescribed heavy pharmaceutical diuretics to reduce a higher than 'normal' blood pressure. With the lowered blood pressure has come lowered sexual ability, and in consequence lowered self-esteem. They don't need any imagined herbal elixir nor some fancied aphrodisiac, but only a return to the blood pressure which was 'normal' *for them*. Nettle has saved many a relationship!

Too low blood pressure carries yet another risk: pressure reduces even further when asleep. In the early morning hours, many an otherwise healthy person has woken gasping for air and oxygen or, worse, has not woken at all. Those people who die quietly in their sleep in the early hours before dawn may have had such severely reduced blood pressure that there was not sufficient arterial flow to keep the heart active.

Positive 'Nettle'

A cup of Nettle tea, or a medicinal dose of this lively plant in tincture or extract form, can send arterial blood out to the body more strongly, especially to the head and the brain. As oxygen is better distributed, skin colour improves quickly. Cheeks go pink, eyes can sparkle out of their previous dead-fish dullness. Concentration improves, so does memory. Hair gains bounce and body, and there's less on the hairbrush each night. One patient wrote to me with an offer to market the marvellous 'hair-restorer' mixture I'd given him to take as an internal mixture (not to rub on). 'I didn't even complain of hair loss at the time,' he chortled. 'How did you know that was my real reason for consulting you! Are you clairvoyant?' 'No,' I smiled. His greying skin, poor cerebral circulation and constant yawning had given me the clues to his *overall* health needs. His renewed hair growth was an extra bonus! Sadly I informed him that my 'hair-restorer' mixture was for him alone. Nettle will only improve hair growth if cerebral insufficiency, with consequent oxygen and iron deprivation, is the reason for the hair loss in the first place. Only a person with this condition would respond with some degree of benefit, and only if the raised cerebral blood pressure was maintained. Both of us would otherwise be in gaol or featured in a current affairs exposé in no time!

Positive 'Nettle' people are aware that physical and mental activity must be maintained not only to stay healthy but to stay *young*. A lowish blood pressure will be no handicap if they constantly raise it by exercise and activity, by new plans, ideas for the future, and the enthusiasm to drive forward. Then the real benefits of low blood pressure become apparent: they can work for hour after hour, steadily and at an even pace. They can also think more quickly and clearly as the activity continues. By the end of a long day they are just beginning to warm up, with pink cheeks and a healthy sweat. It can be a hard job to stop them once 'wound up'! They feel better, fitter and more truly healthy at the end of the day than at its perhaps slow beginnings. 'Harder to start, but harder to stop' sums them up well.

Dosage

Check with your professional herbalist first to establish your blood pressure patterns. While Nettle should always have *some* proportion of Rue prescribed with it, each patient will need slightly different amounts added. Iridology can be a useful diagnostic tool, as the iris shows in many different zones and with different colours in those zones, what type of blood flow and blood pressure is present. It is particularly simple to evaluate cerebral blood pressure from it.

1   Nettle tea as an occasional cuppa is a good pick-me-up, especially for post-period women. Any blood loss is technically a 'haemorrhage' and can lower blood pressure and iron levels for a few days. For those with chronically low blood pressure, Nettle tea every few days may be prescribed.

2   As a mixture ingredient, Nettle is quick-acting, with faster than the usual results from herbal treatment. Energy and oxygen are often interdependent, and both improve with this herb.

3   Nettle ointment is readily available from health stores. Take it with you when bushwalking, and keep it in the medicine cupboard during Australian summers for all the bites, stings, itches, etc., especially if they raise red weals like 'burns' on the skin. If quickly applied, the itch lessens fast, and further application can be made as often as the 'sting' feeling returns.

My own resting blood pressure is approx. $\frac{110}{60-65}$; low indeed. My college students always know when I've forgotten to add Nettle extract to my glass of Lemon juice and other herbs that I sip during a long teaching weekend. Six hours on Saturday and six hours on Sunday, sitting on one high stool all the time, find me yawning, speaking more slowly, with stiff limbs and waning concentration unless the Nettle is added. If they remind me (as they've now learned to do!), I can think, talk and concentrate right up till the last minute of this teaching marathon and then go for a brisk long walk each of the evenings too.

Nettle's greatest use is in making more oxygen available for the vital organs and the major blood vessels. An active and youthful old age is everyone's wish. There is absolutely no need to equate extra years with extra tiredness, apathy and inactivity. Some of our older folks, sitting unhappily on the verandahs of geriatric homes, listless and greyish pale, may have unrecognised needs not for rest and relaxation but for stimulus and renewed activity. If they also have *low* blood pressure, their apparent senility may be from no other cause. Give Grandma or Grandpa a cup of Nettle tea occasionally if you've written them off as in their dotage (always checking on blood-pressure patterns first). Nettles may be just the spark needed to stoke up the fires again!

Oats

Avena sativa

You may be surprised to find that porridge Oats is considered to be a medicinal plant! Grown as a food in cold and temperate countries, it is a staple grain in many cultures. But the seeds, processed into aqueous and water extractions, and the oatstraw (the stem-sheaths and the 'beard' of the grain) are powerful therapeutically.

Amongst Oat-seed blessings are Vitamins B and E in useful amounts, and potassium, calcium and iron are high. The flattened seeds, 'Rolled Oats', are easy to extract from, and also readily digestible. Oat-straw tinctures and extracts contain rich silica sources; silica is essential for tough sheathing of the physical nerves, for nervous system resilience after use, and for the energy of movement of kidneys and bowels. There could hardly be a better combination to keep strong and healthy people stronger and healthier!

As well as its tonic and stimulant properties for muscles and nerve supply to those muscles, Oats is an easy source of vegetable protein for vegetarians. In savoury or sweet combinations, Oats can be the basis for a muesli mixture, for rolled-Oats or Oatmeal porridge, as well as for biscuits, munchies of all kinds, even fruit-puddings. Perhaps its ordinariness has caused us to overlook its strong medicinal aspects.

'Oats' person-picture

Strong, large-framed, energetic and fit, anyone less likely to need 'medicine' would be hard to find!

But 'Oats' has times of physical tiredness, of over-stretched energy, like all of us. You find these people amongst top athletes, with their large muscles rippling, and their trained and fit bodies straining to get just another burst of speed or of endurance. At the time when their 'second wind' is slow to come, when the effort on the heart and blood vessels is greatest, and before they ease into 'overdrive', Oats is the nervine required.

These people may also need medicinal dosages of Oats as they train. Each coaching session demands a little more effort: there are heavier and heavier weights to lift, or higher and higher bars to jump. The daily routine lengthens from one hour, to two, to six. During the conditioning and strengthening period, as the physical challenges grow, Oats in medicinal strength can give muscles the extra bounce and energy needed. Don't forget that the heart, too, is a piece of muscular tissue. It must be tested and tried with heavier and longer loads, gradually applied.

'Oats' is the sportsman and sportswoman. 'Oats' is also the growing child building body tissue with its protein, and with Vitamin E for optimum cell-division. 'Oats' is also the manual worker, the builder's labourer, the ocean sailor and the farmer. Outdoor pursuits occupy this type of person, often when the elements are unfavourable. Cold winds, icy temperatures, a summer heat-wave, or heavy rain may not stop their activity, nor be an excuse to miss a training session. So resistance must be built up, and what lesser mortals would find formidable, these folk must do easily. Often with large-framed and bulky bodies, a sharp wallop across the ear may be their reply if you suggest 'taking a bit of weight off'. If you call them 'fat', you'd better leave quickly while you still have your front teeth. These people know what the fashion magazines don't: to gain strength, one must also sometimes gain size and bulk. They are proud of their strong bodies, and the long hours that have made them that way.

Negative-chronic 'Oats'

We all know that the ageing wrestler may look more like an old punching bag than like Tarzan! Muscles which once were like iron cables have now slackened off. Bellies hang lower over thighs; ankles collapse outwards and twist the pelvis eventually; shoulders droop; even the former height shortens by a couple of centimetres or more as the big muscles of the back sag and allow vertebral compression. Everything points to the ground! Nature's balance acts again: over-development has nowhere to go except into atrophy once the daily routines are no longer adhered to.

My husband was a very large man with enormous shoulders and torso developed by years of boxing, wrestling and weightlifting. As he approached sixty he would look sadly in the mirror: 'If I'd known then how heavy all this muscle is now to carry around every day I would have been content to remain a seven-stone weakling,' he'd sigh. As sportsmen and women grow older, Oats is more necessary than ever. There needs to be improvement in the *tone* of those formerly hard-worked muscles in order to avoid fatigue. Suits which fitted younger broader muscular shoulders droop unfashionably: trousers sag at the rear. A tired older ex-athlete may need Oats in later life much more than in earlier training years.

Sudden exertion can be too great a strain on the heart. The most obvious need for Oats is when one of these formerly strong and fit people, now perhaps well out of condition, decides to show off and repeat, out of the blue, some past physical feat. The puffing and the panting afterwards may be the most obvious result, but the *un*seen effect may be blood-vessel rupture through a too-sudden rise in blood pressure. Major damage may occur.

'Muscle-bound' is no longer a description for the retired athlete, perhaps, but the description is accurate. Muscles used to constant effort and strong contraction may remain tense. Every athlete knows there may be sleeplessness, perhaps, or at best a winding-down period for muscles after the event. This can also be a time for Oats as a medicinal substance, and as a sleep-producer in these circumstances. Adrenally saturated muscles, rapidly flooded with lactic acid, do not contribute to sound restful sleep!

Positive 'Oats'

Even if not athletic and challenging, all 'Oats'-people are strong. The most positive of this type have well-defined musculature, exercised regularly and hard. Whether it's a 250-metre tee-shot, or a rock garden to be built, or even moving house, these people love to use their strength. In fact, they *need* to keep muscles active.

'Oats' women find no problem lifting small children or the weekly shopping bags. 'Oats' Grandpas carry one child on the back, one on one shoulder and another with a bear-hugging arm. 'Oats' shakes your hand with a strong grip — and likes square-dancing! Whether it's on a sailing boat, on a horse or on shanks' pony, 'Oats' will love the challenge. 'Race you home!' they'll yell, at the end of a long active day, and then streak off in front. Every last skerrick of energy is there to be used.

Dosage

1   Eating Oats in the morning can set you up physically for the day. Who cares if you grow a little more muscle-bulk? Your heart will strengthen too!

2   As a mixture ingredient where there is loss of muscle tone through illness, through age or through inactivity, Oats may be prescribed with other nervines like Chamomile, even Valerian. Where continued muscular tension prevents real relaxation and sleep, it is the athlete's remedy.

3   Oatstraw tea may be prescribed where nervous resilience is lacking after physical effort. If you wake up fit and rested after a good night's sleep following a hard and exhausting day physically, then you do *not* need this. But if it takes you days to recover, a cup of Oatstraw tea may be appropriate. Check with your herbalist!

Pennyroyal

Mentha pulegium

As an example of confusion aris-
ing when common names only are used in herbals, the British and
European Pennyroyal is a different plant entirely from the American Pennyroyal. In England, Ireland and Wales the creeping pros-
trate stems lie close to wet boggy ground and, although perennial
by classification, Pennyroyal will die off quickly from drought or
frost, and is perhaps better divided up and replanted at the end of
summer. Its whorls of mauve fluffy flowers climb up the short
flowering stem in the cooler months of the year when other flowers
are scarce in the herb garden. It welcomes the shade of other shrubbery, and must have 'wet feet' often. One of the best clumps I ever
grew was in a house where the laundry plumbing was questionable
and regular floods and excess soapy water bubbled over the concrete step onto the garden. The Pennyroyal thrived! Green and lush,
there it sat content in a scummy puddle. No wonder an old English
name for the plant was 'Lurk in the ditch'!

Because of the undoubted resemblance in effect between
Mentha pulegium and the North American *Hedeoma pulegiodes*,
their considerable botanical differences are often ignored in
popular herbals. The British Pennyroyal was also transported to the
young American colonies and settled in well, contributing to the
continuing confusion.

Many writers on herbs glibly refer to Pennyroyal as an
'abortive' agent: it is unfortunate, but true, that such writers need
deeper and more long-term experience with patients before making
such leading statements. This wrongly-described action of the plant
may then be copied and perpetuated by other writers and collators
of herbal information, and so the misapplied label may stick. If

Pennyroyal produces a period which has stubbornly refused to arrive, the woman concerned was never pregnant in the first place! This herb acts as a uterine tonic, not as a remover of foetuses: when a period is missed for any reason other than pregnancy, Pennyroyal's tonic effect stimulates a lazy, chilled, shocked or hypo-active uterine lining into menstrual shedding again. It is common to find periods late or disturbed during or after travel, after emotional upsets, even after a chill while winter-gardening, sailing or bush-walking: pregnancy is not the most common reason for a missed period!

The uterine lining remains reactive to many external traumas, as well as to menstrual hormones. The good news on Pennyroyal is that, *if* pregnancy is the reason for an absent period, Pennyroyal tea, extract, tincture or oil will *not* produce a period, nor will a newly-attached foetus be harmed in any way from the Pennyroyal dosing.

There is no person-picture for Pennyroyal. It is symptomatic in its indications. The pelvic congestion, the bloating pressure in the uterus, and the resulting hormone-cycle disturbance is, however, to be avoided if possible, if a missed period disrupts natural rhythms. Reproductive and menstrual hormones are the most trigger-happy of all: it is a positive benefit to any woman to re-establish as soon as possible her natural period cycle.

Dosage

1   Pennyroyal tea, a cup daily, if a period is missed for the above reasons. Discontinue as soon as the period arrives. When the following month's period is due, drink a cup of Pennyroyal tea each day, for three days *before* the period's due date, to ensure the regular cyclic pattern remains in its rhythm.

2   For some women, the tea is not strong enough. A dose of *ten drops* of Pennyroyal *oil* has been prescribed, with results within twenty-four hours. But do check with your professional herbalist.

Phytolacca

Phytolacca decandra
Poke Root

$This$ complex plant is to be found in many countries of the world, and Australia has a near-relative, *Phytolacca octandra*, as a well-known weed, especially in areas where poultry farms abound. Hens, pigeons and other domestic fowl will eat its berries, but their flesh may become inedible as a consequence, acquiring strong purgative properties. Commercially, it is to be eradicated if possible!

But herbalists value this plant, and always have done. Its historical and traditional household uses are legion. Its ingredients vary markedly with where it grows, and seasonally too. The dried root is the part most used, but many traditional country recipes and nostrums recommend the ink-black ripe berries to be used as tea.

The plant itself is attractive, though rather rank and untidy in growth. Its reddish stems and rose to bright-green leaves are crowned by berry 'heads' which be₎.ʌ as green, changing to red, purple and to juicy black when fully ripe. All colour stages of the berries are found on the plant at any time, adding to its decorative handsomeness. But it matures as leggy and untidy, even several metres in height, robbing nearby plants of soil nutrients. It is deservedly classed as a 'weed'.

Phytolacca is the prime glandular regulator and tonic in any herbal Pharmacopoea. Pharmacy views with horror its so-called 'narcotic' effect, and has many times questioned its safety. My answer is always that the *tiny* doses prescribed by herbalists throw the Arndt-Shulz law into its reverse position: there may be some pain relief as one of its effects, but there is no *deadening* of sensation, nor inhibition of nervous activity resulting, nor any addictive or over-stimulatory process occurring from its use.

Quantitative analyses of Phytolacca have produced variable results from country to country, as is always the case, but all analyses agree that phytolaccic acid is found in the berries, together with other organic acids such as citric acid. The ripe berry constituents are considerably weakened by heating, or making into a tea, country-style. The root contains Phytolaccin, on which most reference writers differ as to its biological activity and classification. Is it a glycoside, an alkaloid, or neither? As I am neither a chemist, nor a biochemist, I cannot resolve the argument for you. I know only that its use as a glandular tonic, hormone stabiliser, and lymphatic clearer is unsurpassed. There are many and varied sources of potassium in its root.

'Phytolacca' person-picture

Some of us are born with family histories of disease which limit our present health. I often wonder why routine medical consultations today place far less value on family history than formerly. It *does* matter that grandfather may have been tubercular, or grandmother diabetic. It really *does* affect the cells of descendants when syphilis in the family tree has been allowed to run unchecked because undiagnosed. It *does* bring illness symptoms to a later generation when an earlier one has suffered particular types of systemic or venereal disease long ago. We accept that animals and plants cannot grow strongly and in good health if the parent-stock is tainted by certain types of systemic viral, bacterial or fungal symptoms. We find apparent difficulty in accepting that today's 'rheumatism' may echo down from yesterday's syphilis, scrofula or TB in the *human* animal. The complex person-picture for Phytolacca spans several generations. Like Guiaicum (pages 178–82), Phytolacca treats today's resistant symptoms whose primary causes lie back over many yesterdays.

'Phytolacca' suffers aches and pains, which may appear superficially to be 'rheumatic' in origin. These aches and pains have begun at times of glandular stress through rapid or extreme hormonal change. The joint and muscular pains of 'Phytolacca' may occur in puberty ('growing pains') or in pregnancy, after childbirth or with breast-feeding. They can be crippling, causing acute forms of 'rheumatism'. Menopausal hormone changes, slower and more gradual than those of early life, may also precipitate a 'rheumatic' onset. Even very young children, acutely attacked by severe and acute rheumatism — almost out of the blue diagnos-tically — may have their ancestors to blame for their lifelong misery ahead. An excellent term to describe the Phytolacca-needing person is a diagnosis of 'glandular rheumatism'. I personally believe that Rheumatology's present world-wide admissions of inability to find a 'cure' for rheumatism are because they are testing and evaluating *today's* patient-victims, not the real culprits, their ancestors long ago! Some countries, like India, routinely keep ancestors' medical records and histories. Perhaps our generation should question our parents and grandparents, uncles, great-aunts and distant cousins, before they leave us, and write down the family medical history. It may explain otherwise unexplainable patterns of illness now.

'Phytolacca' may have lumpy lymphatic swelling in early life, especially at critical hormonal change periods. Glands may 'come up', and a sore throat and gritty red eyes may accompany a swollen neck, or sensitive armpits, groin areas, etc. It's not 'a virus'. It's an echo from the past. At times of extra loading, exhaustion, shock, change, etc., our ancestors' voices in our genes grow louder!

'Phytolaccas' may also suffer reproductive difficulties all their lives. Natural selection in animals and plants ensures that those units unsuitable for preserving strong genes die off, and do not reproduce their kind. Humans continue to reproduce irrespective of ancestry or, worse, if reproductive organs cannot function well, artifical and high-technology means may be employed. Nature says, 'Not genetically good for the species'; humans say, 'Every person has a right to reproduce.' On what we do to resolve these opposing precepts may depend the healthy future of our species.

So an occasionally 'lumpy' person, with aches and pains worsening at times of special loading or hormonal change, is our basic picture. Added to this must be a tendency to skin sores, pustules and localised eruptions. The scrofulous gene is a strong one still! 'Tuberculosis of the skin' it used to be called. Running open sores, difficult to heal, may also call for Phytolacca internally, or for Phytolacca ointment, externally applied. Where many other healing creams fail, Phytolacca ointment may be the answer. These skin lesions may be latter-day evidence of ancestral ill-health.

Negative-chronic 'Phytolacca'

How much more negative could the 'Phytolacca' person become, you may well ask! Aching, lumpy and with skin breaking out at odd times, surely there is suffering enough. The most negative aspect of a chronic 'Phytolacca' is that symptoms may be so deeply reinforced and part of the birthright that they *resist* all manner of medical treatment, and may also be very slow, grudgingly loosening little by little, under naturopathic treatments as well. There are no quick cures for this person. Sadly, they often visit one practitioner after another, seldom having the patience (understandably!) to wait months, even years, for gradual improvement. In desperation, they may take massive amounts of analgesics, anti-inflammatory drugs, and suppressive or replacement hormones (Cortisone preparations) for the rest of their lives. Amongst the hardest of all patients to improve, 'Phytolacca'-people have my sympathy.

Positive 'Phytolacca'

It is unfortunately true that most 'Phytolaccas' have spent many years on other types of treatment before seeking the help of alternative forms of medicine. How much better to seek treatment of the above kind *before* a chronic pattern becomes deeply established. 'Aches and pains' are *not* to be expected as one ages: this comes as a great surprise to many! Acute rheumatoid onset does *not* descend from the blue on an innocent young child, or a nursing mother. There are always *reasons* for disease, contributory factors and underlying causes. It is the business of herbalists to seek these out as well as to treat present symptoms.

I am glad that Phytolacca *tea* does not exist! This herb should never be self-prescribed. Not only is the dose of extreme importance, but there are certain times of hormonal change when Phytolacca can be protective and others when its internal use may be unduly disturbing — even contra-indicated. It is part of a professional herbalist's training to discriminate, and to assess the timing of treatment, as well as its suitability.

Positive 'Phytolacca' is aware that at times of extreme peaks and changes in hormonal activity, it is necessary to rest more, to free the mind from extra stresses and concerns, and to adjust gradually to the differences in lifestyle such periods will inevitably produce. Shocks also cause *sudden* hormonal disturbances, so all measures to remove shock must be taken quickly. Tears can be great shock removers, followed by talking it all out, then deeply sleeping. Extra Vitamin C at this time helps maintain adrenal balance. Most important of all, positive 'Phytolacca' adjusts to the inevitability of change — even welcoming changes as proof that life never stands still, and that nothing lasts forever — not even any negative influence of ancestors!

Too often I have heard from rheumatoid patients, 'Well, it's in the family, you know so I must expect it'. There *are* ways to gradually loosen such influences, if they are first recognised.

Dosage

1   Leave all internal use of Phytolacca to the professional herbalist's care and caution — and training.

2   Phytolacca ointment may be self-prescribed and rubbed gently but well into 'rheumatic' hands and fingers, joints and muscle-ache areas, if such symptoms fit the above picture. The ointment may also be gently massaged in to any 'swollen gland' areas in neck, armpits, groin, breasts, etc. Applied twice daily, such external use of Phytolacca can reduce the swelling and congestion while the cause-factors are being internally corrected.

Phytolacca and Breasts

Many women, if they still wear a bra, wear one size most of the time, but three sizes larger just before a period is due. Breast enlargement or engorgement precedes a period for many women, who may also retain fluid generally at this time. Such symptoms indicate difficult transition between oestrogen and progesterone hormone change. While being treated internally for this problem, a gentle application of Phytolacca ointment externally twice daily may be advised.

If breasts become lumpy and tight either in pregnancy or with breast-feeding, seek your herbalist's advice on whether Phytolacca is individually indicated, or not.

I recently laughed at one of nature's jokes, which she often scatters about for our mirth if we but know where — and how! — to look. On the *roof* of a tumble-down derelict dairy near Tathra in New South Wales grew a thriving plant of Phytolacca! The plant-seed had found its natural energy-affinity pattern — the breasts, this time of dairy-cows! Even its botanical name means 'plant-milk' or 'herb-milk'. My herbalist friend and his astrologer-wife laughed as appreciatively as I did: it can be a funny learning experience, can life!

Pulsatilla

Anemone pulsatilla

Sometimes called 'Windflower' or 'Pasque-flower', this member of the Ranunculaceae family is different indeed from the ranunculas and anemones of our spring gardens. It grows wild on the poor soils of rocky hillsides flattening down with every breeze, hugging the ground for protection. I saw it growing wild on just such a hillside near the ancient village of Maloola in Syria. Amongst the aged grape-vines, fringed with wild sage, the deep purple cup-shaped flowers moved and blew about, almost too fragile for such a hard location. Several medicinal Anemones grow in England as well as this one, and it also grows all around Europe, Central Asia and Northern India, etc.

Perhaps my original homoeopathic training has coloured my thinking on this herb, but I disagree with many of its attributes and disease-indications as written down by other undoubtedly eminent and respected herbalists. It is mostly mentioned for subcutaneous skin symptoms, for measles, and for slow or debilitating circulation disorders, as well as for inflamed mucous-linings of the respiratory tract. I have found its herbal uses similar in every way to its homoeopathic indications. The dose levels may well be close, and this may also contribute to the similar effects.

Anemonin, a crystalline substance isolatable from the plant after drying, appears to be one active principle pharmaceutically. The whole plant, with its silvery feathery 'tails' blowing in every breeze, is highly toxic when fresh. In herbal medicine, it is only *sometimes* true that 'fresh is best'.

'Pulsatilla' person-picture

'Fair, fat and forty' is one simplistic homoeopathic picture of 'Pulsatilla', written in the generation when females were old at forty. When over-large families were produced and uninspired eating and lack of physical exercise built up avoirdupois early in life, this was all too common a description. The homoeopathic description of 'fair, blue-eyed women of middle age, who wring their hands with their helpless frustration and woe', may not be today's image, but the picture is still recognisable.

'Pulsatilla' often states 'I can't cope!' This phrase may be accompanied by the hands flung up over the head and an abrupt exit — often in tears! The picture may belong generally to what some older males still prefer to call 'the helpless female'. There are undoubtedly times when all of us, male and female, young or old, 'can't cope'. Life gets on top of us. 'At the end of my tether', we describe ourselves. Insult adds to injury, our indignation rises commensurately with the flow of blood to the head and face. A *pink* colour flushes the skin, not the purple-red of anger and violence but the paler pink of embarrassment, helplessness, inability to handle this unfair assault. After all, what did 'Pulsatilla' do to produce the present problem? The immediate reaction for this type is tears, and the need for being comforted and assured of help and strong protection lest cruel fate deal another such blow against this gentle creature. Why, a breath of wind now would be too much!

Just as you offer a cuddle and help to this pink-faced over-sensitive soul, she may smile, wipe her tears away, fly out to the kitchen and cook dinner, singing! At least, this is what some males will tell you. Before feminists out there slap a label on me, let me say *male* 'Pulsatillas' abound too!

Today, more than ever before, male 'Pulsatillas' allow themselves to cry, rush from the room, and generally behave like prima donnas under unfair accusation, malice, spite and cruelty. Hurrah for the equality we've always had, but never owned up to! Males are openly allowed to have their 'can't cope' days too!

'Pulsatilla' episodes may happen when hormone crests slide downhill into hormone troughs. Many women who are not 'Pulsatilla' normally appear to change their whole characters just before a period. Like screaming harridans, they accuse and threaten, cry and yell. Twenty-four hours later they may be their calm, capable, self-assured best again. Like a passing cloud over the sun on a summer's day, their moods can change, almost in mid-sentence.

Other 'Pulsatilla' episodes can happen untypically through the years of menopause, both the male and the female varieties. A formerly happily-married male of forty-five screams and accuses at the family dinner-table, leaves home with one suitcase and runs away to Bermuda with his secretary. A formerly contented placid Mum bursts into tears, tells the family how they've never appreciated what she's done for them all, throws their dessert on the floor, and its container at her husband and rushes out the door to seek a red pant-suit, a lover, and a bit of 'life'. If we've never actually done either, we've certainly been tempted — especially around middle age. The overriding emotion is *hurt*. It's not a violent passion, but its long-term cumulative effects may explode after days, weeks or twenty years. The physical need is to leave the scene of the hurt — explosively!

If these episodes are common in middle life, they are today equally common in teenage years. Your fourteen-year-old throws a tantrum, hurts everyone within earshot with a long-hidden list of their shortcomings, and leaves home. At best, the clouds may blow away and 'Pulsatilla' comes home that night with all forgotten. At worst, the degree of 'can't cope' is so heavy as to be permanent. Anyone who leaves the scene, voice in a rising crescendo of hysteria, is having a Pulsatilla-panic. Because any hormonal see-saws need to be delicately and calmly re-balanced, it is better for Pulsatilla to be prescribed by an objective non-affected trained professional. It could be unwise indeed to self-medicate. Other herbs like Phytolacca, Sarsaparilla, etc., and nervines like Vervain, Scullcap, etc., may be needed too to re-establish a calmer household if a 'Pulsatilla' is in residence.

Negative-chronic 'Pulsatilla'

'I can't stand to see a woman cry' has been the downfall of many a good, kind and compassionate male in the past. Diamond rings are bought to appease, or red roses, or a new house, or a trip abroad. Feeling guilty and self-disgusted, the best of males can be turned into helpless victims by the worst of females. Similarly, a strong and responsible female may be the victim of a 'Pulsatilla' mother, child, or spouse. 'The meek shall inherit the earth' is an apt description of 'Pulsatilla'. All the rest of us give it to them — to stop them crying!

The worst of 'Pulsatillas' quickly realise that tears and a tantrum can get them lots! What was once an episode may become a useful habit! Be aware that it's *your* energy that will be used to correct the situation that's bothering poor little 'Pulsatilla'. Nip such blackmail in the bud early: much 'Pulsatilla' helplessness begins in early childhood.

If 'Pulsatillas' are not fat to begin with, they may soon become so. Masterful inactivity may put on much weight. Hormonal slowing of the thyroid and the adrenal glands may do it too. Many formerly slim and active competent ladies are at the mercy of mercurial hormone breezes in middle years. No one is more disgusted *with themselves* when a sudden inability to cope produces tears in the office, the boardroom or the home. 'It's just not *me*', they assure you and they may well be correct.

Positive 'Pulsatilla'

When hormones are stabilised again, when the clouds have passed, the former competence and responsibility of these women can return. As a practitioner, it's nice to hear *any* patient say 'I can cope again after your treatment'. You know that endocrine balance is improved, hormones are less volatile in their distribution, and stable reactions are ahead. More to the point, the end results of these irrational panics, tears and endless hurts are avoided. Too many teenagers, at the mercy of wildly-changing hormones, have permanently left home. Too many stable marriages and balanced partnerships have been permanently and irreparably damaged not by wilful selfishness but by ordinary folk at the mercy of erratic hormonal imbalances.

Positive 'Pulsatilla' remains calm and stable, recognising that changes are inevitable, sometimes downright upsetting, but needing to happen, and impossible to escape. Positive 'Pulsatilla' buys a size larger in underwear, and apologises to the household or the office *before* any upset occurs. 'Just ignore me if I get a bit sentimental, or tearful, or flustered: it's just one of those things', they'll explain. 'I may be a bit unpredictable for a while until everything settles into the new pattern.' Positive 'Pulsatilla' teenagers ask parents, teachers, counsellors and mates about these new problems. When they hear that everyone else on earth goes through the same emotional roller-coaster ride, they 'cope' much better and follow the advice which has worked for others at times of hormone change.

Dosage   Leave all Pulsatilla treatment to
your herbalist. Not only may you swing your balance systems even
further out of alignment with mis-applied self-dosing, but you may
not be a 'Pulsatilla' person at all, or experiencing such an episode.
There are still selfish lazy passengers in this world, adopting helplessness as their major weapon of defence against having to work,
taking responsibility and generally getting on with things. No
amount of Pulsatilla will 'cure' when the picture is a deliberate and
self-chosen one!

> I have found Pulsatilla useful to prescribe for a certain
> type of both male and female homosexuality. Where
> hormone balances are different from the long-accepted
> norm, both males and females may find it difficult to
> 'cope'. Where such difference is assessed by the prac-
> titioner as causing illness or other distressing symptoms
> such as painful periods, inappropriate body-hair,
> obvious tissue differences, etc. or aggravating other
> symptoms like emotionally triggered asthma, migraines,
> constipation, etc., such stress-symptoms can often be
> mitigated by the careful prescribing of this herb, with
> others. The patient 'copes' better, and any hormonal
> indecision or unpredictability can also be better stabi-
> lised. I do not believe it to be the task of practitioners to
> make moral judgements or give advice along the guide-
> lines of their own beliefs and values. It *is* their task to
> improve the overall health of the patient asking their
> professional aid.

Raspberry leaves

Rubus idaeus

The common Raspberry, one of a large family of Brambles, is mostly considered as a food. Its appreciable quantities of iron and excellent balance of Vitamins C, P and K make it a nutritional package of great value, especially for blood disorders and for circulatory blockage avoidance. Raspberry's *leaves*, however, add folic acid to the above ingredients, and this combination is ideal for all stages of pregnancy, especially as an iron supplement which does *not* constipate. The folic acid helps to keep the foetus well bonded to the placenta, and the placenta strongly adherent to the uterine wall, thereby reducing the likelihood of a pregnancy loss.

Many women become pregnant much more often than they realise! But because of insufficient folic acid they shed the pregnancy in its earliest stages as a 'normal' period. If, on the other hand, a woman who is otherwise healthy in the reproductive organs, and hormonally cannot fall pregnant, a professional herbalist may prescribe Raspberry leaf tea, or Raspberry leaves in tincture or extract form together with other individually suitable herbs to increase the likelihood of a normal pregnancy holding.

Some herbalists advise a cup of Raspberry leaf tea *often* right through a pregnancy. I prefer to respect the laws of inverse ratios of reaction, and advise an *occasional* cup of Raspberry leaf tea throughout a normal, and normally easily-achieved pregnancy. It is only when there is a history of repeated natural abortion, time after time, or great difficulty in holding the pregnancy in the first three months, that I would use the therapeutic levels of dose. It is always best to interfere as little as possible during the course of any ordinary and comfortable pregnancy. While many first-time Mums-to-be want a 'perfect' pregnancy and a 'perfect' child at the end of it, their over-concern, and perhaps today's lack of counselling by experienced older women in the family as was formerly the custom, make them tend to over-medicate themselves during this first pregnancy. Drink too much Raspberry leaf tea and the only result may be an itchy 'Raspberry' rash of pinkish pin-prick spots all over your abdomen. Always remember it is *not* true that if a little is good then a lot must be better! I have more respect for the writers who advise Raspberry leaf tea, say, twice a week during the first trimester and the last trimester of any pregnancy, with an increased intake during the last few days before the expected birth-date — not to cause a tighter placental bond then, but to ensure an easy and whole expulsion of the placenta after the child has left the uterus and is safely in Mum's arms getting to know the outside world. That law of *opposite* reactions from very small to quite large doses is one of nature's most fixed rules!

There is no particular person-picture for Raspberry leaves, except perhaps that unique eternally-female expression on the face as a woman announces 'Dear, I've got something to tell you . . .'. The next step is to keep that facial expression there for the full term of the pregnancy — the combination of pride, wonder, delight and protective concern.

Red Clover

Trifolium pratense

*T*his apparently perennial field-plant is commonly found world- wide, in sandy soils, at high or lower altitudes, and it is difficult indeed to trace its origins back to any particular country, but the European continent records it very early indeed, and I believe that, like Dandelion, it is now a world citizen.

The constituents of Red clover have been well researched, and their long academic names are not our concern here: however, its purplish conical flowerheads indicate its iron/copper compounds. As an alterative, it has specific uses, and needs specific caution in its dose levels. It contains plant-hormones (phyto-steroids) which are quite complex both in their chemistry and in their effectiveness. Not an easy plant to prescribe! Various glycosides are present, making it energy-restorative, and it shows well-recorded evidence of anti-spasmodic effectiveness, especially in that distressing and long-term damaging disease, whooping cough. I can never unravel from its complex chemistry which thread points to its specific action on the spasmodic cough, not only of whooping cough, but on viral coughs too, like those of measles. I suspect that the copper compounds are the beneficial agents here, and I also suspect (but have never found it documented) that cobalt traces, combined with the copper and the iron, act as a savage therapeutic weapon against minute blood-carried pathogens. It may be that the spasmodic cough eases simply because the disease-causing micro-population is decimated.

'Red clover'
person-picture

That often-ridiculed description 'dirty blood' is present when a 'Red clover' picture presents. 'Blood-cleansing', another oft-contested process, is required. The 'Red clover' person may also have deep-seated infection foci like boils, carbuncles, infected sebaceous cysts, infected cystic acne, etc., where the evidence of the 'bad blood' is found just under the skin. Perhaps more useful (and better understood in its indications) in centuries past (Red clover today may need more subtle understanding of when and when *not* to prescribe it) when diseases like scrofula, impetigo, etc. were more commonly found, and when clothing was more voluminous, covering the body more completely than is common today, regular baths were a rarity, and showering and mild sun-exposure all over the body were unheard of. Orthodox medicine often points to its triumphs in eradicating such diseases: the truth is that our higher standards of personal hygiene today, and our understanding of the uses of water in washing the hands, face and body, together with household antiseptics and better plumbing may have contributed the major improvement over diseases formerly called those of 'dirty blood'.

The 'Red clover' person needs iron, with the trace minerals copper (and cobalt?), to spring-clean the blood, and to eliminate via bowels and skin the pathological organisms which threaten to take damaging long-term hold. Repeated localised outbreaks of boils, pendulous cysts around face and neck, or on the body (sometimes the same purplish colour as the Red clover flowers), need the very careful attention of a professional herbalist, and should never be self-treated, nor self-assessed as to causes. Garlic and Echinacea may be added to the prescribed mixture, or other appropriate alteratives depending on each individual case history.

Negative-chronic
'Red clover'

Perhaps one of the most distressing teenage symptoms of basic underlying poor health is the lumpy, red, swollen misery of infected and cystic acne. Such disfiguring symptoms at a time of extreme and rapid hormonal changes and emotional ups and downs as a result, may produce life-long personality disorders. Added to a bruised and fragile self-image that the mirror reflects every morning may be repeated rejections by peer groups and consequent withdrawal and loneliness, even outright anti-social seclusion. Such a teenager may become an ill-adjusted adult, with unpredictable emotional patterns. If these early symptoms cannot be completely removed medically — and they often cannot — a secondary and far more potentially dangerous body-process may begin. Local infection-foci may be walled off by the body — encysted — and left there, latent. These deeper internal cysts may remain for years, only to rupture unpredictably and begin to drain the aged putrid matter back into tissues. The immune system may have a sudden fight on its hands to eliminate these deadly wastes quickly. The patient may at such a time feel, and be, very ill indeed! The rupture of an ovarian cyst is a process to be avoided, hence the popular resort to surgery to remove such cysts whole. There may be other times, if better health causes more positive and improved elimination, when the contents of a cyst may begin slowly to drain through the cyst-sac, and it collapses and is broken down and gradually reabsorbed and eliminated. Cysts *internally* may be present for years, unsuspected: skin cysts are far easier to see and treat early.

Positive 'Red clover'

There is hardly a human alive today who knows of the word 'cancer' and does not have an occasional fleeting fear of its lodgement in body-cells and the slow unobserved activity of 'free radicals'. 'Have I got it?' or 'Will I get it?' is a question often asked in consultations. No one but God knows, and no one but nature, acting then *against* life, can determine when, if ever, such an anti-life process may begin.

Positive 'Red clover' is aware that unless life's 'rubbish' is eliminated promptly and completely, the odds against good health are higher. The body cannot tie off little cyst-bags full of waste matter and pathogenic material if there is no 'rubbish' left each day. The first and most obvious naturopathic step towards cancer prevention is to remove negative body processes which may otherwise contribute to ideal conditions in which free radicals can clump together, proliferate, and set up a focus-area which is hostile to human health. They may then actively overcome the former healthy cells of the area.

Positive 'Red clover' makes sure that all organs of elimination work strongly and regularly. Lungs, kidneys, bowels and skin all appear to be stimulated in their waste-removal processes by this herb. Prevention is its strong point: if actual cysts are present, benign or tending otherwise, the herb *may* be included in therapeutic care, *but with the utmost caution*. It takes a very experienced herbalist indeed to understand the potential dangers of a *sudden* release of putrid material into tissues and bloodstream. I have no time at all for — nor respect for! — any 'herbalist' who states, 'It's all natural and good, you know: herbs can't hurt you.' Such inexperience can not only produce patient-discomfort but a poor prognosis for the patient's continuing good health. Like any other profession, herbal medicine improves in safety and efficacy in direct proportion to the *experience* of the herbalist concerned. Early unbridled enthusiasm for all things 'natural' needs to be tempered by the grey hairs of caution and long and painfully-gained experience.

Dosage

1   Red clover tea *occasionally* may be drunk as any other herb tea. Do *not* assume that ten cups a day will remove any threat of later free-radical activity! You may just feel really uncomfortable, with elimination organs working overtime.

2   Long-experienced professional herbalists introduce Red clover as a mixture-ingredient in very small quantities indeed, only increasing the proportion if absolutely necessary. Those who are more towards the radical left or the radical right of the profession may adopt the view that powerful elimination must always be the aim, and the poor human involved must just grin and bear it! I disagree with both extremes, mainly because better results can be achieved without such heavy-handed determination to 'fix' patients, no matter how. Slowly and cautiously is the way to treat with Red clover!

Many years ago now, I suffered severe mastitis following the birth of my second son. In hospital at the time, I was unable to refuse massive antibiotics by injection and by mouth, and my youth deferred to the authoritarian might of modern medicine. (Today I would just sign myself out immediately, and go home to my Garlic!) A small 'lump' remained in the breast, and this was explained to me then as 'scar-tissue'. I accepted this and forgot all about the matter.

Sixteen years later I was taking a short course of Red clover tea for a clump of boils which appeared on my leg. To my amazement, I experienced three days of real and debilitating elimination, during which my arm numbed, and the breast-trauma area of sixteen years earlier stirred up, becoming very painful indeed.

When I realised the implications, I put myself to bed and added other alteratives to an internal mixture to clear what was obviously now not 'scar-tissue' but a small residual cyst. In a few more days not only did I feel quite recovered again, but the entire breast-'lump' had disappeared altogether!

Do not underestimate the effect of alteratives: blood-'cleaning' must always be the final process to complete and remove all traces of prior infection and to remove the possibility of residual waste-matter being permanently encapsulated and left *in situ*, only to cause possible trouble years ahead.

Rosemary

Rosmarinus officinalis

*I*n an earlier work (*The Book of Herbs*, page 159) I have written of the home uses of Rosemary oil. Professionally, there are some added indications.

Many therapeutic plants recently evaluated by pharmaceutical standards could be labelled 'toxic' at some stage of growth, in some particular part of the plant but not another, or in overdoses. It is at present being made very clear by our profession to various pharmaceutical investigative bodies that part of the training and education of a professional herbalist is to discriminate in and practise with such qualified information. It is surely unfair, as well as unreasonable, to restrict the access by herbalists to their tools of trade. Especially is this so when the pharmacists concerned have had no training in how *herbalists* use these plants, sometimes quite differently indeed to the way pharmacy insists we do! Rosemary is a case in point. While Rosemary oil is universally accepted, even by pharmacy, in cosmetics, perfumes, lotions and creams for external application, Rosemary *leaves*, consumed to excess internally, can cause dizziness, circulatory surges, even palpitations, and are rightly described as '*Verboten*'. Any pharmaceutical attempt to classify the *whole* plant Rosemary as 'toxic' would be laughed out of court, but it is sad that other extremely beneficial and useful *whole* plants like Comfrey, Sassafras, Hawthorn, etc., are being progressively removed from access by herbalists and by the public, because some so-called 'dangerous' attribute or dose-level can be pharmaceutically produced as 'proof'.

There is no obvious person-picture or Rosemary-type. Its use as an oil is well known in its external application for sore and over-used muscles after prolonged or unusual muscular exertion. For gardeners, tennis players, golfers, and lifters of heavy objects at home or at work, a little Rosemary oil rubbed straight away well into the over-used muscle-bundles can remove the likelihood of stiffness and soreness in the following few days. A few drops added to a long soaking hot bath can be just as effective.

A drop or two of the oil may at times be added by herbalists to an internal mixture to treat spleen congestion or chronic hypertension which has caused spleen enlargement and engorgement. It is occasionally used the same way for a spleen enlarged by malarial attacks. But the oil can also penetrate well and quickly through the skin, reaching superficial blood vessels and relaxing their tension. A few drops rubbed well into forehead and temples can remove the muscular tension and consequent eye-strain of long hours at the wheel of a car, driving in poorly-lit streets, or even in busy city traffic with its constant delays and frustrations. If you accumulate a permanent frown as part of your facial expression, try a finger-tip of Rosemary oil rubbed in well (carefully avoiding the eyes themselves!) and feel how better blood supply and less tense muscles improve your wellbeing.

Rue

Ruta graveolens

*F*or all circulatory disorders of the veins, Rue is a classic and essential partner therapeutically for Nettles (pages 230–5). Ideally, when any circulatory adjustment is called for, it is advisable to balance both veins and arteries together to avoid change in one causing uneven rhythms in the other. Rue is for the 'blue'-blood, to ensure strong and regular pumping back towards the lungs of blood which has already visited the cells, dropping its oxygen about, and now needs to return for cleaning and re-charging. Sluggish venous return may put an unnecessary loading on kidneys and heart, and this becomes more of a problem if a too high arterial pressure is also present. One half of the blood going too fast and the other half too slowly means that pressure-'walls' will occur, with the risk of rupture of vessels both minor and major.

Rutin, its best-known glycoside, is also known sometimes as 'Vitamin P'. Now established as one of the best and most actively beneficial herbs for venous congestion and for consequent varicosity, Rue must live down its mediaeval reputation and a more recent — and wrongly assigned — reputation as an abortive agent. Pennyroyal (pages 240–1) gained such a reputation too. If either of these herbs produces a period which has been missed, the woman concerned was not 'suffering' from pregnancy but from pelvic venous congestion and stasis, which prevented the normal uterine shedding of a period. However, I would *not* prescribe Rue for pregnant ladies in the last few months of their pregnancy, only because *any* treatment which may cause rapid pelvic changes in pressure is undesirable then.

I disagree entirely with a statement made about Rue in *The Encyclopaedia of Herbs & Herbalism* edited by Dr Malcolm Stuart (Orbis, 1979). (If Dr Stuart was the 'Editor', as stated, who actually *wrote* this book? Whose personal *experience* is found in this collated miscellany?) Dr Stuart states that, 'Rue must only be used by medical personnel'. Such a leading statement would bring down the wrath of experienced herbalists over the ages in every part of the world where this delicately beautiful but foul-smelling plant has been safely prescribed by them. I would join their ranks as a herbalist who has never found any abortive or related effects from the prescribing of Rue, nor does it act 'principally on the uterus'. The person-picture below elucidates further.

Rue contains Vitamins P and K, supporting the clotting and anti-clotting substances of the blood so that clots are not dangerously or inappropriately formed, but there's no unstoppable haemorrhaging either. Blood viscosity is balanced when these two mechanisms are also in balanced partnership. Two unusual organic acids, caprinic acid and caprylic acid, which are also found in whole cow's milk and in coconut, help the liver and are similar in effect to that of Evening Primrose oil, protecting and 'lubricating' the continuous movement of blood-platelets over one another, discouraging 'sticking' of platelets. Oenanthylic acid, a substance created when wine 'ages', is also found. The whole plant above the ground is used, or sometimes the leaves only.

If you grow this delicately-formed but hardy annual, or biennial, in your herb garden, be aware that it may cause a local dermatitis-like reaction on skin-contact, and never touch the eyes directly after handling the fresh plant. These irritating propensities are greatly diminished, almost totally removed, when the plant is dried; after extraction by water/alcohol blends from the dried plant-material, these effects are entirely absent.

'Rue' person-picture

'Rue' suffers from general venous congestion which shows obviously in the blood vessels of the eyes, especially if angry or frustrated and helpless, without releasing such pressures on the outside world. Keeping the lid tightly on a pressure-cooker of unspoken emotions, 'Rue' may appear to be always under control, even phlegmatically calm under stress. If you could see inside them, congested blood vessels would be throbbing under enormous pressure, and both systolic and diastolic blood pressures could be alarmingly elevated.

'Rue' may show a reddened back of the neck when embarrassed or made to look foolish, reflecting a surge in cerebral blood pressures both venous and arterial. They may also become constipated from time to time as rectal veins enlarge and haemorrhoids obstruct the lower bowel internally as well as showing painful enlargement externally. Female 'Rue' may suffer pelvic congestion before a period, with pressure and bloating discomfort; all these symptoms release as the flood of menstrual blood eventually lowers the pressure in the area. Both male and female 'Rue' will be lucky to avoid varicose veins in the legs at some stage of their lives. The preventive use of Rue in an individual mixture may need to be a long-term affair, and may be partnered with counselling and advice on acceptable other ways to discharge pent-up emotions and, most important of all, to use *actions* of some kind to lower arterial and venous blood pressures uniformly, and to discharge emotional pressures.

Negative-chronic 'Rue'

Potentially, this person lives with a time-bomb, and is perhaps the most at risk of all patient-types to sudden circulatory disasters. Internal haemorrhages as blood vessels collapse under constant high pressures may be life-threatening. A stroke may result, causing crippling incapacity for many years, if not permanently. There may be portal-vein congestion overloading the heart and causing great pressure changes in the lower limbs and trunk. Venous congestion in the legs may bulge the large veins out into twisted, tortuous, purple ropes which throb and give pain after long standing or long sitting. Such people can die from the inside, eventually, as the constant high pressures finally explode weakened major blood vessels. The sad truth is that the majority of this type chronically hide the extent of their internalised angers and frustrations, and therefore medical treatment may be too late to repair the tired blood vessels involved. Spotting them in earlier life, and taking preventive steps thereafter, is the better way to avoid the fatal heart infarction, stroke or other internal haemorrhage at perhaps an unduly early age.

Some of this potential damage later *is* within 'Rue's' ability to control earlier. The most extremely negative of them nurse and feed their angers, enjoying, in a perverse way, the adrenal 'highs' produced. Businessmen and sportsmen and women should take heed. An artificially produced adrenal-'hype' in order to succeed in a challenge or a confrontation may become a lifetime habit.

Positive 'Rue'

Aware that all of us will experience anger sometimes — frustrated helplessness before the tax department, the boss, or the courts; an unfair business deal; broken emotional promises or aggressive hitting out at those we love which reflects only our own present stresses — positive 'Rue' takes *action* to release pressure in other acceptable non-damaging ways. One positive 'Rue' I know goes rock-fishing alone at night, the pounding of the waves overriding his own circulatory pressures and stresses of the week. Another sails his boat offshore and screams out terrible fates ahead for all his business competitors. He returns to shore like a lamb, calm and de-pressurised. Many positive 'Rues' climb mountains, or *walk* for kilometre after long kilometre, coaxing their circulation into rhythmically keeping time with their stride, and safely removing accumulated pressures. Some of them punch a bag in the gym, others lift weights, or build brick walls or stone-fences. Any *rhythmically* repetitive activity can gradually and safely act as pressure-valve release for the whole system. It's not only hard or regular activity needed, it's the *rhythmic* swing of the pace, and the repetition of the movements, that bring about a slow, and therefore safer, pressure release.

Some sit on beaches and look at waves breaking again and again on the shore. One female patient picked up her knitting every time a family row brewed up at home 'Otherwise I'll desperately want to shout, hit them all, scream out my boredom and frustration and upset the very people I love the most,' she told me. 'The rhythm and repetition of my knitting seems to calm me down somehow.' I prescribed Rue tincture, with other herbs, in her individual mixture against the day when she had no knitting handy to pick up! (Her family thought her a most placid and calm anchor in their tempestuous household!) Her symptoms needing my help already included occasional constipation for three or four days, and a large varicose vein behind one knee. Her eyes grew red as she described to me her general family problems and worries. Rue, with some Nettle added to preserve the balance, could help her understand her own need for a more powerful de-pressuriser than knitting!

Dosage

1   Rue tea is not a pleasant experience! Nor is the taste of a leaf or two of Rue in the salad bowl at all acceptable! The foul aroma of this plant is matched by the equally foetid taste.

2   More acceptable as a tincture or extract, the tiny doses pre-scribed may be further diluted in a half-glass of water. If I take a Nettle–Rue combination after maybe an episode when a member of the press has reported me less than accurately, or there is profes-sional argument needing my mediation, I still like to follow the bitter taste of the Rue with an orange or a dried apricot, or a taste of honey. It is unlikely indeed that overdosing with self-prescribed Rue will occur: it is self-limiting because of its taste.

St John's Wort

Hypericum perforatum

This common weed is often declared 'noxious' to livestock by departments of agriculture worldwide. A plant beloved of European and North American herbalists and naturopaths today, it is used extensively in Germany. Its history as a 'sacred' herb dates back to the distant past in Nordic and Baltic countries. Mediaeval popular names often reflected the medicinal worth of plants: some of the most valuable were given the names of saints. Unfortunately, far too many referred to St John, and it is difficult indeed to sort out *which* St John is referred to! Worse, there can be later confusion as to which plant is referred to in herbals. For this reason, I prefer to call it Hypericum, for more exact identification.

The plant is a short thin-stemmed nondescript perennial, carrying five-petalled yellow flowers with tufted stamens. (There are hybridised garden varieties of Hypericum available, with bigger much more decorative flowers but, as always with hybridised plants, lacking any medicinal value.) If cattle graze on pastures which contain it, their hides can become photosensitive and large patches of de-pigmentation may render the hides of little commercial value. For pastoralists, it is *not* a blessing! To the sick patient, however, it can at times appear miraculous in the changes wrought. No wonder it gained sanctification!

Its contents of stearic and palmitic acid, essential fatty acids for liver and skin health, are joined by the minerals calcium, magnesium and phosphorus. I believe it also will be found to contain zinc, and possibly other trace minerals as well, especially those involved in endorphin production which is the body's natural response to lower pain. The deep red oil found in the transparent oil glands in the leaves is used alone, for skin application. The traditionally trained herbalist treats causes, primarily, so internal medication with Hypericum may well be concurrently undertaken. The indications for this plant are when there is nervous over-stimulation or excitation which may also involve pain, inflammation, etc., with the evidence of such trauma found *on the skin*. Think of all the disease conditions in this classification: measles, shingles, viral rashes, prickly heat, eczema, insect stings and bites, even 'allergies' can fall within its sphere of usefulness. Irrespective of whether blood vessels, torn tissues, etc., may contribute to the disease pattern, the definition holds: an *over-stimulated* nervous condition with its evidence on the skin.

'Hypericum' person-picture

In iridological terms (*Iridology*, Nelson, 1980), Hypericum is indicated for the people whose extreme whiteness of fibres in the iris reflects a highly reactive nervous system to tiny stimuli. Even a mosquito bite may raise a lump in seconds, reddish and painful, and continuing for days. These people are often 'sick' from a nervous system which is too *strong*, not too weak. Every stimulus encountered produces immediate and acute response. Unlike the slower 'Slippery Elm'-type, 'Hypericums' are quick to do everything. Quick to grow, quick to mature, quick to dive headlong into life, their co-ordination may sometimes suffer with the speed of their nervous energy, and occasional clumsiness may mark them out. They put off, if possible, any experience where physical pain is known to be involved. Dental appointments find them apprehensive, to say the least, with vividly recalled memories of past pain. They put off such appointments often, preferring to have all their teeth pulled out with general anaesthesia if at all possible. Injections are also avoided. In fact, any *sharp* pain experiences are so vividly recorded and recallable that they may refuse altogether a possible second experience. As children they may have to be dragged screaming to the dentist or to a medical treatment previously painful. Do not call them 'silly' or 'cry-babies': they really have a very low pain threshold, and their nervous systems record any pain at white-hot levels.

Strangely, they carry emotional suffering well! More than most people, they take decisive and speedy action to settle problems with others. The telephone is in their hands in seconds, and some poor creature at the other end hears, 'Listen, what do you mean by calling me a liar', or similar, shouted down the mouthpiece. These people are *speedy*. They gallop through the day, their agile minds often leaping ahead of them and causing the above unco-ordination. Often intellectually bright, they enjoy their education only if the teacher is not boring or slow. Heaven help such a teacher: 'Hypericum' as a child can be precocious! In later life 'Hypericums' seek new experience and intellectual challenge. They choose their friends not for their sterling worth or moral support, but for their *stimulating* company. Good or bad, it doesn't matter, but *indifferent* is a sin!

'Hypericums' have intensely reactive five senses. With hyper-acute hearing, a sensitive palate, and a sense of smell that finds spring a heady season, they suffer most of all with touch-sense. Wearing nylon underwear can cause a red hot rash, or choosing plastic shoes for their style only can make them brain-tired in an hour. Garden plants may raise blebs and blisters on contact; walking on pebbly beaches may be torture. Hyper-acute are their reactions to contact between their skin and any other substance, living or man-made.

Negative-chronic 'Hypericum'

Leaping up to turn down the stereo-player which is just a fraction unbearable in volume, negative 'Hypericum' may trip over the table leg and crash to the floor. The enforced rest nursing a sprained ankle makes them amongst the most difficult of all patients to please. The open window is too cool, the closed window is too hot; an exact gap of 10 cm is just right! Soup is too heating but a salad is too cooling, 'Let's have a warm baked rice pudding,' they suggest. If you are vainly trying to keep your temper, don't bother! They *know* they are being pernickety and difficult, but it springs from a *physical* hypersensitivity, not an emotional one. Rant and rave at them for being a pain in the neck, and they'll agree with you. But the skin rash is real; the weeping eczema is obvious; the tears in the eyes from the pain of shingles, or the measles virus is unbearable, almost. The skin application of the thick, dark, maroon Hypericum oil can be kindness indeed. The pain and irritation subside somewhat, and as the pain drops the behaviour improves. Calling for an interesting book to pass away the time spent immobile, an easier-to-please patient saves the household from mass walk-out.

Positive 'Hypericum'

*A*lways more reactive to physical nerve stimulus than most people, healthy 'Hypericum' takes some keeping up with! They smell the roses, watch the sunset, then dash off to write a poem about it. They often *cry* at beauty, because the experience for them is almost painfully deep. A friend's kind help, and they feel unbearably touched, experiencing keenly the loving concern behind the action. They often see further and deeper than most people. They live life to the full, devouring new learning, new experience, new ideas and stimulating conversation — albeit with a rash from strawberries or an itchy wrist from a metallic watch-band. They may appear to suffer from skin allergies but they only experience hyper-reactivity to almost *any* stimulation. Taking internal Hypericum (the whole-plant tincture or extract) can damp down the over-stimulated nerve signals to avoid short-circuiting. Even the most healthy of 'Hypericum'-types occasionally needs solitude, or a dip in a mountain stream, or baring their bodies to the gentle winter sun. The touch-sense may need a rest, using the various 'touches' of nature to produce it. Warm sunshine, a grassy lawn, a dip in the ocean, a rainforest walk, and 'Hypericum's' restless nervous energy is cut down to manageable size again by the touch of the vastly greater energies of nature.

Dosage

1   *Never* used as a tea, and rightly so.

2   Hypericum oil may be applied at home to any itching painful skin rash, bite, sting or healing burn. *Gently* does it!

3   For more professional treatment of cause-factors and underlying hypersensitive reactions, seek the aid of your professional herbalist. As all 'Hypericums' are super-sensitive physically, dose levels must be low initially, only increasing if tolerated. Too high a dose, and you may cause the reverse procedures. An angry 'Hypericum', throwing the arms about and flailing the furniture, is to be avoided if possible!

Homoeopaths prescribe high potencies of Hypericum as a symptomatic pain-reliever. Especially good for dental and post-surgical pain, Hypericum 6^C and up to Hypericum^M potencies may be advised. It is *always* best to consult an objective professional rather than make a subjective diagnosis. When I'm feeling out of sorts, I don't diagnose and prescribe for myself, I ask one of my trusted associates to assess from an outside standpoint, and to prescribe for me. Self-diagnosis is economical, but misguided and foolhardy. Unless you are a möbius strip, you cannot be inside yourself and outside yourself at the same time!

Sarsaparilla

Smilax ornata

A natural partner for Pulsatilla (pages 247–51), Jamaican Sarsaparilla is considered the best of several different Sarsaparillas, each with some medicinal value. (Although exported *through* Jamaica initially, this Sarsaparilla is native to Central America.)

The roots of this plant are the parts used. Dried and pulverised, they yield their properties to extraction by water/alcohol, the very long thin roots providing by this means a unique-tasting medicinally active solution.

Sarsaparilla waxes and wanes in popularity. A century ago there was hardly a household in Europe, Great Britain and the Americas without Sarsaparilla cordial on hand to offer to weary or hot travellers and friends on a summer's afternoon. It may well have been one of the first commercial marketing successes of the herb-world. Reputed to cure syphilis, it took off in popularity and zoomed to the top of the therapeutic charts. Perhaps there were guilty consciences amongst those genteel and demure ladies on the lawn, attended by their correct husbands! Sarsaparilla consumption certainly was high!

At one time in most medical Pharmacopoeas, Sarsaparilla has lost its commercial backers today, although in Australia there is still one cordial manufacturer who makes it, and a large pharmacy chain makes a 'Sarsaparilla compound' which is used as an internal 'tonic' for teenage acne.

Recent analysis has shown Sarsaparilla roots to contain oestrogen, progesterone, and testosterone, the male and female hormones. But taking Sarsaparilla roots extract, or the medicinal tincture, should not leave you undecided between Arthur and

Martha hormonally! My oft-repeated testimonial to the synergistic action of plant-drugs, and the body's ability to absorb and distribute needed nutrients whilst eliminating unneeded substances found together, still stands. No woman has ever grown hair on her chest from taking Sarsaparilla, nor has any man gained a high-pitched voice! Whichever hormone applies will be selected, and others discarded.

Traditionally, the use of this plant was pronounced as 'alterative'. Hormones were regarded as unadjustable in its heyday. If you couldn't conceive, then that was surely your destiny: if a male was infertile, then there was a family 'taint' somewhere. Today, our prejudices are of a different kind. It's 'right to life' or 'right to choose' today, and with just as vehement a polarisation as earlier. So it may be that Sarsaparilla's popularity will return: herbalists prescribe it for hypo-function of the reproductive system in male or female. Whether it be a low sperm count or previous tissue damage in the male, even after a reversed vasectomy or a mature-age circumcision, any physical impediment to the reproductive organs may need Sarsaparilla to be prescribed. For the female a partial ovarectomy, the removal of one entire ovary, a Fallopian tubal-ligation reversal, even a vaginal pH condition hostile to male sperm, may need treatment with Sarsaparilla in the general mixture.

Reproductive-system organs are peculiarly sensitive to shocks, intrusive surgery, and to deep-seated instinctive attitudes, acquired beliefs, restrictions, guilt and social traumas. The last and most evocative of our primitive racial survival instincts still present with us, our '*right*' to reproduce our species, may result in the death of our overloaded and polluted planet! Still each female demands to carry a child, and each male celebrates his male 'success' at the birth of his first son. All the rational discussion and the hostile factions arising for and against the reproduction of our kind will take many moons to unseat our *instinctive* responses on this subject, which have nothing to do with what *ought* to be, theoretically.

When a female asks a herbalist to help her achieve a healthy pregnancy in spite of massive physical reasons why this may be difficult, Sarsaparilla, together with perhaps Phytolacca, Raspberry leaves, etc., may be prescribed. Those readers with a pharmaceutical bent may theorise that this apparently contradictory hormone content will never be effective. Empirical medicine, the medicine that stands on *results* not theories, proclaims the effectiveness of this herb: there are many humans alive today whose landing-ground was eventually prepared by the use of such plants. We always have a little celebratory giggle in the dispensary when one of my associate practitioners proudly announces, 'I just got another one pregnant!' If the practitioner happens to be a male, he quickly adds 'Good old Sarsaparilla!' and avoids our raised eyebrows!

More of an episode in life than a person-type, Sarsaparilla also acts as a tonic to the liver, and is truly alterative in its effects on the blood. If a poor health history runs in both family trees of the couple who are now distractedly seeking every means of conception available, Sarsaparilla's alterative effects may remove the last lingering ghosts of great-grandfather's syphilis and its carry-on effects, with different but related traumas as a legacy for his heirs. There is no blame attached to the poor would-be parents now, but a syphilitic gene often causes sterility in both male and female descendants generations later.

Dosage

1   A mild glass of Sarsaparilla cordial has a pronounced blood-cooling effect in hot weather. It can be drunk by all age groups.

2   Sarsaparilla is not used as a tea at all.

3   In tincture or extract form, and in proportions different for each individual, it is prescribed for many and varied hormonal-insufficiency symptoms, and also prescribed at times of extreme hormonal change like puberty and menopause to make the transition more easily and more speedy.

> For teenage acne, Sarsaparilla is often prescribed with liver regulators like Dandelion, Fenugreek, etc. Even Sarsaparilla tablets, taken alone, can help the hormone changes take place more positively without a long post-puberty pattern of 'spots' until age thirty-seven! If you still 'break out' on the face before a period, or suffer spotty eruptions around the neck and the hairline past the twenties, Sarsaparilla may be needed to help your hormones 'decide' on their levels of production.
>
> Menopausally, Sarsaparilla may also be needed for the same reasons, to help bridge the inevitable changing of gear hormonally. Menopause can be a longer and more gradual process than puberty, but perhaps older folks are better able to cope with these later changes. Or

perhaps *not*? It is always a joy to lessen the hot flushes, the emotional fluctuations, and the headaches, sleepless times and adrenal slumps of menopause. Perhaps women notice it more, as the absence of a period cycle is for them a major change. But middle-aged males can also benefit when Sarsaparilla is indicated. Their hormones may be less obviously reactive, but perhaps because of this, their adrenal-energy slumps, emotional outbursts, even self-damaging behavioural changes, may be harder for them to understand and to come to terms with.

Scullcap

Scutellaria lateriflora

*H*erbalists have railed against each other over this plant since its quite late introduction into medicinal use. As recently as 1983 an English visiting medical-herbalist raised again the old argument: was the 'Scullcap' in our extracts and tinctures really Scullcap? Had another plant been substituted? Were we giving our patients the wrong plant? Did we know our business anyway? For years the controversy has arisen and died down, only to re-surface when different herbals give conflicting information, and some conscientious student or practitioner compares them. Even the botanical name is under query. *Potter's Encyclopaedia of Botanical Drugs* spells it 'lateri*folia*', usually thus dubbed when the *leaves* of the plant are the medicinal parts to be used. But most other reliable Pharmacopoeas name it as 'lateri-*flora*', with the flowers the useful parts. It complicates even more when several other British and European Scullcaps are used (*S. galericulata*, *S. versicolor*, and *S. canescens*) especially when the 'official' variety is a North American native. So there is reason for all the confusion, even amongst professionals! It's comforting to know that *all* the varieties have similar medicinal qualities.

Pharmacognosists have extracted from all of these Scullcaps a substance called scutellarin. While for many years this principle was believed to be inert, there is much evidence to the contrary today. Seldom, if ever, does nature manufacture *useless* ingredients: it's up to us to find out more, that's all.

The Scullcaps are somewhat self-effacing in growth, most of

275

them being small or semi-prostrate. Tending to prefer boggy soil in Australia and damp edges of shrubbery, rather than open ground, their growth here is a little more difficult unless you live in cool humid zones geographically. In Europe and in the USA, they seem to grow more happily in open sunshine. (Many plants from the northern hemisphere differ in their growth habits and preferences when grown in the southern hemisphere. Plants react more obviously and quickly to changes to geomagnetic energies than do people.)

The 'whole herb' is used in making medicinal tinctures and extracts. This term always refers to the parts *above* ground, and is traditionally picked for processing just before the flower-buds open. Any plant at this stage has its greatest energy concentrated in the green leafy parts. So it seems the academic argument as to whether it is 'S. lateri*flora*' or 'S. lateri*folia*' is a too pedantic one!

Perhaps the botanical and the Latin confusion needs further explanation here. Scullcap is spelled 'Scullcap' not 'Skullcap'. Its name has absolutely nothing to do with cranium bones nor with a Hebrew homulka, despite what some dictionaries mistakenly say. *Scutella* means 'a little dish', and refers to the shape of the saucer-like lower lip of the flower, with a lid, or cover, suspended above it. However, when its medicinal applications are described, you could perhaps be forgiven for associating it, if not with the human *skull*, then perhaps with the human *brain* in some of its useful properties.

The plant contains a volatile oil, Scutellarin, and several bitter glycosides. There is tannin, a little fat, and the usual plant-sugar and cellulose. The bitterness of the herb is immediately obvious from tasting the extract, so its action is going to be to stimulate gastric mucosa as well as tighten and tone various tissues. Its greatest use, however, is as a nervine. Not until recent years has Scutellarin been found to stimulate not only the absorption and use of Vitamin B_3 (that essential member of the B-group which protects and gives resilience to the nervous system as a whole) but Scutellarin can also play a role in regulating the balance of two vital hormones, adrenalin and noradrenalin. These two hormones perform complex balancing of a *glandular* function which often appears to be more of a *nervous*-system function. If you have an imbalance between the two hormones, you can appear to be nervously distressed when in fact you are hormonally disturbed. The following person-picture of 'Scullcap' may suit a patient in overall terms as a general personality-type all through life, but many of us can experience 'Scullcap' episodes under extremes of adrenal response.

'Scullcap'
person-picture

Classic 'Scullcaps' are tall, and often painfully thin at some stages of their life. They are intellectually bright, often brilliant, but in this facile mercurial mind can also be found a mental laziness unless constantly stimulated. At school, they can be written off as 'daydreamers' and dullards, or even as *too* smart for their own good. Their schoolwork can show flashes of brilliance when they're 'hot', but all too often when boredom sets in they find clever ways of avoiding study, repetition work and teaching which they feel is beneath their interest.

They are 'ideas' people. Their minds leap about like Harlequin reflecting broken images of flashing thoughts in three-way mirrors. But between these periods, long mental-deserts may stretch out. When this happens, they can become *agitated*, irritable, cantankerous, self-pitying and even downright cruel. The answer to their problems is often a new challenge, a fresh stimulus mentally, even a change of job or change in type of job. 'Scullcap'-persons relish the new and the different. Their minds are quickly able to commute between one idea and the next. Perhaps unfortunately, the need for 'something new, something different' may not bring with it consideration for the effect on the world at large of their brilliant ideas. Values, safety, moral restraints, caution, even cost, are words seldom in the vocabulary of the typical 'Scullcap'.

As well as being generally long and lean, they are *leaners* too. They slump their long bodies into a semi-reclining chair if possible, or lean against door-jambs or walls, or even bus-stops. They prop one hip up on the kitchen table while talking. They seem often to be bone-tired, with *ennui* and a deep sigh as they change their conversation position. One very typical sign is shaking hands, especially if apprehensive, excited or over-tired. Some of the most extreme of the type have a triangulated upper eyelid that droops sharply down to the lateral, or outside, eye-corner.

Many tend to live in the fast-lane, burn the candle at both ends, dance all night and sleep late. There can be an appearance *difference* about them which may be real, or may be contrived to startle or to cause comment.

They can generate ideas, plans, advertising slogans and business ventures that no one else has ever attempted because the *idea* is new. They are sometimes to be found in the forefront of scientific research in many fields. They are often found in television commercials! They slope around university campuses in their dozens, talking about what's wrong with 'the system' — *any* system — so long as it can be debated, discussed, organised theoretically — and then too often forgotten altogether when yet another idea is born.

Negative-chronic 'Scullcap'

Here is a walking 'nervous breakdown' which has nothing whatever to do with the nervous system and should more accurately be called an 'adrenal collapse'. The functions of the adrenal glands are variously affected by anxiety, over-concern, apprehension and real fears. At first, there is adrenalin called out into the bloodstream to fight against the real or imagined challenges, to harden up muscles and send blood to vital areas of head, heart, etc., and to leave non-essential areas like the digestive tract alone during the period of the challenge. However, if challenges appear every few minutes or every few hours (as in wartime or in bushfires or even in after-Christmas sales crowds or football grand-finals), the adrenal glands work overtime. Constant over-stimulus will eventually produce adrenalin-noradrenalin imbalances and one or both adrenal glands may capitulate under the long-term overload. A 'nervous breakdown' lies ahead some-where for this type of person if the stresses and loadings are maintained.

In the early stages of negative-'Scullcap', there may be increas-ing dependence on cigarettes, coffee, alcohol, even stimulant drugs, to maintain an adrenal 'charge' in the face of increasing anxiety, tension and actual fears. When someone tells me they're suffering from 'stress', what they are describing is exhausting adrenal glands.

After all the coffee and stimulants to keep them 'high', the next casualty is sleep. Many resort to 'downers' of some kind to achieve sleep at all. Some rely on sedatives, tranquillisers, etc., and then deplore their chronic lack of energy during the day. Others who persevere with poor or broken sleep soon develop even shakier hands and a greater need for some form of stimulant-crutch during the day.

Negative-'Scullcap' may also suffer from headaches or migraines: tension-headaches, so-called, but hormonally-caused. Real blinders these can be, and increasing irritability and tem-peramental storms can follow. I often think of 'Scullcap' as the media-remedy. All those operatic prima donnas, highly strung actors and actresses, script-writers and popstars, disc-jockeys and comperes; every one of them is adrenally-saturated when working under on-stage pressures and adrenally-exhausted after the show.

Creative people often suffer the same way. Artists have black depressions then fear, apprehension, even terror, when their works are assembled for public show. Fashion designers and models drink black coffee to keep the adrenaline high as the autumn collection is launched. All these people under challenge and pressure meet it with adrenal-hormone response.

Positive 'Scullcap'

I know a brilliant sculptor, acclaimed world-wide, who is yet a classic 'Scullcap' — but in the positive aspect. His ideas decorate buildings with flashing brilliance and fantasy-shapes, but he *grounds* the energy of these ideas by producing working drawings with painstaking care and attention to detail, then brings reality to the dream using considerable practical engineering knowhow. His ideas are *earthed* and *accomplished*, not just talked about. But hands which may shake everywhere *except* on the drawing-board, and a tendency to light sleep, plus a magnificent '*ennui*', proclaim the classic 'Scullcap' picture.

Positive 'Scullcap' regulates the adrenal flow with practical action and real performance — then sleeps — albeit lightly! When Scullcap is prescribed as part of a mixture for this person-type, there is relief from the razorback ride of ups and downs, and energy maintains a more even and regular flow-pattern. The 'highs' become times of real creative and intellectual progress, but the 'lows' are accepted as a need for rest, sleep, contemplation and calm renewal. Sleep comes more readily and is a little deeper. This person can turn 'off' now as well as 'on'. Apprehensions can be dismissed by action, and any idea can now be extruded from the churning thoughts these people hold in their minds, and can be put into practical form. The white-hot mental activity eases to more productive levels.

All of us have times in our lives of shock, anxiety, sudden reversals and challenges. Such confrontations may make urgent demands on our adrenal-hormone responses, and Scullcap may be prescribed as one ingredient in a herbal mixture appropriate to that person at that time, although the patient may not be a classical 'Scullcap'-type. Many armed forces personnel have showed need for Scullcap in the wars of our last few generations. Constant fear; waiting in trenches or in the jungle for an enemy attacking without warning, is a Scullcap-episode. 'Shell-shock' it was called, or 'gone troppo'. Constant adrenal overloads caused adrenal collapse. Tears, shaking, inability to sleep or eat, fantasies and nightmares,

all signified the same need for peace and quiet, rest and recupera-
tion, and freedom from challenges for a long time. Scullcap could
have been a part of their rehabilitation.

But the super-positive 'Scullcap', never needing to take this as a
remedy, is a joy to be with. At seventy they are running about like
teenagers, full of plans for the future. They buy all the latest gadgets
and are innovative. They *relish* challenges! They love to fight, especially for an apparently lost cause, or to protect others. 'You old
war-horse', I prodded one of them, 'you're itching to get a challenging job somewhere on some committee where you can bowl them
over with your energy and push through your new ideas into
action.' He grinned at me. 'You're damned right', he bellowed. He
sleeps with a clear quiet mind, then wakes at six and leaps out to
start the day with enthusiasm. He's never had a headache in his life
and his hands are rock-steady. My Scullcap bottle would stay
unopened on the shelf were this man ever my patient!

But for the rest of us, the adrenalin may pump more slowly,
and we may at some time in our lives need Scullcap's restorative
effect. It is not, strictly speaking, a sedative, nor is it a tranquilliser
to blunt our sensitivity and reduce our stress-reactions. It is a re-
balancer of adrenal hormones, and of all the body processes that
adrenal distress disturbs.

Dosage

1   It is not possible to buy Scullcap tea, and it is probably just as
well.

2   The dosage of this herb must be carefully evaluated and
prescribed, and needs a trained professional assessment. Because
Scullcap people are too facile in their adrenal output, the dosage
must be carefully determined in order to *calm down* the balance,
not set it too quickly or too strongly into motion in the opposite
direction. There may be breaking down of the Scullcap's effect by
adding other nervines to the patient's mixture, or there could even
be just a trace of Scullcap added to any mixture prescribed for
different illness symptoms where that patient is Scullcap-type
anyway. Don't assume you need Scullcap in large doses every day if
you fit the above pictures: leave it to an objective assessment by a
trained herbalist. It's often better to 'see yourself as *others* see you'
— and an objective aspect is especially needed in prescribing
Scullcap.

Senna

Cassia acutifolia
C. angustifolia

*F*ew indeed are the pharmaceuticals containing only plant substances which have been allowed to remain in the British Pharmacopoea! European Pharmacopoeas contain more, but I feel in my bones that their days may also be numbered. A preparation made only from Senna pods, ground up and compressed into tablets, is one survivor in our current Pharmacopoea. (Incidentally Australia does not have an *official* Pharmacopoea, but follows the British one closely. 'Mim's' publications of therapeutic drugs are the nearest thing we have in Australia to a standard pharmaceutical reference work.)

Senna is, and always has been, one of the safest and most consistently effective of all plant laxatives. Herbalists put it atop their laxative lists: it can be prescribed for children, and for travellers of any age whose temporary constipation is due to time-zone changes and body-rhythm interruptions. It is perhaps the one medicinal-strength laxative which is prescribable for pregnant women, if needs must. It is useful to produce normal bowel rhythms again after fasting before surgery, especially abdominal or lower-bowel surgery. It is kind to haemorrhoid sufferers and those with recent haemorrhoidectomies. What a relief to have almost nothing cautionary to write about a plant's medicinal uses!

Just to spoil my euphoria, I'm sure, one recent herbal medicine student detailed to me the new medical evidence that young women, pigheadedly striving to be fashionably emaciated, are overdosing on pharmaceutical tablets of Senna! To what lengths will wrongheaded vanity and the need for acceptance by the herd drive our impressionable young? I sometimes despair of my ongoing battles and professional disagreements with some medicine and pharmacy doctrines ever being resolved: I *always* despair when fashion is my adversary! If grown, otherwise-responsible adults continue to appreciate bony skeleton-like female bodies as their beauty ideals, anorexia here all our daughters come! I agreed with my husband in his appreciation of 'feelable females'. I'm sure bone-against-bone contacts between the sexes must lack something!

Senna may be combined with other laxatives like Cascara, Aloes, etc. when a dry or inflamed bowel is the reason for constipation.

Like all classically trained herbalists, I do not continue to relieve symptoms only without searching for prime causes. Laxatives should only be given over short periods of time for the stimulus to produce necessary evacuation. Reasons for the constipation continuing may run the whole gamut from temporary anxiety or spatial change, to major bowel obstruction by tumour, etc. Laxatives should *always* be a temporary measure. High in iron, in energy-stimulant glycosides, Senna is not habit-forming nor do you need an increasing dose to produce the necessary peristalsis.

CAUTION

Do not use the pods of the common almost-weedlike yellow garden Cassia in mistake for Senna pods. The yellow pea-flowers of the garden variety are different from, though distantly related to, the medicinal type, but the pods of the garden Cassia will give you nothing but griping diarrhoea — at best!

Slippery Elm

Ulmus fulva

The dried, powdered inner-bark of the Red Elm of North America has been thankfully used not only by herbalists but by orthodox medicine and pharmacy for the greater part of a century. As a weaning food for young babies and also as an easily assimilated and soothing gruel for the aged, its safety and efficacy cannot be doubted.

The mucillage which is its greatest contribution therapeutically is of a unique kind, absorbing intestinal fluids, and swelling up a little; but at the same time this mucillage is highly nutritive, containing calcium compounds, especially calcium phosphate, which are readily absorbed. For the very young and the very old, needing extra calcium for developing bones or for ageing bones, Slippery Elm Powder is an ideal dietary additive to porridge mixes, muesli and to today's nutritive blender drinks. Do not be heavy-handed with it! Its unique taste, a cross between mouldy cocoa and rancid malted milk, makes it self-limiting as a food. It also is difficult to blend with just water, remaining in gluggy lumps. Although some packet-instructions suggest its use this way, it blends more easily with sticky or fatty substances like yoghurt, or mashed banana. It has a strange effect on fats in the intestines, too, surrounding fatty excess and moving it along with the Slippery Elm mucillage towards easy bowel excretion.

'Slippery Elm' person-picture

A stress-*swallower*, 'Slippery Elm' swallows everything — pride, insults, injustices, undeserved criticism, sadness, shock, loss, etc. Their life experience is *digested*, literally. They may comment, 'That's a hard truth to swallow', or 'I can't *stomach* this guy at the office', or they *feed* on their angers. They hesitate: 'Give me time to *digest* what you've just told me.' It may be a good 24–30 hours before they give you their conclusions — digestion time! In with the food at mealtimes go the hurts, the slights, and the experiences of the day, good or bad. It is absolutely essential for those people to eat in calm, happy surroundings with cheerful compatible people: a 'business lunch' for them can be a health hazard. Otherwise, for maybe a day afterwards, they may rumble, and, wind blowing up, and down, reach for bicarbonate of soda, fizzy alkalising drinks, or their pharmaceutical tablets for stomach 'nerves'.

I assessed one current-affairs host as reacting this way on daily stress loadings. 'Doesn't everyone?' he flung back at me. Such people find it hard to believe that there are different people who eat and drink and are merry, taking their stresses in muscles, in central nervous system, in adrenal glands, but *not* through the intestinal tract. Often irritable by nature, 'Slippery Elm' goes through unpredictably different effects from the *same* food, depending on the circumstances in which it is eaten.

Negative-chronic 'Slippery Elm'

If year after year the stresses are unrelieved, even ignored, this type of person can ulcerate through the entire digestive tract. Some do it high up, and a peptic or gastric ulcer causes pain, wind and dietary limitation. Others ulcerate at the duodenum, the site for *competitive* challenges. Others blow their stresses out lower down, and ulcerative colitis may be their lot. The worries may not drop until the rectum is reached, and acid burning and itching may occur there. These people burn holes in themselves internally: their rather grim facial expressions may reflect not only real intestinal pain, but a growing dissatisfaction with the life experiences they are swallowing. They can be terrible to work for! A family argument at the dinner-table last night, followed by a sleepless night of popping digestive aids, finds them grouchy, miserable and taking it out on all around them the next day.

By nature, they seldom settle any differences and arguments quickly. Also by nature, they may not admit to their own shortcomings at all, preferring to blame cruel fate rather than taking any blame themselves. In character, therefore, they often blame their *food* for upsetting them. Off they go to allergists, nutritionists, and anyone who promises a dietary regime which will remove the intestinal discomfort. One such clinic patient drove us all to despair. With increasingly long — and different! — lists of foodstuffs to which he showed 'allergic' responses, he grouched and grumbled his way through the consultations, accusing us of ineptitude, poor training, inexperience and more. 'You should be able to fix my problems', he challenged. 'No, if *you* fix your life's problems, we will have no job left to do', I responded. He would not, or could not, understand, and left us for another naturopath who gave him quantities of tablets, rigid dietary guidelines and a whole list of prohibitions. She failed, as we had. At last report, he was back to a medical regime that virtually anaesthetised the digestive tract so that it wouldn't register the continuing pain and distress actually happening still. No doubt he now *feels* fixed!

On top of the food-plus-stress may go alcohol. This can rapidly worsen the entire problem. 'Slippery Elm' people seem to prefer wines as their tipple. They will give you all the reasons in the world why a glass of wine aids digestion, even quoting the biblical 'Take a little wine for thy stomach's sake.' They then drink heaps! Typically, they do not suffer morning-after *headaches*, but stomachs may be tender for days. A little good food, in pleasant company and surroundings, may be the best hangover cure for them.

Positive 'Slippery Elm'

Don't we all 'swallow' hurts and troubles occasionally? Sometimes it's salutary to hear and swallow some unpalatable truths about ourselves! Seeing ourselves as others see us may be a necessary lesson. The positive people of this type still digest rather slowly such an honest appraisal. A day or two later can see them apologetic, eager to discuss further any need for their personal changes in behaviour or attitude. They then *do* change — and so does their life-experience which should now be easier for them to 'chew over', digest and remove. Still they will say phrases like 'Leave me to chew over this proposal for a day or two', or 'Give me a little time to digest this new marketing approach.' But they keep their real eating away from this process. If a 'Slippery Elm' person says, 'Just give me a light meal tonight dear, I've got some things to think through', this healthier approach shows awareness of their own personality traits. Don't put down in front of them an overflowing plate, a bottle or two of wine, and three courses to follow later! In accordance with their natures, they may swallow the lot rather than complain!

Positive 'Slippery Elm' can be a really nice and easy person on the outside, uncomplaining and soldiering on. On the inside they are a mass of quivering marshmallow, sensitive, sometimes even fearful, with intestinal linings which redden, swell and give discomfort as Life passes through them. Listen to their food preferences for the day: you will learn whether life has been easy or hard for them recently.

Dosage

1   In household use, a teaspoon of Slippery Elm powder, mixed with yoghurt or a mashed banana, can soothe intestinal discomfort after too-hot curry the night before — or too much alcohol! It is always better to anticipate nature's ways, so it can be even more effective to take this dose *before* the meal at the curry house, and before the Christmas party, the New Year celebration or the family birthday. Even before a trip around our Australian vineyards, or a wine-tasting night, can be much more effective than afterwards!

2   When ulceration and tissue damage has already occurred, the dose may be increased to one dessertspoonful daily, mixed in the same manner. As Slippery Elm powder will remain protective for approximately thirty hours, it is not necessary to take it three times daily.

CAUTION

As Slippery Elm powder absorbs intestinal fluids to some extent, taking too much can leave the intestines and lower bowel drier than is advisable. If constipation results on taking Slippery Elm, reduce the dose greatly, and consciously drink far more fluid.

Thuja

Thuja occidentalis

No matter how I caution against self-diagnosing, there will always be those readers who feel it's all easy, and can't do any harm, and will be tempted not only to self-diagnose but to choose which herbs to treat themselves with, ignoring all my pleas otherwise. For this reason alone, I will not mention here any internal uses of Thuja. Even experienced professionals are occasionally surprised by unusual patient-reactions to this herb.

However, as an ointment externally, it is our major fungicide. For all fungal infections of the skin, and for some viral–fungal combinations like plantar warts, its action is predictable and positive. Pronounced 'too-jar', this handsome conifer grows in time to a very large tree. I saw a magnificent and massive specimen in the garden of Dr A. Vogel at his Teufen Clinic, high in the Swiss Alps. There are many developed hybrids, or garden varieties, in cultivation but, as always, losing their medicinal value in this process.

There are several fungal and other infections which affect the hands and the feet particularly, those areas often exposed more than the rest of the body to moisture. Such medicinally named diseases are paronychia (fungus under the fingernail bed), tinea (the itching miseries between the toes, and elsewhere), and plantar warts (the viral–fungal focuses which grow *inwards* from the skin surface, and otherwise may need surgery to remove) and all respond well to regular and continued application of Thuja ointment, or to Thuja tincture dabbed on after every exposure to moisture.

Many of the people who contract these fungal infections may have constantly wet hands and feet. Most susceptible are housewives, young mothers, public swimming-pool staff, and gardeners. One patient with paronychia under both thumbnails worked at the fish-markets, de-scaling and boning fish under running water. *Fresh*-water funguses respond well to Thuja. At *salt*-water public pools, the staff may escape, but if the dressing booths are wet constantly with *fresh*-water after showers, they may not.

Purely symptomatic in its indications, Thuja ointment should be locally applied, freshly each day, immediately after shower or bath. On a clean dressing, a little dab of the ointment, or drops of the tincture, must be in contact all the time. It's not enough just to rub a little in or dab it on. Contact must be maintained continuously.

Dosage

1   Apply the ointment on a clean dressing once daily for approximately six to eight weeks for plantar wart treatment. *Do not* dig at or pull away any skin which may appear to be loosening or rising away from the surrounding skin during this time. Just keep applying the Thuja dressing. When permanently removed after treatment ends, you'll see the skin gradually resume 'normal' texture and surface. The plantar 'wart' does *not* lift out whole. In fact its title 'wart' is a misnomer. All you do with the Thuja is penetrate into the area, killing off the virus—fungus and leaving the normal tissue to recover its former character.

2   For paronychia, dab Thuja tincture on to the nail-bed edges after exposure to water. After washing up, washing hands in the bathroom, using cleaning fluids, etc., give another quick application.

3   Many Thuja ointment labels contain advice to rub it in to painful rheumatic joints, especially in hands and fingers. Consult with your herbalist on whether this advice is applicable to your particular kind of rheumatism, and to the reasons for its onset.

Thyme

Thymus serpyllum
T. vulgaris

Many of our culinary herbs today were earlier used in food not only for the taste, but for the medicinal effect. There can never be a sharp cut-off point between culinary herbs and medicinal herbs. Thyme, part of most *bouquet garni* blends used in cooking, and added dried to prepared seasonings, is powerfully therapeutic. As a germicide, it stands almost equal with Garlic as an antiseptic. As a carminative, it ranks with Chamomile. Even as an anti-inflammatory agent it is strongly effective. It's not coincidental that the Christmas poultry has been seasoned with Sage, Thyme and Parsley since ancient times. Powerfully protective and therapeutic, these herbs could be called the 'big three' of herbal medicine.

Thymol, one of Thyme's aromatic resinous oily ingredients, is a germicide more effective than carbolic acid but without its dangers. Both externally and internally, Thyme tea is sufficiently concentrated to be effective, but as a tincture or extract only very tiny doses are required. Thymol is especially effective against streptococcal infection in throat and progressing to kidneys. Many tonsillectomies may have been avoided by the use of Thyme as a tea, as a gargle, or in an internal mixture.

In my teaching and in media work, I must often talk for hours. Regularly, every few weeks, my second-year students listen for six hours on Saturday and six hours on Sunday, their writer's cramp painful to behold. Without what they refer to as my 'life-support system' on my table, I would not be able to speak on Monday! No, it's not Scotch and water; it's lemon juice, with chopped chunks of rind and pith soaking at the bottom of the glass, and Thyme extract, Yarrow, etc. added. My voice is still strong on Sunday evening, and I do not suffer the relaxed throat and inflamed vocal chords called 'clergyman's throat'. I now carry a little container of my 'brew' to all public speaking engagements. How I suffer if I forget it!

Dosage

1   Preventive treatment with Thyme tea gargled then swallowed down should be health maintenance for all those who shout at football matches, yell across the paddocks, or sing grand opera. For all of us, an occasional throat or laryngeal infection may occur or tonsillitis. Make a cup of Thyme tea as soon as symptoms are noticed; don't put it off.

2   In an internal mixture, Thyme can be beneficial not only to the throat but also to the spleen. What acupuncturists call a 'wet spleen', pulpy and enlarged, can begin better blood-handling with this herb. I have absolutely no idea why!

Uva-ursi

Arctostaphylos uva-ursi

The popular name 'Bear Berry' apparently refers to this plant's habitat in mountainous parts of the far north of the northern hemisphere. (Many plants thrive in widely separated continents but in the same latitudes. Perhaps receding ice-ages encouraged this global 'layer' principle.) Many European herbs date their mythically distant reputations from the Celtic era. Those fierce fighting mercenaries, craftsmen and bards once covered most of Europe and spread well into Baltic countries too. Uva-ursi's history is ancient indeed, and its growth and traditional uses follow closely the lines of Celtic expansion. In one of the last remaining strongholds of things Celtic, the mountains of Wales, Uva-ursi's shiny green leaves cover rocky outcrops and boggy places still.

Its traditional uses give us some insight into the common disease symptoms of this era: the formation of stones in organs was apparently prevalent, as it was also in ancient Egypt and around the Fertile Crescent of the Middle East.

Uva-ursi combines astringent and demulcent constituents — a rare blend. It is both tonic and stimulant, but also soothing and calming. Most herbal writers mention its effectiveness against kidney-stone pain, its cleansing and toning of the bladder with swift return to comfortable urination, and its traditional addition to treatments for gonorrhoea, soothing irritable genito-urinary tract inflammation. I have, in common with many other herbalists, found it equally soothing and tonic when gall-stones are the problem to be treated. High in organic acids, especially gallic acid, Uva-ursi also contains a glycoside called Arbutin which gives the plant its tonic effect.

'Uva-ursi' person-picture

If you are one of the fighting Irish, you'll have quite a deep-seated respect for the secretive Welsh! Every military policeman knows the *different* ways nationally gathered brigades will react off duty. The Irish fight easily and naturally all the time, the Scots threaten and hammer at you with their long arms and their large size. But the Welsh, aah, the Welsh! They sing as they decapitate you suddenly, then disappear into the green valleys and the hills like images out of your dreams. Strong Military Policemen shudder when a brigade brawl erupts in a Welsh pub! 'Uva-ursi' persons smoulder with age-long resentments about being underdogs, with fighting continuously all their lives against long odds. 'A chip on the shoulder' may also indicate stone in the kidney or bladder, or the gall bladder. On the defensive always, 'Uva-ursi' assumes that everyone else is out to get him, or her. They are seldom lukewarm: they either love you or hate you and there's never much in between. Fiercely loyal to their friends, relatives and the 'tribe', they stand united in little groups against the outside world and what it can do to them. They remember all past humiliations, and woe betide you when *they* become the boss, or the union representative! These people can harbour grudges, and enjoy getting their own back.

Negative-chronic 'Uva-ursi'

Suffering always from past injustices, negative 'Uva-ursi' may have difficulty leaving the past and living in the present. Things may have been bad back in the mountains centuries ago, but today, with a car in the garage, with a well-fed and well-dressed family around and a little put by in the bank, things are really not so tough. It is only with reluctance that negative 'Uva-ursi' can be persuaded to smile. Rock-like facial expressions do nothing but add to the grim determination underneath. Don't stare too hard at them in a public place, or you may find yourself confronted by an angry bear, asking 'What are you looking at, buster; something funny about me, is there? Am I holding my knife wrong?' — and it's on again!

To hurt *someone else* seems to be their instinctive reaction, if any reaction at all be grudgingly shown. At other times it's like contemplating the Grand Canyon's walls.

They can be *very* selfish, and *very* self-centred. 'Don't talk to me about *your* troubles', they may say, and refuse altogether to admit anyone but them may have any. 'I've got troubles of my own', they'll fling over their shoulder as they leave. Those around them often live in fear of their tempers, which can be violent, especially after alcohol affects the liver, gall bladder and the kidneys. Not the best of flatmates, employees or bosses! Kidney stones or gall-stones add obstruction and pain to the outflow of bile, and of fluid wastes. 'Excrement on the liver' may be an apt description of their physical symptoms. Lower-back pain results, or griping indigestion, with acid reflux especially when trying to sleep.

Positive 'Uva-ursi'

When positive, these people have shorter memories for past injustices, and look to improvement for the future. Just because grandfather died poor is no real reason for you to walk over all business limits, cheat your partner and tell lies to the Stock Exchange in your personal vow to die rich — to even up the score. While negative 'Uva-ursi's' plot and plan and use much of their life-energy in evening up old scores, positive 'Uva-ursi's' bury the past and leave the revenge to fate, God or the Devil. They know that while there is always an *effect* of the past in the present and the future, it halts humanity — and consolidates calcium deposits — to dwell there too often, or to let it ruthlessly restrict their outlook on life today.

Dosage

1   Uva-ursi tea is comforting and demulcent when kidney stone or gall-stones block or restrict the passage of fluids past them. Many patients have found that the tea alone has obviated the need for surgery. It is still best to have the tea-dosage assessed for you professionally.

2   In tincture or extract Uva-ursi may be added with Buchu, Dandelion, etc. to mixtures where both liver and kidneys show impeded function due to gall or kidney blockage. For gonorrhoea, an individually-tailored dose of this and other herbs is useful to relieve the irritation and reduce the discharge.

Valerian

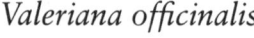

Valeriana officinalis

One of the most valuable of all herbs for the professional, but also for home use, Valerian's folklore is rich with mediaeval overtones. Not only was it supposedly the lure used by the Pied Piper of Hamelin to attract all those troublesome vermin to follow him to their deaths by drowning, but it has been associated with strange cat behaviour over the centuries too. Echoes of witchery again! Or is it all explainable?

Although the botanically 'official' label is the one most commonly used in its identification for medicinal use, there are quite a few different varieties with different habits of growth in various localities and other countries. It is not native to Australia, and indeed can be difficult to grow here. It prefers a lime-rich, moist soil, with its roots in shade, and some sun, preferably gentle morning sun, on its erect flowering stems. The basal rosette of palm-like leaves throw, like the dandelion, numerous variations in shape, numbers of pinnate divisions of each leaf, and quite marked variations in colour density. Botanists have decreed, as botanists will, that some of these differences in form are so great as to need differentiation of variety and a new name. Added to the plant's personal idiosyncrasies and varietal characteristics is the usual variation in oil content. Moisture needs play a large part in the chemical production of the iso-valerianic acid present in its oil. Valerian, like people, shows individually different results depending on its childhood and environment!

The 'root', or more specifically the rhizome of the plant, is the medicinal part. Some herbalists like to use it fresh, and manufacturers make the tinctures or extracts from the freshly-dug rhizome. Others, like myself, prefer the ancient tradition of drying the root first, even for a whole year's cycle, before extracting its somewhat different chemistry after this maturing period. In 1907 work done on the *fresh* root showed the presence of different biologically-active substances including a glycoside, another alkaloid and some resinous matter, all of which change chemically as any drying progresses. However, the drying root also develops active medicinal substances as the enzyme activity transforms it, and in the process of 'dying' slowly it develops iso-valerianic acid in which oily liquid is found the characteristic foetid odour — Valerian's trademark. Both forms of processing have their adherents amongst today's herbalists.

The oil of Valerian also contains pinene (as found in Pines, Conifers, etc.) and acetic and formic acid to stimulate nerve fibres into the active mode, while the valerianic acid (which is found in many other plants of the nervine-class) calms and stabilises the energy so obtained. It must be classed as one of the greatest nervines, in either method of preparation. In minerals, Valerian is blessed with magnesium and phosphorus in excellent proportion and large quantity. As a plant-source of magnesium phosphate, it is arguably the best.

Dioscorides, painstakingly observant, found this one easy. Like Middle-Eastern scholars before him, he named it 'Phou' or 'Pfu'! Perhaps he borrowed the onomatopoeia from the Alexandrine Egyptians who were great at it, especially when a little play with words, meanings and sounds could lead to a literary pun or a papyrus-picture joke. Certainly the smell of Valerian root is unforgettable! It has been known to escape even from screw-topped glass jars in kitchen cupboards, and your refrigerator will never be the same again if you store it there. A cellophane bag is best (not plastic). Seal this with a twist-tie, then pop it all in a glass jar which can be tightly sealed and leave it in a cool (not cold) kitchen-shelf corner. I can perhaps better describe its odour to you as a blend of ripe Stilton cheese and recently removed jogging shoes. Don't start your friends off into new home herbal-medicine experiences by recommending Valerian tea as their first exposure to it!

Its body action, either fresh or dried, can best be described as antispasmodic and sedative. It is, indeed, one of the fastest acting of sleep-producers for the person-picture type following. It is a herbal tea to be taken at nighttime, not first thing in the morning or during a busy day. Its professional uses are far more complex, and when prescribed in a mixture for illness-symptoms as described below, it may be necessary to take a three-or-four-times-daily dose of the extract or tincture.

'Valerian' person-picture

The 'Valerian' person is well controlled. *Well*-controlled may be a misapplied adjective for some; *tightly* controlled applies to most. It just depends on how highly you value being perceived to be cool at all times. Friends and family may think of you as 'cold' rather than cool; undemonstrative or unresponsive, and certainly uncommunicative. Almost the opposite of the 'Chamomile' person, the 'Valerian' picture is one of monosyllabic answers, intense willpower, and a poker-face. 'Valerian' natives will *never* let the world see them out of control, or showing emotions. It's not that they don't have them; it's just that they are none of your business! Often they are intensely passionate people, with fierce loves and hates, but they'd rather just sit there, fists gripping their armchair and knuckles white, telling you they *are* relaxing. Under a deceptively calm exterior, carefully and painfully acquired, may be a boiling cauldron of tensions and spasms, and physical or emotional pain that would make a lesser mortal complain and yell and dramatise, but you'll never hear it from the Valerian-type. 'It's just mind over matter', they'll inform you when you're being particularly obnoxious, temperamental and vocal about it. They have no patience with 'wimps'; they admire achievers and tough cookies and corporate raiders, and probably — secretly — John Wayne. Secretiveness always marks them. The one person at the party who won't tell you his or her Zodiac sign is usually 'Valerian'. Anything which may penetrate the thick skin and defensive self-control is shunned. Heavens, what business is it of anyone's what emotions, feelings, hurts, panics, disappointments, jealousies or resentments they have on the boil? Nor do they show *happy* reactions much either. Whether they'd make good spies is problematical, as although they look like the world's best survivors, impervious to pain and 'cool' at all times, the *passion* of their basic nature may burst through the protective layers at the wrong time.

So 'Valerian' people won't give much away, in any sense. They can be called 'mean' by their enemies, and 'careful' by those who love them. They can test you out to find any weaknesses in your character or the stories you're telling them, and will have as their friends only the strongest people they can find. Often relentlessly hard on themselves, they can be found in weekend army camps, body-building gyms, and jogging at dawn. They *will* overcome any weaknesses, and that's that.

Negative-chronic 'Valerian'

As such tightly controlled people punish their bodies, they develop a fearsome ability to maintain muscular contraction and tension. Even when asleep, and apparently resting, you'll find them with arms or legs crossed tightly, and even their facial muscles contracted into a tight frown. Some grind their teeth in their sleep. *All* of them wake *tired*; as if they've been running around the block all night. And it's not far from the truth! Maintaining muscular contraction, even through the sleep process, is hard work! Even getting to sleep in the first place may for them be an exercise of will. 'Big toe relax', they command: 'next toe relax . . .' and they *order* themselves to sleep instead of giving in and letting Morpheus slide over them in apparent victory. Many are *afraid* to sleep, especially in strange surroundings.

In fact, fears of all kinds can be the basic reasons for a 'Valerian' person's tension. Fear of failure, fear of weakness, fear of loving and being rejected; 'fear of financial ruin' one diagnostic repertory finds inherent in them. To overcome these fears, they develop awesome programmes of control.

As you can imagine, such muscular contraction can squeeze blood vessels and pinch nerves. Blood pressure can rise alarmingly as a 'Valerian'-person fights to maintain control and outward calm. 'Essential hypertension' is common, and the load put on major vessels like heart, liver, even kidneys, can be considerable. Spleen can take a beating, too, and enlarged spleens can be found in middle to later life. The blood flow to the brain may be the most at risk. Strokes can occur after a lifetime of such tension, and they may even occur from early middle age onwards, apparently in the prime of life. *Pressure* of many kinds, emotional, physical or circumstantial, can be reflected in even tighter control and alarmingly sudden pains, spasms and 'tightness' and constriction feelings. Almost all 'Valerian'-persons have a 'heart attack' scare at some stage of their lives as a quick clutch of pain or breathlessness *causes* fear and apprehension, and makes the spasm stronger and stronger. Heart attacks may actually occur, too. Many of us have had experience or knowledge of a relative or friend whose heart locked tight, never to move again, under continued stresses and emotional tensions. Perhaps if there had been *less* control, more tears or bad temper or anger, or even love and tenderness expressed when felt, the cardiac seizure may never have occurred.

So symptoms needing Valerian include muscular tension, either chronic or recent, and the result not only of physical trauma but also of emotional or environmental pressures. 'A nagging wife' used to get the blame: 'he was nagged to death' is perhaps a Valerian occurrence. Excessively strict discipline can be a cause, but so can *self*-criticism and being a too-hard taskmaster on yourself. 'Relax!' yell your friends, and you tighten even more in fury at their uncalled for interference.

High or fluctuating blood pressure is one Valerian indication, but so is pain, whether the person be 'Valerian'-type or not. Chronic or severe acute pain can *cause* spasm and tension as well as being the result of these. A broken leg yesterday can call for Valerian tea tonight and for quite a few nights to come if necessary. Even during the day, you can break the rule and have a cup if strong pain occurs. It won't then matter so much if you also have a doze afterwards, relaxed and pain-free.

The chronic pain of deep-seated rheumatic arthritic diseases calls for Valerian, too, especially if the person is a 'Valerian'-type — and many rheumatoid arthritic patients are! Gritting their teeth against the ever-present agony, they smile bravely and few around them realise the depth of their suffering. It is, of course, also possible that 'Valerian'-people are arthritis-prone anyway. Keeping a stiff upper lip under all pressure and adversity may win you a Brownie badge, but it may also accumulate tension and pressure, where bone-end grinds hard on joint socket, or where blood vessels inflame and run red-hot with the burning miseries of rheumatism. *Over*-controlled people are much more likely to earn such diseases as a reward for their bravery!

Positive 'Valerian'

Sure, there's achievement going on here, and plenty of self-pride in accomplishment, but positive Valerian *relaxes* easily when it is all over, and is not ashamed to feel fear under stress and pressure — but conquers the challenge anyway. Here are the soldiers who can cry and talk after the battle, and the achievers who tell you openly of their earlier fears which they have beaten with action, not suppression. Here are the humble heroes who say 'I don't know how I did it: I was dead-scared.' Positive 'Valerian' *relaxes*, sings rude songs, laughs and talks and cries without embarrassment or fear of ridicule. Positive 'Valerian' exhausts the muscles with active challenge then sleeps like the household cat, loose-limbed and spread all over the bed. Tomorrow may bring another battle, another challenge, but tonight we sing, dance, make love and flop asleep. Aches and pains seem to be rare: blood pressure is often on the *low* side, and positive 'Valerian' tells lots of jokes and true stories at his or her own expense. A failure may be turned into a funny story at dinner, or tossed aside with 'Gee, I was an idiot today; I must have looked a right Charlie.' No superhuman expectations here! And no counting sheep or some quick Yoga exercises needed either!

There are few cautions in taking Valerian except the general ones applying to all medication: *don't* assume that if a little is good, a lot will be better (it may work in the *opposite* end of the rule and keep you awake!). Don't self-medicate, and then wonder why you're walking around dizzy and slightly nauseous the next day. It still needs a professional herbalist to assess your dosage levels, and to begin *gradual* Valerian exposure. If you happen to have *very* low blood pressure, a sensitive liver and sluggish bile-ducts, then Valerian may not be for you. It can tend to stimulate bile-flow strongly, and can also cause more bile production. Hence the nausea and stomach distress if it is contra-indicated.

If you are the Valerian-needing type, you may feel absolutely 'exhausted' as you begin taking your prescribed mixture in the first few days. What you're experiencing is not exhaustion but *relaxation*. This may be a foreign feeling indeed as you flop from chair to bed with apparently no 'energy'. Persevere, (you're good at it!). This is what other people feel: it's called 'relaxed'! For the first time for many 'Valerian'-types, sleep can come easily, and you wake with true refreshed energy after *restful* sleep. This unfamiliar feeling will pass in a day or two, and you'll find yourself waking more easily and leaping out of bed without an effort of will or self-disgust at your 'weakness' in failing to sleep as you needed to.

Dosage

1 A cup of Valerian tea after a highly-pressured day of challenges and battles can suit just about all of us, with the provisos listed above. But if you find yourself not able to sleep without it, then a more professional assessment of your whole health history is required. Home-remedies are fine up to a point, but nothing replaces that first objective and trained assessment of you by an experienced herbalist.

2   In nervine mixtures, Valerian acts as a pain-reliever and anti-spasmodic so three times daily doses of extract or tincture may be prescribed. However, *prolonged* dosing with Valerian can be contra-indicated: the *good* herbalist will have been removing the *causes* of your pain and tension so, while Valerian is an anodyne, antispasmodic and nervine, it is mostly used to remove symptoms, not causes. Other nervines may be prescribed with it to help calm down nervous excitability, and there may also be mineral-rich herbs needed too, especially those high in silica, calcium and zinc, to complete the recovery pattern.

Vervain

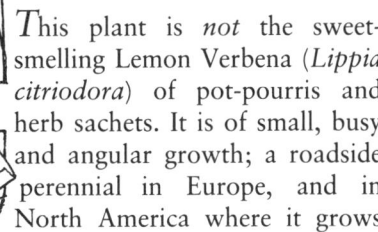

This plant is *not* the sweet-smelling Lemon Verbena (*Lippia citriodora*) of pot-pourris and herb sachets. It is of small, busy and angular growth; a roadside perennial in Europe, and in North America where it grows larger and is more commonly called *Verbena hastata*. The small flowers are pale mauve, on thin wiry stems. As with so many mauve-flowered plants, its physiological activity is nervine; and it is tonic and astringent. Its history parallels that of Uva-ursi, being a medicinal herb beloved of the early Celtic cultures through Europe and across the Baltic countries, even into the Ukraine. In very old traditional herbals, it is credited with beneficial effects on as widely separate diseases as colds, worms, scrofula and visceral obstruction! Such claims are often the basis for medical and scientific scoffing today — until the underlying person-picture of 'Vervain' is exposed.

Several glycosides give it tonic and energy-raising properties, so there is certainly a little 'lift' gained from its use, improving many illnesses where general debility and low nervous energy contribute to symptoms. But worms? And scrofula?

'Vervain' person-picture

The classic 'Vervain' is conscientious, always busy and somewhat irritable. In fact, they feel downright uncomfortable with nothing to do! While watching television, and supposedly relaxing, there is always knitting, or vegetables to be peeled for dinner, or embroidery, or a *list* of some kind running through their mind. They leap up in the middle of the gripping movie drama to put the rubbish-bin out, iron a shirt for tomorrow, or look up a reference book to settle a point in today's office argument. Their minds leap about, crossing off jobs to be done, one after another. Seldom is there a day that dawns without a *list* in their mind of targets to be achieved before evening. They may be workaholics, happy only when doing something constructive.

They pick at themselves with their fingers, scratching at an itching spot or a pimple. They fiddle with their own fingers, pulling at nail cuticles and picking at loose skin, small abrasions, healing cuts, etc. They never leave themselves alone! They scratch, rub and change position; their feet tap, or set up a rhythmical swing from a crossed leg. They pat hair into place and check the alignment of their clothing whenever they leap from a chair or desk to *do* something which has just crossed their mind.

They are *detail* people. Every small detail must not only be planned, but carried out, finished and then happily crossed off their list for the day, the month or the year.

Ill-health of many different kinds may follow this constant activity of the peripheral nervous system. 'Hypericum' people site the origin of their hypersensitive reactions in cranial nerves or spine: 'Vervains' suffer from *surface* and *peripheral* nervous-system *irritations*, rather than generalised pain. Neuralgias are common, and skin itchiness even more so. When they undress at night, it can be heaven to scratch at odd spots unreachable during the day. With a look of bliss, they dig fingernails into the shoulder, or round the back, rubbing at small tension spots and local 'itches'. Scratching at themselves seems to be the most obvious general trait!

All this constant nervous activity, leaping up and down as yet another duty, chore or detail comes to mind, can cause restless tiredness and general irritability. They may be hard to live with, especially if you are a lackadaisical slob! Many skin irritations they suffer are of the dermatitis-type, on hands especially. Their fingernails would be anathema to *Vogue*!

Negative-chronic 'Vervain'

If the pattern is not recognised and treated early, ingrained fussiness and criticism of everyone else's shortcomings may make them lonely people! Working back at the office increases. 'No-one else does it properly', they scowl. They toss and turn restlessly in bed, and some have even been known to get up and go in to the office at 2 a.m. to finish something that has been preventing their sleep. Others keep a note-pad by the bed or in the car, jotting down 'things to be done' as they cross the mind. Different from 'Hops', who pre-manage and organise, sometimes quite impractically, even negative 'Vervain' is a *practical* person, a worker and a self-stresser. The inevitable occurs: a premature heart attack, adrenal exhaustion, migraines, broken marriages and bitter disappointments in those around them who may not feel that constant *work* makes one acceptable to others and therefore to be admired by them. Under every workaholic's irritable skin is the need for their dependants and the world at large to say 'Aren't you *wonderful*! We can always rely on you, you are so responsible, dependable, conscientious and trustworthy.' Instead, a Friday-night migraine and a lonely weekend at home, washed out — but still working! — may be their only reward. While the family go the beach, negative 'Vervain' cleans out the kitchen cupboards, and becomes bitter and resentful of others' fun. In naturopathic terms, when resentments harden and become fixed and obstructive, so do inorganic calcium compounds! Those kidney stones, which by tradition improve when treated with Vervain, may take twenty years a-coming. Hardened resentments can cause body concretions in gall bladder, kidneys, even in arteries. Arteriosclerosis may also lie ahead for the sober and serious negative 'Vervain' whose work ethic is top-heavy and precludes an equal amount of fun, relaxation or an occasionally unplanned day from balancing up homoeostatic scales. 'All work and no play' produces a surprising range of illness symptoms, most of which can disappear when on holidays. Unfortunately, negative 'Vervain' may seldom take that holiday!

Positive 'Vervain'
The world runs on oiled wheels if you have one of these around! Always on time for dinner parties, always with an appropriate gift for the hostess and an enquiry after her Mother's rheumatism or the swimming-pool's filter-trouble, positive 'Vervain' makes a marvellous guest. They love to fix things: their good health shows that they balance fun-work with serious-work, and know when to pick up a hammer and quietly fix something rather than criticise the householder as a slob while detailing all their own meticulous perfection.

Positive 'Vervain' has a strong heart, and often lives to a venerable age — with a conscience which is cleared of obligation every day, before seeking sleep. When the 'list' is crossed off for the day, positive 'Vervain' sleeps as soon as the head hits the pillow, with a child-like smile. They wake, refreshed with a typical phrase — 'Well, what's to be done today?' You do them no favour not to have an answer ready!

Dosage

1   Vervain tea is rare, and seldom prescribed.

2   In medicinal mixtures for this type, Vervain may be prescribed with Alfalfa, Dandelion, etc. The major vitamin needed is the whole B-group. 'Vervain's' annoyances are small, not major. Even the most negative of them copes with major traumas, shocks, adverse conditions and challenges, with great competence and almost eagerness.

'Vervains' I have known

My Grandmother, who knitted a pair of soldier's socks each day during the Second World War, while she rocked her chair to and fro and ran the whole household gently and with foresight in every detail. She lived ninety-four years, still working.

A doctor-friend who made a comprehensive 'travel-list' which he offers to friends so they don't forget some detail which may be overlooked in packing, in accommodation arrangements, and in household safety while absent.

Years ago, when my practice had developed so that bigger premises were needed, I did all the cleaning myself at the weekends to save dollars earmarked for the bank. On Monday morning, glowing with righteousness and an obvious list of cleaning jobs crossed off the previous day, I was confronted by the pointing finger of a *negative* 'Vervain'. 'There's a dead leaf on that plant', she said impatiently. 'I would have thought you, a herbalist, would have removed that.' Not a word about the shining floor, the polished office and the vase of fresh flowers on the counter! A few weeks later, I was sweeping the footpath outside the rooms (a job which should have been done by others) and she caught me again. 'Don't you know a broom should always be pushed away from you, not towards you?' she lectured, flashing up the stairs in her perfectly pressed suit. We parted company permanently a short time later!

Another positive 'Vervain' who is retired and in his seventies, helps pensioners in his district repair their homes, with no charge for his labour. 'I like to keep busy', his clear blue eyes twinkle as he says it. And his health is excellent!

Violet leaves
Viola odorata

For those who like a little metaphysics with their physic, the common Sweet Violet is an ideal plant to explore more widely and deeply. (I cannot resist at least one foray into things wonderful: if the pharmacognosists rail and rant, they have done it before, and will doubtless continue.)

One of my most personally fascinating discoveries, after more than three decades of work with medicinal plants, has been the *patterns* nature puts energy into, and how related energy shapes, colours, even odours, have affinity and easy interaction between animal, plant, human, etc. The growth pattern of Violets is strange. Gardening readers will have observed how a Violet-patch planted in one spot will 'walk' to another some distance away next season. The original source plants may be lost, withering away and infertile, but the creeping root-stolons travel away from the parent patch, relocating and sending down roots elsewhere. In Europe, and back through myth and legend, the Violet has symbolised death of one kind but rebirth in a different dimension. Even the odour of the Violet is chameleon-like: it can overpower other scents while losing its own! As an absorber of stale odours, of the unpleasant smell of decay, even of the odour of Death itself, it is gently overpowering, sacrificing its own pure perfume in the process.

Some years ago, while preparing a lecture on the lymphatic system, I was struck by the pattern of resemblance between the creeping linked-beads of this system with its root-nodes and runners, and its 'patches' at points of major lymphatic collection under arms, at the groin, etc. Suddenly, some of the ancient texts made sense: the medicinal uses of the Violet, flowers, leaves and creeping roots had previously been obscure to me but if the plant cleared lymphatic blockages, and renewed normal lymph flow, then the ancient writer's observations made sense. When I discovered that an alkaloid similar to Emetine (found in Ipecachuana) had been extracted in recent times from the plant — by a pharmacognosist, no less — the relationship was complete. Even as recently as 1931, Violet leaf tea, for lymphatic cancer of the throat, was listed in the British Pharmacopoea!

Ancient herbalists practised empirical medicine: if something worked it was tried again, and again, and with variations. The 'rule' soon became evident, and the use of a plant in particular symptomatic pictures was established.

One intriguing ancient custom also tantalised me: Violets were carried at funerals of children or of those who had died too young, cut down by mysterious blood diseases without apparent pre-illness occurring. Was leukaemia, or something like it, about in mediaeval times? Did more primitive people sense more, feel more, and understand better, than our higher intelligence and clever technology is providing for us? Have we almost lost the ability to read nature and learn from her about ourselves?

There is no person-picture here to limit your horizon. Go out and look at the world around you, at the clouds and the insects, at the new moon and the path the setting sun makes across the water. Look at the *geometry* of nature — 'earth-measurement', the word means — and judge whether mankind's newer standards are accurate enough and honest enough.

Dosage

1   I would not self-prescribe Violet leaf tea, extract or tincture, as seldom will the need for the plant's use be evident to the person concerned. The lymphatic circulation is the quiet underground stream, cold and hidden, tumbling through caves and pools, its eventual outlet as a spring or stream kilometres away from its secret source. Lymphatic nodes which slow down, enlarge or block altogether may be collecting wastes from a primary focus of trouble in the body which is quite different and remote.

2   Violet leaves tincture or extract is prescribed herbally when there is lymphatic stasis, blood-component changes, and for some causes of spleen enlargement. The iris of the eye, more than any other diagnostic tool, can clearly demonstrate with particular signs and colours when, and where, lymphatic drainage is less than ideal, so that *early* treatment may be taken to clear such stagnant pools and restore the flow.

It's hard not to wax poetic about the Violet: 'modest' violet, 'shy' Violet. Changes in the quality of elimination following its professional prescribing may make the patient blush! 'Where did all that muck come from?' many a patient has asked me. 'Inside you', I reply, 'and you never knew it was there.' 'Better out than in', as my Grandmother used to say!

Wintergreen

Gaultheria procumbens

Oil of Wintergreen is added to almost all embrocations, balms and rubs when deep muscular pain is to be treated. The characteristic and powerfully penetrating smell of the oil wafts from every gymnasium, every football dressing-room, and from every sports-medicine clinic. The same penetrating power takes Wintergreen oil's soothing warmth deep into big muscles of the back, the legs, the shoulders, through fascia and connective tissue where less strong aromatic oils cannot penetrate. For lumbago, for 'gardener's back'; for ceiling-painters and garbage-men; for anyone where heavy lifting may over-strain or athletic goals may lead to deep muscular spasm and pain, Wintergreen's oil is only for *external* application.

The plant is native to Canada and northern USA, and has entered both pharmaceutical and herbal Materia Medica comparatively recently. The leaves are the medicinal part, salicyclic acid being found therein. The pain-relieving action of this compound is well documented and accepted in all forms of medicine. Resinous substances also are found in the leaves. The anti-inflammatory effect is quickly observable, and the consequent pain relief a blessed relief indeed.

Oil of Wintergreen adheres so strongly to the skin that it may be difficult to remove it from the hands after massaging a patient with it, or after self-application to painful rheumatic nodes and joints. First rub on another bland oil like Almond or Safflower, and the Wintergreen will then remove more easily. *Do not touch eyes or nostrils* or other sensitive body areas with hands which have just used Wintergreen! Pain relief will be obvious for some hours. Last thing at night even the most stubborn muscular or rheumatic pain will improve from a Wintergreen rub, so that sleep will come more easily. Use old bed linen, though! That penetrating odour may persist even after a trip through the washing machine.

Dosage

External application only. A few drops is all that is needed, rubbed well in to painful and inflamed areas. Once daily is usually enough, but if the condition is severe, twice daily may be necessary.

Witch-hazel

Hamamelis virginiana

A well-marketed herb last cen-
tury, Witch-hazel was found in every household medicine cabinet
for the treatment of bruises, bumps and blows with blunt instruments. It is an excellent vulnerary, stops external and internal
haemorrhaging quickly and seldom if ever needs to be used over
more than a day or two for this type of injury. Like Yarrow (*The
Book of Herbs*, page 199) it is highly astringent, but where Yarrow
is more useful against fast arterial bleeding, Witch-hazel is more
specific for venous seepage, and the crushing of small veins which
lead to purple bruises later.

Witch-hazel lotion is also useful for reducing the swelling
when a blunt object hits, or is hit by, a human, and there is bone-
impact. The most common site for Witch-hazel's use on children
seems to be the head and face. Small children bump into furniture,
fall down steps, and an 'egg' appears in no time. Apply a cotton pad
soaked in Witch-hazel lotion, or tincture of Witch-hazel, to the
spot, and hold it in place for a few minutes while you cuddle and
soothe the hurt child. Older children run into tree branches, bark
their shins against rocks, and get hit by soccer balls, cricket bats —
and other children! Use Witch-hazel *as soon as possible*: it works
better the faster it can be applied. Hours later it is of *some* use: days
later its effect is much less, and repeated applications may be needed once or twice each day for bad sprains and strains with bruised
and swollen areas of tissue.

For varicose veins which ache and throb at the end of a tiring
day, saturate a narrow length of old soft sheeting with the Witch-
hazel lotion, and wrap it around the vein area on the leg. Do this
while the leg is *horizontal*, not elevated or dropped. This removes

all gravity pressure, and allows the astringent and penetrating fluid to shrink the vein a little without too much change in blood flow. Half an hour is all that's needed.

Use the same Witch-hazel lotion saturating cotton pads to cover the closed eyes for quarter of an hour at the end of a tiring day driving or if winds have caused irritation from fine dust. Even if vanity wants to lose the wrinkles around the eyes which may age you more than you care to admit, the same weekly fifteen minutes of shut-eye, with cotton pads with cool Witch-hazel applied, can tighten sagging skin and add renewed twinkle. Once a week is fine — and safe: twice a day is far too often and you may only give yourself a headache, not a Mona Lisa expression!

Haemorrhoids are varicose veins of the rectum, and Witch-hazel ointment is needed here for local daily application to shrink these bulging blood vessels and relieve pressure and pain.

Witch-hazel is used *externally* for almost the same symptoms for which Rue is prescribed *internally*. Because Witch-hazel has such a powerful astringent action, I hesitate to use it internally, preferring Yarrow for internal astringency in haemorrhages after surgery, ulcer-seepage, etc.

Although Witch-hazel is a symptom reliever only, there is a sad person-picture which may at times apply. Battered babies, beaten wives and children, prize-fighters and footballers, all may show on the skin the purple bruises, 'black' eyes and contused tissues after blunt-object force. *Bones* are often deeply hurt as well as skin, leaving later possibility of weakened tissues which can lead to arthritis, even to bone cancers. Prompt treatment is needed for these people: don't wait a week or two before seeking help if life's bumps and blows rain down upon you. The fluid which quickly cushions the area may remain; the swelling may overload or tear lymph vessels. Later, much later, a permanent weakness may be the end result.

Prescribing

I imagine you have picked out on your way through this book some 'person-pictures' which fit you, your family, your workmates, even public figures. Do you just take one herb alone, or is each mixture composed of several, or many? Do you take it permanently, or for a 'course' of treatment, or every day three times, or in a tea occasionally?

If you've been driven to distraction by my constant admonitions to leave it to your professional herbalist to decide, there is a reason. Finding the appropriate remedy-list is comparatively easy; deciding on the *proportions* of ingredients in an extract or tincture mixture is much more difficult. In the accuracy and balance of these proportions lies the key to major and lasting improvement.

It may have only taken you a few hours or a few days to read this book: it takes two to four years of training at herbal colleges to become a diploma-level graduate. There is much more to the safe and efficacious use of herbs than reading a 'do-it-yourself' book only. There must be thorough grounding in how the structures and functions of the body work, how they are improved upon and how they are injured or destroyed. There must be training in differential diagnosis — what 'pain' indicates a strained inter-costal muscle and what a heart condition, and how to differentiate by asking the right questions. Evaluative techniques for dealing with patient-personalities must be taught and environmental and attitudinal factors which make people sick must also become familiar. Job-related disease, postural stresses involved in work, and the emotional climate of the person must also be considered. It takes *twenty* years before it all flows easily, and a lifetime before the experience gained should be taught to others authoritatively. Not until then can the underlying patterns be seen for what they truly are.

At every patient's reply to a consultation question I jot down a possible herb, nutritional supplement, or other remedy. At the end I may have nineteen herbs and fourteen foods noted down! Then begins the culling process, where accuracy can improve, or decrease, depending on my final choices.

Some herbs on my list may have tick after tick beside them, as reply after reply showed need for this one plant. Others may overlap in the way in which they change body conditions, so the least applicable are discarded. Some remedies for particular 'person-pictures' may be obvious in the first few minutes of consultation. Other deeper cause factors may show through slowly, or not until the second visit when the patient trusts you more and begins to tell the *real* story. Still other herbs will be chosen to relieve present distressing symptoms.

I seldom use more than five herbs. More indicates a need for better and sharper discrimination and more confidence! New practitioners always over-prescribe, seeing too many side-tracks, red herrings, and little details. The older hands go for the bottom line. On a really good diagnostic day, one or two herbs, chosen with painstaking questioning and exhaustive elimination, may work wonders. It *is* essential to work as simply as possible in final mixture ingredients so you'll know what plant is producing what change in each patient. If you include nine, or fifteen, or more than twenty herbs, as some 'herbalists' do, you're admitting to shot-gun therapy because you figure you can't help but hit *something* which will improve. And how will you learn which herb in practice does what, growing in experience as you do?

In herbal medicine tradition, herbal 'Simples', one herb at a time, are used by the most experienced of all. On a rare day when I have prescribed only one herb as a hundred per cent of the mixture, I give a little salute to the shades of Dioscorides, Galen and to Imhotep — the greatest of them all.

A Word to
the Wise

Some readers read the last pages of a book first, 'just to see how it ends'. I want to end on the same note as I began: the practice of herbal medicine needs training, education, care, accuracy and attention to detail. 'Nature medicine' is not as easy in its application today as its title would suggest. When humans were closer to the animals, leading simple lives of struggle, subsistence and survival, our *instincts* chose the plants for food, for drink and for medicine. There were resemblances between the patterns, in the colours and shapes found in nature, and the old brain, the subconscious and superconscious seat of racial memories, made instinctive choices. Mind you, there is no record of how many times humans made themselves ill, or even died, from a hasty or wrong choice! But racial experience grew, and we learned from the mistakes. Inbuilt into our inherited cell-memories, we began to collect a body of evidence on what was 'good' for the organisation of cells called a 'human', and what was harmful; what berries, fruits, seeds, etc., killed or caused uncomfortable symptoms, and which others were compatible nutritionally for us, renewing our energy, promoting endurance, and prolonging that indefinable quality of life called 'good health'. This process took aeons of time to evolve and become imprinted generation after generation.

Then along came intellect. 'Rational' decisions began to replace instinctive ones. Teaching by others on how nature *should* be began to replace how nature *is*. Science began to make *its* laws, and they increasingly did not coincide with the real and established laws of the universe already operative since our world began to support life. Theory replaced practice, and intellect replaced instinct. Thinking overruled knowing; book-learning, especially in young formative years, ousted experience as the best-preferred of life's teachers. Personal observation, that most essential of diagnostic tools, almost died out medically. Statistics were 'in'; 'average daily requirements' of all sorts of nutrients were established as the new 'rules'. 'Recommended daily doses' for *everyone* were the new law. Individual differences were irrelevant: everyone was required to be the same as everyone else. Even the small flock of sparrows in my garden right now proves again to me that in nature, all are *not* equal! One needs — and gets! — twice his share of seeds, another stands back until the aggressive leaders have taken their fill. Yet another decides it's worms today, and seeds some other time. In nature, every plant, animal, bird and human is *different*! This irrevocable law knows nothing of 'average' requirements, nor of 'standardised' doses. Every human being will need different amounts and types of medication for the same disease, because their individual reasons for the symptoms they describe as 'illness' are also different.

The successful practice of herbal medicine is reserved only for those who *know* deeply and instinctively that everyone is different. Certainly, there are professional herbalists who 'go by the book'; measured identical quantities are dispensed, and some improvements and changes occur. They learn the long names of all the alkaloids and the glycosides found in plants: they put a batch of herbal extract or tincture through spectro-analysis machines and can then, to three decimal places, tell you its constituents and how theoretically, the patient who takes this herb should react. But when a sick old lady, or a worried young mum, or a middle-aged businessman consults you across your desk, your knowing how to spell 'glycoside' or 'Scheuerman's Disease', will help you not at all! It's a sick *person* sitting there, not a statistic or a theory! You must relate all your advice, your therapeutics, your changes to be made and your prognosis to a *human being* who will most certainly tell you of the improvements, or otherwise, at the follow-up visit. It's no use consulting a textbook to see if your diagnosis was 'right' or your treatment matched the 'average daily dose'. Theory falls over, whimpering, when practice shows otherwise!

Be *wise* first, and clever only later, if at all. Your patient wants a headache-cause removed, not an ego-exercise from you about your theoretical, correctly spelled student days. Let patients teach *you* by their results whether the system you follow works and is a valid one. If it is, they will beat a path to your door; if it is *not*, all the gold-edged diplomas on your wall, which cost you dear in time, effort and money, are worthless.

Don't be found at the other extreme of herbal medicine, either! The *under*-trained herbalist has an even more profound problem: it is simply not enough to want to 'help people' by telling all within earshot what has worked *for you*. Rushing about with a paragraph on 'Red Clover for Acne' in the weekly health column of your newspaper may find you being sued by irate parents of a teenager who has taken twice the amount, three times too often, and now has pustular eruptions on neck and arms as well as no sign of improvement in the original acne! Restrain your wish to 'help': you may not only be hindering instead, but *all* herbalists will suffer by reputation because of your enthusiastic, but incompletely informed actions. Heaven preserve me from amateur herbalists! When the headlines blaze in the Sunday papers, all my profession suffers too and, worse, the image of 'cranks' and 'weirdos' surfaces again. Contain yourself: after all, why would students undergo years and years of professional training if it was all so simple?

This is not to say that self-prescribing of Garlic oil capsules for a cold is to be frowned on, or putting a little dish of Horseradish relish on the table for your spouse with hayfever is irresponsible. It *is* to say that that 'cold' may be an early hepatitis for which Garlic is contra-indicated, and the 'hayfever' may be a symptom of nasal polyps which could need surgery!

Diagnosis is the difficulty. Finding out the true causes of the symptoms, and the appropriate individual treatment required, is a job for well-trained herbalists, not for amateurs, or for those misty-eyed caring souls who want just to 'help humanity'! Then, and not until then, can you, the patient begin to understand your real needs, which plants to use, what dose to take, in what form, and how often.

I have deliberately broken one of my former and early precepts as a herbalist by the above cautionary advice. When I began to carry out the knowledge of my grandparents and my parents (over thirty years ago now) the use of plants as medicine was almost unknown in this country, and all we pioneers had first to educate, under the astounded and hostile gaze of the whole world, it seemed. Today herbal medicine is not only accepted and in new popularity, but the media has popularised it too to the current level of 'ordinary'. Every second magazine has a 'Herb Corner' column, health stores sprout in every suburb, mothers in the home or workforce, and fathers too, teach the children the health benefits of parsley, in tabouli or as a garnish, and the need for Dandelion 'coffee'. In Victoria alone over 390,000 patient-visits in one year to various 'alternative' medicine practitioners were recorded as part of their State's comprehensive and voluminous *Inquiry into Alternative Medicine* completed by the All-Party Social Development Committee in late 1986. The only bad news here is that most of the other Victorians are self-diagnosing!

Undertake a professional course of training if you want to be of the greatest benefit to your fellow-man and woman, using herbs to keep them well, as well as to treat their illnesses.

In spite of all these above warnings delivered each year to my new class of keen embryo-herbalists, one of them thought she knew better. She later told me her following experience. 'It was such a lovely little blue flower on the bush', she looked at me dreamily. 'It couldn't do any harm looking so pure and innocent, and I felt I had been led to this place to find it and discover a new plant that would revolutionise herbal medicine and bring suffering mankind closer to a spiritual one-ness with the universe.' She ate a few handfuls of the blue flowers — and experienced nothing but griping diarrhoea for several weeks afterwards! As I keep on explaining, Vincent Van Gogh studied the formal rules of painting for three years before he picked up brushes and created 'Sunflowers' in twenty minutes. There are no short cuts, nor is there any room for the 'guru'-image or the ego-needs of the individual practitioner. Knowledge validated by many centuries of experience is passed down and on to others for further exploration from their experience in turn. There is no such course as 'Instant Herbal Medicine'! Those of you who have been frustrated by my advice, at the end of almost every herb named in this book, to 'consult your professional herbalist' now realise why I have not, contrary to my earlier books in some ways, always recommended 'self-help' with these herbs, especially in their extract or tincture form.

Students and patients have for many years asked me to write a herbal medicine textbook. Such a work would fill the shelves of the Bodleian Library! I can only *begin*. I vowed I would begin it only at eighty-five years of age, because I would need the time to learn enough, or at least enough to be valid from experience so that nature's rules shine through. I have been prevailed upon to begin earlier: I stress the word 'begin'. There are hundreds of thousands of plants from the land, from the sea, and even epiphytes from the air, which have been used medicinally throughout the world since man's earliest appearance on earth. 'New' herbs may also be added as gradual evidence builds up in time on their results. While it would be silly to ignore work already well documented, and which has stood the test of efficacy in time, *judicious* book-learning can help put you in touch with great minds who lived when the world was younger, so it cannot be entirely ignored as the basis upon which to build further knowledge, and to prevent one herbalist's work being duplicated by another unnecessarily.

In light of this last chapter, perhaps you should now read again the first long section of this book. Any knowledge you gain from it should then be more wisely used.

Gaining knowledge is one use of mind: wisdom in its application is another. 'A word to the wise', they say, 'is sufficient.' I fervently hope so!

Index